SCARNE
ON
CARD TRICKS

by John Scarne

A SIGNET BOOK

NEW AMERICAN LIBRARY

TIMES MIRROR

SIGNET TRADEMARK REG. U.S. PAT. OFF. AND FOREIGN COUNTRIES
REGISTERED TRADEMARK—MARCA REGISTRADA
HECHO EN CHICAGO, U.S.A.

SIGNET, SIGNET CLASSICS, SIGNETTE,
MENTOR and PLUME BOOKS
are published by The New American Library, Inc.,
1301 Avenue of the Americas, New York, New York 10019

First Printing, February, 1974

1 2 3 4 5 6 7 8 9

PRINTED IN THE UNITED STATES OF AMERICA

*Dedicated to my friend
Dr. Ben Braude,
magic's most enthusiastic hobbyist*

CONTENTS

The details and descriptions of all the tricks in this book were written by John Scarne. Many of the tricks are Scarne's own creations. Where a performer is listed here, it indicates that he was the originator of the trick, performs it frequently, helped to improve it or avows that the trick is a favorite of his.

Publisher's Introduction

Before the curtain goes up and John Scarne steps onstage to show what can be done with a deck of cards, with no manipulative skill whatever, the publisher will deal a few words of introduction from the top of the deck. To most readers of this book John Scarne needs no introduction. But a good book travels far and lives long. And so, for the sake of those to whom John Scarne is just a name, here are some facts.

One of John Scarne's businesses is teaching card and dice players how to get a better run for their money, and how to avoid being fleeced by crooked gamblers. His two earlier books, *Scarne on Cards* and *Scarne on Dice*, have been hailed by experts as the standard reference books on their respective subjects. And *Scarne on Card Tricks* has already been hailed by top magicians as sure to be the standard book on non-sleight of hand card tricks.

His other business is fooling the public as a card manipulator; his hobby and favorite indoor sport is fooling magicians. And just to rub it in, he doesn't do it up on a stage surrounded by a crew of assistants and a ton of mechanical apparatus. Instead, he works his card miracles under the very noses of the magicians, using nothing more than a borrowed pack of cards, ten steel-spring fingers, and a pinch or two of diabolically contrived misdirection. If you think all these nice words are just something a press agent dreamed up, listen to what Scarne's competitors, the magicians themselves, have to say.

The late Nate Leipzig, a gentleman of the old school, was always considered top man with a deck of cards, but when he was at the height of his fame, Leipzig wrote these words about Scarne: ". . . he is the most expert exponent of wonderful card effects and table work I have ever seen in my life." Leipzig himself climbed the heights with sleight of hand, with nothing but his fingertips to climb with. As long as he lived he was the greatest of magicians' magicians and the most widely respected man in the field—perhaps all the more respected because at the climax of his career he could point to John Scarne in Fairview, New Jersey, and tip his top hat.

John Northern Hilliard, for years the manager of Thurston,

the magician, and one of the best American authorities on the history of magic, has added his compliments. He lists Scarne as one of the greatest magicians of all time. "I have seen all kinds and conditions of magicians," he wrote, "but I have yet to see anyone who surpasses Scarne in originality and sheer skill of hand . . . his skill is unbelievable."

Dunninger, the world-famous mentalist, says: "John Scarne is without a doubt the greatest card manipulator in the world."

Scarne is the highest paid card manipulator in the country today, his fees running as high as $1,000 for one evening's performance. He appeared at the White House for the late President Roosevelt on numerous occasions. At present, Scarne has taken to the lecture platform where he lectures on crooked gambling and performs his famous card tricks.

During World War II, at the War Department's request, Scarne acted as card and dice consultant to *Yank,* the Army newspaper. He also toured hundreds of Army camps and Naval bases during the war, doing card tricks for the G.I.'s, and answering their questions about all forms of gambling.

Scarne has been called into consultation as a card and dice expert by the Federal Bureau of Investigation, the New York City Police Department, and law enforcement agencies throughout the country. He has also lectured to many magicians' conventions on how to perform card tricks.

In addition, Scarne has given lessons in card tricks to such notables as the Prince of Wales, Orson Welles, Joe Di Maggio, Joe Louis, Milton Berle, James J. Braddock, and countless magicians who seek him out almost daily for his advice.

Articles about Scarne have appeared in *Esquire, True Detective Magazine, Newsweek, Time, Science Digest, The Saturday Evening Post, Life, Look, The New Yorker, The American Magazine, Police Gazette, Yank, Infantry Journal, American Weekly, New York Times Magazine, Parade,* and the *Reader's Digest.* Every major newspaper in the United States has carried articles on Scarne, as have English, Canadian, Indian, Australian, and Latin American publications. Columnists Walter Winchell, Bob Considine, John Lardner, and many others have occasionally devoted their columns to a description of Scarne and his exploits. The late Bob "Believe It or Not" Ripley found in Scarne a never-ending source of material.

And now the curtain goes up, and John Scarne will do the talking.

A New Era in Card Tricks

Five years ago, I decided that the card trick enthusiasts deserved a better grade of card tricks than they had been accustomed to performing. On the whole, the tricks performed by the non-sleight of hand card enthusiasts at that time were so simple that the secret was easily discovered by the person or persons they were intended to mystify.

Then and there I decided that something should be done to remedy this situation, and that is when I started to write this book. There is no doubt in my mind that almost everyone likes to see a good card trick, when presented entertainingly. The latest statistics show that of the fifty million Americans who play cards, approximately two million attempt to perform a card trick now and then. Add to this number the hundred thousand amateur and semi-professional magicians in this country and we find a good proportion of the American population interested in performing card tricks. In all likelihood these figures are gross underestimates. My experience has shown that there is an almost universal interest in card tricks, and rare indeed is the man who has not at some time in his life attempted to perform a trick with a deck of cards.

My first step in developing a new era of card tricks was to consult some of the world's outstanding magicians, including Dunninger, Cardini, Dai Vernon, John Mulholland, Francis Carlyle, Blackstone, Harlan Tarbell, and many others whose names are listed in this book. These men felt virtually the same way I did about the state of non-sleight of hand card tricks, and were most co-operative in supplying one or more of their favorite tricks for inclusion in this book. However, in almost every instance these consultations followed the same pattern. After describing or performing the trick, the magician invariably said, "You see, John, this trick is a good one, but it requires sleight of hand to perform."

In any event, I asked for, and received, their permission to include these effects in this volume. My next step was to remove all need for manipulative skill from these tricks. I spent hours on each one, devising new methods of execution to replace the sleight of hand used in the original tricks. The next move was to

3

test the individual tricks in their new form. Each trick was performed before a critical group of magicians, and all weaknesses were removed. Some of my most gratifying moments—during the course of writing this book—occurred when I went back to the magicians who contributed the tricks and performed them, using the new methods. That these men could not believe that no sleight of hand was involved in the trick was the supreme accolade.

I have also included approximately thirty original tricks of my own in this book. These tricks, I am certain, set a new high mark in non-sleight of hand card tricks. They have been tested by me over a five-year period, and I have fooled some of the world's leading magicians with many of them.

Remembering that many good effects have been ruined by a poor presentation, I then sat down and wrote little stories (known as "patter" in the magic world) to accompany most of the tricks. The patter serves a two-fold purpose; it makes the trick more interesting to the spectator and it gives a logical reason for the use of those subtleties which have replaced the sleight of hand.

In order to eliminate the sleight of hand in most card tricks, I had to devise many new principles, heretofore unknown, such as:

1. New mathematical formulas.
2. New dodges and subtleties.
3. New ruses, to help the performer apply psychology as an aid to deception.
4. New means of misdirection (the art of diverting the spectator's attention away from the secret).
5. New simple moves that appear to the spectator to be clever sleight of hand.

In learning to do these tricks, the reader must bear in mind that although no manipulative skill is necessary to perform them, they must be studied carefully before being performed in public. In learning a card trick, the scientific approach should be employed. First, pick out a trick that you like particularly. Study it for a day or so, learning the patter and presentation, and then perform the effect without an audience until you no longer have to think about each step. Then, try the trick on one of your closest friends and get his reaction to it, for very frequently a spectator will see more flaws in the presentation than the performer himself will. After you have corrected any flaws in the trick, perform it again for your friends until you have completely mastered it. You are then able to perform for a perfect stranger without any fear of embarrassment. Next, pick out another and follow the same procedure until you have learned several card tricks. Blend these tricks into a routine, so that each naturally follows the preceding one, and you will have added that professional touch to your performance.

A few words of caution and we will be able to go on to the description of the tricks themselves. For your first tricks, don't select any that require two packs of cards, or one which entails memorizing several things. Select a more simplified trick—there are many in this book—and gradually work your way up to the more complicated ones. In general, the simpler tricks will be found in the front part of the book, the more complicated ones toward the back. But this is not a rule, for I have not followed any set pattern or order in listing the tricks. Read them all.

Learn to use patter with your tricks; that will make your performance more entertaining to your audience. It is not expected that you will memorize the patter in this book; the patter has been included only as a guide to you in preparing your own.

When performing, be natural. Naturalness cannot be achieved by memorizing your patter, but by having just an outline of what you wish to say.

Do not perform all the tricks you know for the same audience at one time. Present just a few tricks, well performed, and retire. Assort your tricks intelligently. Plan a varied routine consisting of dissimilar tricks, with no two of them using the same principle. Don't let appreciation or applause induce you to perform as an encore a trick you haven't perfected or one too similar to a trick you've already done. Leave them wanting more.

Never reveal how a trick is done. A good card trick is like a precious diamond: it must be guarded very carefully. When you have mystified your audience with a card trick, you will usually be met with the question, "How did you do it?" Don't tell! If you do, your standing as a performer will drop.

After completing a trick, you will frequently be asked to "Do it again." Never repeat a trick for the same audience at the same performance, for this can easily lead to exposing the secret. The value of a trick lies in its mystification. If you repeat a trick, you are no longer entertaining your audience, for they will not be mystified by the second performance. On the contrary, they will be attempting to figure out how the trick was done, and the psychology of deception will not be present. Second, it isn't very comforting for a performer who has just completely awed his audience to repeat a trick, and to have some smart alec learn the secret and reveal it to the rest of the audience. So I repeat, *never repeat a trick for the same audience at the same performance.* This book certainly contains enough material for an evening's entertainment without the performer's having to repeat himself. When your audience is baffled, they will credit you with possessing manipulative skill which is not yours; and they will spread your reputation as a card trickster. But if they know how you do your tricks, when your name is mentioned they will reveal your secrets.

If, while you are performing, you should run into a smart alec who consistently annoys you, ignore him. Should he become insistent about being permitted to shuffle and cut the cards at times when this would not be practical, merely say to him, "I'm doing this trick my way. If you care to do a trick, *you* can do all the shuffling and cutting you want." Hand him the deck. He will usually be caught completely by surprise by this action, for even if he knows a card trick, it will not compare with the tricks you will learn from this book. Should he continue to annoy you, place the pack of cards back into the card case and say, "That's enough card tricks for today." Your audience will be angry with him, and instead of being the center of attraction as he wished to be, he will be the object of everyone else's scorn. Remember, if your performance is good, the audience is on your side and will resent anything or anyone who interferes with the show. Should you see someone else doing a card trick, pay him the same courtesy and consideration as you would like others to pay you.

But that's enough of my chatter. Get yourself a pack of cards, and let's go on with the tricks.

JOHN SCARNE

Fairview, N.J.
August, 1950

1. CALLING THE CARDS

PRESENTATION AND EFFECT

A spectator shuffles a pack of playing cards very thoroughly and hands it to the performer, who spreads the deck face down all over the table. He mixes the cards all around, and invites the spectator to help him. Now he explains that he has X-ray vision. He can see through cards—knows what denomination and suit each one is, even though they are face down and all mixed up. To prove his statement, the performer asks a spectator merely to point to one of the face-down cards on the table, and he will name it. The performer asks another spectator to make a list of the cards he calls, and then, when several cards have been called, the performer will give the cards to the spectator to verify whether they were called correctly. Needless to say, the performer calls every designated card correctly, and never makes a single mistake. Checking the list with the card proves this.

THE SECRET

The spectator shuffles, then hands the deck to the performer. Without being observed, the performer must look at the bottom card of the deck and remember it. He spreads the cards face down all over the table, keeping his eye on the location of the bottom card at all times. If the spectator helps mix the cards, the performer must be especially careful in following the location of the bottom card whose face he is remembering. When the spectator points to the first card, the performer names the card which was on the bottom of the deck. He now picks up the card pointed at, looks at the card as he does so, but does not let the spectators see it. The spectator points to another card, and the performer calls the card which he has just picked up and looked at, which was the first card pointed at.

Example: The bottom card of the deck was the king of spades. When the spectator points to the first card, the performer calls out, "King of spades." The other spectator writes this down. The performer picks up the card pointed at, looking at it as he does, and sees that it is the 3 of diamonds. The spectator points to the second card; the performer calls out, "Three of diamonds." The other spectator writes this down. The performer picks up the card and sees that it is the 6 of spades. The spectator points to the third card, and the performer calls out, "Six of spades." The other spectator writes this down, and the performer picks up the card, looking at it as he does so. The cards the performer picks up are placed one on top of the other, forming a deck. The performer must make sure that he does not allow the spectators to see the cards as he picks them up.

After doing this several times, the performer announces that calling as many cards as he has ought to prove that he has X-ray vision. Then he says that he will pick out *one last card* himself

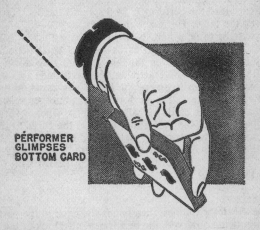

PERFORMER
GLIMPSES
BOTTOM CARD

and call it, just for fun. Here is where the trick comes in. You realize, of course, that the performer has not been calling the card before he picks it up, but has been calling the card he picked up previously and is holding in his hand. To straighten this out, the performer decides to pick the last card. He makes sure to pick the card that was at the bottom of the deck at the start of the trick, whose location on the table he memorized. When he points to his "located" card, he calls out the name of the card he last picked from the table, which was the last card the spectator pointed at. Following our example above, we know that in this case the card at the bottom of the deck, whose location the performer knows, was the king of spades. We also know that "king of spades" was the name the performer called when the spectator pointed to the first card on the table. Therefore, when the performer picks the king of spades from the table he must put the card with the group he has been picking from the table as though it were the first card called. If he has been putting each card picked up on top of the previous card, he must put the king of spades on the bottom. If he has been putting each selected card below the previous card, the king must go on top. This done, he can be sure his group will match the list made by the other spectator.

2. ACES FROM THE POCKET

PRESENTATION AND EFFECT

The performer invites a spectator to shuffle thoroughly and cut the cards. When the pack is handed back to the performer, he places the pack in his coat pocket, and mentions that he is going to attempt to find the four aces while the pack is in his pocket. He puts his hand into his pocket, and after quite a bit of fumbling, produces one of the aces. This is continued until all four aces are produced by the performer.

THE SECRET

This trick is merely a bold maneuver on the part of the performer, who has already taken the aces out of the pack and placed them in his pocket. After the deck has been shuffled and cut, it is placed into the pocket alongside the four aces.

To be more convincing, this should be done after another trick. A good one to follow this with would be "Calling the Cards."

3. THE UPSIDE-DOWN DECK

This trick comes from Francis Carlyle, one of the best card men in America.

PRESENTATION AND EFFECT

The performer holds the deck in his hand and requests the spectator to cut the deck at approximately the center of the pack. The performer and the spectator each hold half the deck. The performer selects a card from his half of the deck, and looks at it. He requests the spectator to select a card from his own group, and to look at it also. The performer and spectator exchange selected cards, but do not look at each other's card. The performer now holds the spectator's selected card, the spectator holds the performer's selected card. Each inserts the card he holds face down into his portion of the deck. The spectator is instructed to shuffle the cards he holds.

The performer asks the spectator to hand him about half of

the cards he holds. The performer reverses this group, turning them face up, and places them on the bottom of his own group, but leaves about one third of the narrow edge of this group uncovered. Taking the remainder of the spectator's group, the performer reverses them so that they are face up, and places them on top of the groups he holds in his hand, but does not cover them completely. He allows all three groups to be seen; the spectator's face-up cards on the bottom, the performer's face-down cards in the middle, and the spectator's face-up cards on the top. After the cards have been shown, as described above, the performer squares up the deck, and goes into his spiel, as follows:

"Ladies and Gentlemen, I am now going to attempt a remarkable feat that requires considerable manipulative skill. I not only am going to have the entire pack straighten itself out, so that all the cards will be facing the same way (all face down), I am going to go much further. I am going to have the two selected cards reverse themselves in the pack, so that they will be the only cards face up in the deck, whereas the rest of the pack will be face down."

The performer asks the spectator to name the card he selected. Then the performer names his own selected card. The performer then snaps his finger, and says, "Presto" (or waves his hands over the pack, murmuring a few magic words). Spreading the cards from hand to hand, it is found that all the cards are face down with the exception of the two selected cards that are face up. Truly a remarkable finish!

THE SECRET

The performer has a card reversed (turned face up) on the bottom of the pack. He has memorized the face of this card. After the spectator cuts the deck, the performer immediately selects a card from his group. Holding the selected card, face down, in his right hand, the performer requests the spectator to select a card from his own group and to note its value. While this is being done, the performer reverses the group of cards held in his left hand, so that the bottom card which he memorized is now on top. By reversing the cards, the performer faces all his cards up, except the top card, which is face down.

The performer and spectator exchange selected cards but do not look at them. Each inserts the card he holds into the group he holds. The spectator shuffles his group. (This is done so that the spectator may not judge the whereabouts of the card he inserted in his group.)

The performer takes half the group from the spectator, reverses the entire group, and places them face up on the bottom of the group he holds, leaving about one third of the group protruding. Taking the spectator's remaining cards, he reverses them, and places them face up on top of the cards he holds, but allows all three groups to be seen.

The trick is now completed except for the fact that the performer does not call the card he selected, but instead names the memorized card that was placed on the bottom of the pack.

It is suggested that when doing this trick, or any trick where a card or cards are reversed in the deck, you never use a pack of cards with an all-over design on the back. Use a pack with a white border. The reason for this is that it is easy to spot the overturned card in a pack of all-over design.

4. TRAVELING ACES

One of magician Charlie Nagle's favorite tricks.

PRESENTATION AND EFFECT

The performer places four aces in a row, face up on the table. He then deals one card face down on top of each ace, but lets the ace still show. He deals two more rounds of face-down cards on top of each ace until he has dealt three indifferent cards. The aces are turned face down, but are kept in their original position (an ace being the bottom card of each of the four groups). The four piles are placed one on top of the other, and placed on top of the rest of the deck.

The performer deals the top sixteen cards into four groups, dealing one card at a time to each group in poker-dealing fashion. The fourth pile naturally is comprised of the four aces. This pile is marked by turning the bottom ace in the group face up. One of the other three piles is selected by the spectator, and the bottom card of that pile is turned face up.

Now the performer states that wherever he places the face-up ace, the rest of the aces will travel to join it. The performer transfers the face-up ace to the pile selected by the spectator by placing it face down on top of this pile. The face-up indifferent

card at the bottom of the spectator's selected pile is transferred to the top of pile where the face-up ace was.

The performer snaps his fingers and says, "Aces travel." Upon turning up the two heaps, the aces are found together in the spectator's pile, and the pile where the aces were thought to be in the first place is found to contain four indifferent cards.

THE SECRET

The cards are dealt out, as stated, up to the point when the sixteen cards are redealt off the top of the pack. The first four cards are dealt out to form four separate piles, the fourth card dealt being an ace. The performer deals the fifth card off the deck, holds it in his hand, and remarks (pointing to the fourth card dealt), "That card is an ace."

As a rule, someone will say either, "It is not an ace," or, "It should be an ace." But, regardless of what they say, you do a little cheating at this point by placing the card you are holding in your hand (which was to have been the fifth card dealt) underneath the deck, which you still hold in your other hand. Do

12

this as quickly as possible, then instantly turn up the fourth card on the table, which is the ace, as if to prove that the ace was really there.

Now continue to deal the cards face down, beginning with the first group, one card at a time to each group, until there are four piles comprised of four cards each. Of course, we know that the fourth pile has one ace at the bottom and three indifferent cards on top. Since we put the fifth card on the bottom of the deck, we changed the position of the cards, so that the third pile has an indifferent card at the bottom and the remaining three aces on top. The first and second piles are both comprised of four indifferent cards.

The performer must now force the spectator to select the third pile. This is done as follows: Ask the spectator to point to two piles out of the first three. Should the spectator point to piles one and two, the performer removes these two piles, leaving pile three. Should the spectator point to two piles, one of these being pile three, the performer takes away the pile which was not pointed at. This method is repeated with the remaining two groups, and the third pile is forced on the spectator. Then the bottom card of pile three is turned face up.

The only piles remaining are three and four.

The performer exchanges the upturned ace for the face-up indifferent card in pile three, as explained in "Presentation and Effect." Upon turning the cards in pile three face up, we find that the aces have "traveled."

Seldom will a spectator notice the performer placing the fifth card on the bottom of the deck. His mind is on the ace, and he does not know what you are up to until the effect is completed.

5. DUNNINGER'S MENTAL CARD TRICK

I asked my friend Joseph Dunninger, the famed mentalist, for a trick for this book. He gave me this, undoubtedly one of the most talked of card tricks ever performed. This trick has been sold for as much as $200.

PRESENTATION AND EFFECT

The performer shuffles the pack of cards, or permits a spectator to do so. The performer selects a card from the deck, or has the spectator point to the card he wants the performer to select. This card is taken from the pack and placed in the performer's pocket without anyone's looking at it.

The performer produces a crystal ball wrapped in a handkerchief. Removing the handkerchief, he proceeds to polish the crystal ball with it. He then asks the spectator to look into the crystal ball, and to concentrate. Soon the spectator sees a card appear in the crystal. He is asked to call out the name of the card he sees.

The performer takes the selected card out of his pocket, and it *is* the one just named by the spectator.

THE SECRET

The requirements are a deck of cards, a handkerchief, a small crystal ball, which can be purchased in most novelty stores, and a miniature card about the size of a postage stamp that can also be purchased in most novelty stores.

Paste this miniature card on the crystal ball, then wrap it in the handkerchief. Before the start of the trick, take out of the

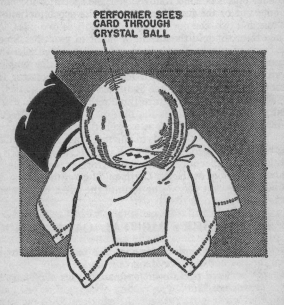

PERFORMER SEES
CARD THROUGH
CRYSTAL BALL

deck the card that matches the one you have pasted on the crystal ball, and place it in your pocket.

When the trick is being done, it doesn't matter which card is selected, as this card has nothing to do with the trick. The card you need for the trick you have stolen from the pack and placed in your pocket before the start of the trick.

You then produce the crystal ball wrapped in the handkerchief. While pretending to wipe the crystal ball, be sure that you have the miniature card to one side and that it is covered by

14

the handkerchief. Expose about half the top of the crystal ball.

Now you request the spectator to look down into the crystal and tell you if he sees a card there. Naturally, he replies, "No." (If you are holding the crystal as described above, he will look from top to bottom, and cannot see the card because it is on the side.)

Turning the crystal, so that the card is on the bottom, you turn to the spectator and suggest that he concentrate more deeply, that the materialization will then become more apparent. You ask the spectator to look into the crystal again, and he is completely entranced when he sees a card which is magnified many times its size by the crystal. The spectator is asked to name the card he sees.

When he names the card, the performer turns the crystal ball, so that the card goes to one side, and the spectator sees the card vanish.

The performer reaches into his pocket and produces the card which matches the card seen in the crystal, leaving the selected card in the pocket. Of course, the spectator thinks you have produced the card he asked you to select at the beginning. This makes the trick a big success. The spectator never dreams you have produced a card you secretly pocketed before the start of the trick.

6. BEHIND THE BACK CARD TRICK

A favorite trick of magician Carmine Laino.

PRESENTATION AND EFFECT

The performer shuffles the pack, then holds it behind his back. He requests a spectator to cut the cards anywhere he desires and to look at and memorize the card he cut to (bottom card of the cut group). Then the spectator is requested to replace the cut group on top of the deck.

The performer looks into the spectator's eyes and states that the spectator's eyes still have a picture of the card he just looked at. The performer looks through the pack and finds the spectator's card.

THE SECRET

When shuffling the cards, the performer must be sure to take a peek at the bottom card of the deck and to remember it. The spectator cuts a group of cards and is told to look at the card he cut to. The performer turns to face the spectator and asks, "Have you looked at the card yet?" This is the secret. While turning, the performer takes the bottom card, which he knows,

15

and places it on top of the cards he holds. When the spectator says, "Yes, I've looked at the card," he is instructed to place his group on top of the cards held by the performer. This means that the card the spectator looked at will be placed on top of the card the performer is keeping in mind. Therefore, it's very simple to find the spectator's card. The performer, looking through the cards, knows that the card the spectator looked at is above the card whose face he has memorized.

7. SCARNE'S PREDICTO

PRESENTATION AND EFFECT
The performer removes a pack of cards from the card box, and places them face down on the table. The performer produces a small business card about half the size of a playing card. If he has no business card, he may use a small piece of paper. He announces that he will write a prediction on the card, but will not tell what he has written just yet, as the prediction is what he is going to compel the spectator to furnish. After the prediction is written, he requests the spectator to cut the cards by raising the cut portion only about two or three inches above the rest of the deck. While the spectator has the cards cut and raised up as described, the performer places the business card between the two cut portions of the deck (in other words, he places the business card on top of the cards on the table). Then he instructs the spectator to replace the cards he holds on top of the pack. The performer cuts the pack several times and squares up the pack.

The performer announces that if he has been successful he has compelled the spectator to cut the cards so that the business card is resting between the ace and 10 of diamonds.

To prove his statement, the performer deals the cards one at a time face down onto the table, until he comes to the business card. The performer takes the card above the business card, the business card itself, and the card below it from the deck and places these three to one side. He then continues to deal out the remainder of the deck, which proves to any skeptics that he had only one business card in the deck. Upon turning over the business card, it reads, "You have placed me between the ace of diamonds and the 10 of diamonds." The two cards are turned over. We see the ace of diamonds and the 10 of diamonds, bearing out the prediction.

THE SECRET

Before the start of the trick the performer gets two business cards exactly alike, or he may use two identical pieces of paper.

16

On one of the business cards he writes, "You have placed me between the ace and 10 of diamonds." Looking through the deck, he finds these two cards, and places the business card between them. He has the ace face down, the business card with his writing face down (printed side up), and the 10 face down. He is careful to have the business card completely covered, so that it is not sticking out the sides. Then he places these prepared cards face down near the bottom of the deck, about five cards from the bottom. Then he places the deck back into the card box.

The other business card, which is identical with the one he just prepared, is the card the performer will pull out of his pocket and use when doing the trick. Therefore, he must remember to write on the same side of this card as he did on his prepared business card which is already in the deck. The opposite side of

VISITING CARD ADHERES TO FACE OF CARD

this business card must be prepared before the start of the trick —by placing a piece of beeswax on it, which will cause it to stick to the face of the card above it when it is inserted in the deck. You can see now, that since the cards are being dealt face down, this card will be undetectable because it is stuck to the face of one of the cards. The only business card that will be found is the one which the performer prepared.

At the beginning of the trick, the performer produces the business card, writes the prediction on the unwaxed side, has the spectator cut the deck by raising the cut portion about three inches off the table. The reason for not lifting the cards higher is we don't want the spectator to see at what card he is cutting the pack.

Then the spectator replaces the cut portion on top of the deck. The performer in the act of cutting the cards must really press them together tightly, so that the waxed card will stick to the one above it. Now when the cards are dealt out, we will find the first business card between the two cards predicted. Since it is identical, the spectator thinks this is the only one used. Now our trick is a success.

The performer may predict any two cards he desires so long as he prepares himself for this trick as directed above.

8. THE FOUR ROYAL FLUSHES

PRESENTATION AND EFFECT

The performer removes a deck of cards from the card case, cuts the deck in two, riffle shuffles both halves together, has a spectator cut the cards, and squares up the deck.

The performer states that he only needs the high cards (10, jack, queen, king, ace) for this experiment. He then turns the pack face up, and deals the cards into two groups, high cards and low cards. The low cards he deals face up, the high cards he deals face down. After the cards have been separated, the performer asks the spectator to cut the high cards as often as he wishes, and to deal out four poker hands face down onto the table. Upon turning over these poker hands, we find that each hand is a Royal Flush.

THE SECRET

Prepare the deck before the start of the trick, as follows: First, take out all the high cards (ace, king, queen, jack, 10) of each suit and arrange them in the following order: four aces, four kings, four queens, four jacks, four 10's. The four aces must be arranged—first clubs, then diamonds, then hearts, then spades. Kings, queens, jacks, and 10's must be arranged the same way (clubs, diamonds, hearts, and spades).

Place this group of twenty arranged cards on top of the pack and put the pack back into the card case. When ready to perform, remove the cards from the box, cut the pack into two

18

equal halves, and riffle shuffle the cards once (try to give them a good riffle shuffle).

This shuffle takes away all thoughts of a previous stack, although the stack remains. What actually has happened is that the twenty high cards have been shuffled into the low cards, so that when the performer separates the low from the high cards, he is actually taking the high cards out of the pack exactly as they were stacked. The spectator's cut does not alter this setup in the least.

9. EGG A LA CARD

Paul Clive, the popular English magician, gets the credit for this mystifier.

PRESENTATION AND EFFECT

The performer removes a deck of cards from the card case and requests a spectator to call a number between 10 and 20. The performer deals the cards face down one at a time onto the table, forming a pile, until he has dealt the number called by the spectator. The performer picks up this group of cards, and says he is going to add together the two digits of the number called. Then he again deals the cards face down onto the table from the group he holds, until he reaches the card whose position in the group is the same as the number he arrived at. This card he then places to one side to be used in this experiment. He puts aside the remainder of the deck.

For example: The spectator calls out number 18. The performer deals eighteen cards face down into a pile. He picks up the eighteen cards and adds the two digits of the number: 1 plus 8 equals 9. The total being 9, the performer deals nine cards one at a time face down into a pile from the group he holds. The ninth card he places to one side, announcing it will be the card used in the trick. Neither the spectator nor the performer has seen this card.

The performer passes around a hard-boiled egg for examination. The egg is then handed back to the performer.

The performer rolls the egg back and forth across the selected card. While doing this he utters the magic words, "Hokus pokus alla gazam." Then he states that the egg will name the card selected. Putting his ear close to the egg as he rolls it back and forth, the performer claims he hears the egg say, "Shell me, shell me." The performer shells the egg. On the white of the egg is found written the name of the selected card. Upon turning over this card, we find the egg named it correctly.

19

The performer must force a card on the spectator. This is done as follows: The deck of cards is prepared previously by placing the desired card at number 9 from the top of the pack. Regardless of what number the spectator calls out between 10 and 20, follow the directions described in the presentation and you will always select the ninth card from the top of the deck for use in this experiment. Truly a great force.

The egg must be prepared as follows: Dissolve one ounce of alum in one pint of vinegar. Dip a small brush into this solution and print the name of the card you are going to force (ninth card from top of deck) on the egg shell. Let the egg dry until no signs of writing remain. Then boil the egg for about ten to sixteen minutes (preferably sixteen), and let the egg cool off. That's all there is to it.

You are now set to perform "Egg à la Card."

10. THE TURN AROUND CARDS

PRESENTATION AND EFFECT

The performer deals eight cards off the top of the pack, face up, to form a row on the table. He informs the spectator that when he turns his back he wants the spectator to turn one or more of the cards around (end for end), and when this is done the performer will turn back to face the spectator and name the cards that have been turned.

THE SECRET

The pack has been prearranged by placing the following eight cards face down on top of the deck: 3 of clubs, 6 of spades, 5 of clubs, 9 of spades, 7 of clubs, 6 of hearts, 3 of spades. He must place these cards so that the stems on the spades and clubs on the pips in the center of the cards are all facing the same direction, and the point of the center pip of the heart card is facing the same direction as the stem of the spades and club cards. Now, when he deals these cards face up onto the table, the center pips will all be facing the same way. He must make note of their direction. When the spectator turns some of the cards around, it will be easy for the performer to name the turned cards, as the center pips will be facing the opposite direction of what they were formerly.

The performer may use other cards than those mentioned, particularly odd-numbered cards.

11. IT'S A NATURAL

This unusual trick, using a borrowed deck of cards and a packet of matches, is the joint creation of the writer-magician, Martin Gardner, and his magician associate, Bill Simon.

PRESENTATION AND EFFECT

The performer borrows a deck of cards and a pack of book matches. If they are not available, he uses his own. The performer requests the spectator to shuffle the deck of cards thoroughly and to cut the deck several times. Then he is instructed to deal seven cards face down onto the table. The performer looks through the seven cards.

The performer studies the seven cards for a few moments, then writes a prediction on a piece of paper, folds it, and puts it to one side. He does not allow the spectator to see what he has written. The performer squares up the seven cards to form one group, and places them face up in the center of the table.

Now, the performer requests the spectator to remove one by one as many matches from the packet as he desires, and to place each match on top of the group of seven cards. (He may remove one or all the matches, or none of them. How many he uses is left to the spectator's discretion.)

The number of matches the spectator removes determines the number in the group of seven cards at which we find the card predicted by the performer. Counting to the number designated by the matches, we find the card the performer had written on the paper at the start of the trick.

THE SECRET

The spectator may shuffle or cut the cards to his heart's content, because the seven cards can be selected at random. When the spectator deals seven cards onto the table, the performer

21

studies them for a minute and memorizes the card which would be third from the top if the cards were placed face down. This is the card he notes on the piece of paper. He folds up the groups of cards and places them face up in the center of the table. That's all there is to it; the rest of the trick depends upon the number of matches the spectator decides to use.

The only preparation necessary for this trick is that the performer must make sure the packet contains exactly eleven matches, no more and no less. If the spectator's match box contains more, the performer uses enough matches in the act of lighting a cigarette to leave only eleven remaining. If the packet contains less than eleven matches, the performer uses his own, which he naturally prepared beforehand.

The performer does not state what he is going to do at the start of the trick, therefore he may make use of the matches in any logical manner he sees fit. For this purpose, the inventors of this trick have worked out twelve methods for locating the predicted card regardless of whether all, some, or none, of the matches were removed by the spectator.

After the spectator has torn off a number of matches, the performer counts these matches to himself. That's all there is to it. The rest of the trick is worked by the performer using either the number of matches torn off, or the number of matches remaining in the folder; and by counting from the top of the cards face up, or from the top of the cards face down. The reason for placing the seven cards in a pile face up on the table is so that it will not seem unnatural to count the cards face up if it is necessary.

To make it easier for the readers to follow, let us illustrate. Let us say the performer noticed that the 2 of spades was third card from the top of the seven-card group when the cards were placed face down. This is the card he notes on the piece of paper and puts aside. He then places the group of cards face up on the table.

Now the performer must memorize the following so that he will count the cards correctly regardless of the number of matches used.

Spectator tears out eleven matches. Performer counts the matches, and says, "You have removed eleven matches, therefore eleven is our key number." If the spectator removes no matches, the performer states, "Since you have removed no matches, let's see how many are in the packet." Finding eleven, he says, "Our key number is eleven."

In either case the performer takes the group of cards, still face up, and counts to 11 (by placing the top card of the group on the bottom with each count). The 2 of spades will appear after the eleventh card is counted.

If the spectator tears off ten matches, the performer picks up the group of cards and turns them face down. Then he counts down to the tenth card, which will be the 2 of spades. (He counts by transferring the top card of the group to the bottom with each count.) If one match is torn off, he counts the number remaining in the match book—there are ten matches left—and counts to ten, as described above.

If the spectator tears off nine matches or two matches, the performer does as follows. If two matches were torn off, the performer turns the group of cards face down, counts off the top two cards, and turns over the third card, which will be the 2 of spades, as predicted. If nine matches are torn off, he counts the number remaining in the match book, finds that two matches remain, and counts as described above.

If the spectator tears off eight matches or three matches, the performer does as follows. If eight matches were torn off, the performer counts the matches remaining in the match book. There are three matches left. He turns the group of cards face down, counts down, and turns over the third card, which is the two of spades. If three matches were torn off, he counts as described.

If the spectator tears off seven matches or four matches, the performer makes use of the four count. He picks the cards up and counts them face up. He counts off four cards, and the fifth card will be the two of spades.

If the spectator tears off six matches or five matches, the performer makes use of the five count. He counts the cards face up, and finds the two of spades at the count of five.

12. THE TALKING CARD

My acknowledgements to Al Altman, motion picture producer and magician.

PRESENTATION AND EFFECT

The performer removes a deck of cards from the card case and deals ten cards in a row face down onto the table. He deals from left to right, the first card being the extreme left, the tenth card being the extreme right. Placing the remainder of the deck to one side, he tells the spectator to remove one card at a time from the extreme right, and place it on the extreme left. The spectator may move from one to nine cards, as many as he desires. Then he is to slide the row over so that the row of ten cards will be in the same place and will look exactly the same as it was before any cards were moved. When the spectator understands the instructions, the performer turns his back, and the spectator moves as many cards as he desires as instructed above. When the entire row is in its proper place, the spectator informs the performer it is all right for him to turn back to face the audience.

Now the performer looks at the row of cards, and concentrates. He turns over (face up) one of the cards in the row. The number of pips on the card is equal to the number of cards the spectator moved. For example: The spectator moved three cards, the performer turns up a 3-spot. No matter how many cards the spectator moves, the performer will always turn up a card equal to that number. The spectator is told to be especially careful, in an effort to fool the performer. After the spectator has done this once, and the performer has turned up the right number, the spectator may do it again and again, and each time the performer will turn up the right number. This trick can be continued as long as the performer sees fit.

THE SECRET

The performer arranges ten cards—from ace through 10, using all the suits—and places them face down on top of the deck. The 10 is the top card, below that the 9, and so on down to the ace, which will be the tenth card in the deck. When the performer removes the deck from the card case, he is ready to perform, having already prearranged the cards. He deals ten cards off the top of the deck face down in a row, starting from his left and ending at his right. Naturally, the 10-spot is at the extreme left (being the first card dealt); the ace, at the extreme right (last card dealt.)

To illustrate the trick: The spectator moves five cards *one at a time* from the right to the left. The performer turns up the end card at the left. This card will be the 5-spot. The performer turns the card face down again, and leaves it in its same position in the row. The spectator tries again. The second time, the performer turns up the *sixth card* from the left in the row. The card turned up, following the example above, will be the 2-spot, which will prove to be the same number of cards the spectator moved. The third time this is tried, the performer would have to turn up the *eighth* card from the left in the row.

This effect can be repeated as often as desired, but the performer must always total the number of cards moved to determine which card to turn up. In the example given above, the first card the performer turns over is the one at the extreme left. This is always the correct number moved by the spectator the first time. The second time, the performer turns over the sixth card from the left because he knows in this case that five cards had been moved at first—he goes one higher than that and turns over the sixth card. Following the example above, the sixth card is a deuce, meaning the spectator moved two cards. The performer adds: five cards moved the first time, two cards the second time, total—seven cards moved altogether. Therefore, the third time the performer turns up a card, always counting one higher, he turns up the eighth card from the left. This will be found to be a 4-spot, the same number the spectator moved. If the performer desires to continue, he adds: five moved the first time, plus two the second, plus four the third time, total—eleven cards moved altogether. The next time the performer turns up a card, counting one higher, he would have to turn up the twelfth card. When his total is over ten, he drops the 10 and counts the remainder, therefore he moves the second card from the left. This method has been explained in detail so that the reader will see clearly how this system of counting works. However, when performing this trick, the performer just remembers his last total and adds the last number of cards moved. That will be the number of the card from the left to be faced. He doesn't have to remember how many cards were moved each time as long as he remembers the correct total and adds the number of the last card turned up.

13. YOU DO AS I DO

A specialty of many of America's top magicians.

PRESENTATION AND EFFECT

The performer produces two packs of playing cards, hands one to the spectator, keeps one for himself. As he hands the

pack to the spectator, he tells him, "Success or failure of this experiment depends on you." The spectator is instructed to duplicate the performer's every move. The fact is stressed that if two people do exactly the same thing, or as close to the same thing as possible, they must naturally arrive at the same conclusion. "However," the performer warns, "any deviation will cause failure."

The performer starts to shuffle his pack, and requests the spectator to do likewise, following as closely as possible with his own deck. At the completion of the shuffle, they exchange decks, the performer handing his to the spectator, the spectator handing his to the performer.

The performer selects a card from the pack he is now holding, and requests the spectator to do the same with the deck he holds. Each looks at the card he has selected and memorizes it. Each places his card face down on top of the deck he is holding.

Now the performer and spectator each places the deck he holds on the floor or on a near-by table. Each cuts his own deck. Each places the bottom half of the deck on top of the top half which he has just cut. They exchange decks. The performer takes the spectator's deck, the spectator takes the performer's. Each looks through the cards and picks out the card he selected before. Each places the card he has taken out of the deck face down on the floor or table, whichever is being used in this experiment. The performer announces that if the experiment has been successful—because they have both done the same things —the two cards selected must also be the same. The performer turns over the two cards selected and we find they are identical.

THE SECRET

While the performer shuffles his deck at the beginning of the trick he must make sure to see the bottom card of the deck. The packs are then exchanged. The spectator now has the performer's deck, on top of which he places the card he has selected. Then the spectator cuts the deck. By placing the bottom half of the deck on top of the cut half, the spectator is placing the bottom card, which the performer has seen and has memorized, on top of the card he selected. Now they exchange packs again. All the performer has to do is go through the spectator's cards, and when he finds the card that was at the bottom of the deck, he knows that the card under this is the one the spectator selected. The performer removes this card from the deck, pretending that it is the same card he selected. You can see, therefore, that it is not necessary for the performer to remember the card he really did select, as it has nothing to do with the trick and will only confuse him. The spectator who knows nothing about how the trick is done looks through the performer's deck and picks out the card which he had selected. This is how we find two identical cards at the conclusion of the trick, the performer proving that "You do as I do" works.

14. YOU DO AS I DO
(Using one pack of cards)

Sometimes two decks of cards are not available, so if the performer would like to get an effect similar to "You Do as I Do" (performed with two decks) this trick will do exactly that for him, allowing him to use one deck. The method and patter come from the brilliant mind of Al Baker, "The Dean of American Magicians," in collaboration with Dr. Ben Braude, the clever New York amateur magician.

PRESENTATION AND EFFECT

The performer shuffles the deck of cards (or allows the spectator to do it) and requests the spectator to hold his hand out palm up. After the shuffle, the pack is placed face down on the spectator's outstretched hand.

The performer says, "I am going to attempt to put you under my direct physical and mental control." The performer then cuts off the top half of the deck, keeping it for himself, leaving the bottom half for the spectator. The performer instructs the spectator to follow his every action and to "Do as I do" as exactly as is possible. The performer announces, "I am going to select a card from the group I hold; look at it and remember it. I want you to do the same with your group." After each has looked at his own card, the performer says, "I am going to place my card face down on top of the group of cards I hold. I want you to do likewise." Then the performer cuts his group of cards, and instructs the spectator to do the same, saying, "Cut your group so that the card you selected will be completely lost." After the cut, the performer and spectator exchange groups. The performer takes the spectator's cards, the spectator takes the performer's.

The performer tells the spectator, "I want you to look through the cards you now hold" (performer's original group) "and to pick out the card which is closest to the card you selected and are remembering. For example, if the card you selected before was the deuce of spades, look through your cards and pick out the deuce of clubs. This is the card most similar because they are both deuces and are both black. If you cannot find the deuce of clubs, pick out the deuce of diamonds because that is the next closest. The suits run: spades, clubs, diamonds, hearts. If you haven't the deuce of clubs, or diamonds, pick out the deuce of hearts. If you have no deuces at all, the card nearest to the deuce of spades, which is your selected card, is the ace of spades because it is the next lower numerical value of the suit you selected. Thereafter, the cards would run: ace of spades, ace of clubs, ace of diamonds, ace of hearts. When you have found the card most like yours, take it out of the group and place it face down on the table."

The performer must make sure the spectator understands what he is to do before proceeding with the trick.

While the spectator is looking through his cards to find the card closest to the one he selected, the performer looks through the cards he holds and removes the card the spectator originally selected. This he places face down on the table.

The performer then says, "Remember what I told you before, that I would get you under my complete physical and mental control. Well, I did just that when I selected my card first, forcing you to select a card most similar to mine. Of course, you didn't realize you were doing this, but now it will be proven."

The performer now names the card originally selected by the spectator, and turns it over for all to see. Then he names the card the spectator placed on the table, announcing it was the card selected by the performer. Turning this card over ends the trick with a very dramatic result.

THE SECRET

The performer shuffles the cards and makes sure he sees and remembers the bottom card of the deck. He may allow the spectator to shuffle if he thinks he'll still be able to see the bottom card of the deck without arousing suspicions. The performer places the deck in the spectator's hand. He cuts off the top group for himself. He selects a card, looks at it, places it on top of his group, and cuts the pack. The spectator does the same. So, when the spectator cuts his cards, the bottom card of the deck—which the performer is remembering—will be on top of the spectator's chosen card. The performer has no need to remember the card he selected, as it has nothing to do with the trick. All he has to remember is the bottom card of the deck.

Then the performer and spectator exchange decks. The performer instructs the spectator to pick out a card most like the one he chose. While the spectator is doing this, the performer looks through the cards he holds and finds his key card (bottom card of the deck). Directly below this is the card the spectator selected. The performer places the spectator's card face down on the table. Still looking through his cards, the performer sees what cards he holds that are most like the spectator's chosen card. In this way he knows what cards the spectator has that are close to the chosen card, and by the process of elimination he will know what card the spectator placed on the table. Knowing this, he pretends it is the card he picked out, and that he forced the spectator to pick a similar one.

Example: The performer looks through the group he holds, and below his key card is the 6 of clubs. This then is the spectator's card. The performer sees that his group also contains the 6 of spades and the 6 of diamonds. He knows then that the spectator holds the 6 of hearts. Now he can name both cards on the table. If the selected card is the 6 of clubs, and the spectator holds the 6 of spades and the 6 of hearts, he would put down the 6 of spades, since it is black and most like the card he chose. Knowing this, the performer can call the card correctly.

15. HEATH'S MASTER SPELLER

The principle of this remarkable card trick is credited to Royal Heath, the broker magician. Therefore, I call it "Heath's Master Speller." However, a few additional twists have been added by the author.

PRESENTATION AND EFFECT

The performer removes from the pack thirteen cards of the same suit (from ace through king), or he may instruct a spectator to remove them. The performer places the thirteen cards face up in a row on the table, and explains the effect as follows: "These thirteen cards can be arranged in over 6,227,020,800 different ways." The performer takes the 9 and 8 and states that they can be arranged two ways, 9 and 8, and 8 and 9. Adding the queen, he explains, the three cards can be arranged six ways; and he illustrates by arranging the three cards in several of these combinations, such as queen, 9, 8; 9, queen, 8, etc. The performer continues by saying that four cards can be arranged in twenty-four ways, five cards in one hundred and twenty different ways. The entire thirteen cards can fall in any one of 6,227,020,800 different arrangements. "Regardless of the number of different arrangements of these cards," continues the performer, "I am going to pick these cards up and place them into a magical sequence that will permit the trick to be concluded successfully, regardless of the spectator's selection."

The performer picks up the thirteen cards and forms one pile, placing them face down in the center of the table. The performer announces that he is going to have the spectator cut the packet, and whatever card the spectator cuts to will be the card used in the trick. He states, "Regardless of which card you cut to, that is the card we are going to spell out to locate the thirteen cards in their proper sequence from ace through king."

The performer requests the spectator to cut the group of cards any place he desires. The spectator may cut one card, a few cards, or lift the entire group of thirteen cards. The spectator cuts the cards off the pile by merely lifting a card, or group of cards, off the thirteen-card packet. The performer immediately faces up the bottom card of the cut group, and instructs the spectator to note the face-up card, and to place the cut group back on top of the face-up card. For example, the face-up card is the king. Therefore, the performer will spell out K-I-N-G to locate the cards in sequence. As the performer spells, he removes one card for each letter from the top of the group and puts it on the bottom of the group. After he has spelled out king, he turns the card, which is on top of the group, face up and places it on the table. It is the ace.

He spells out king again, removing one card, for each letter spelled, from the top of the group and placing it on the bottom of the group. He turns the next card face up, and it is the deuce. He spells king again, turns the next card face up and places it in

5 – 3 – 10 – 7 – A – K – J – 4 – 6 – 2 – Q – 9 – 8

the center of the table—this card is the three. The performer continues spelling out king and turning up cards until all thirteen have been accounted for. And we find that the cards were turned up in sequence from ace through king.

The cards must be arranged as follows: 5-3-10-7-ace-king-jack-4-6-2-queen-9-8. The 5-spot must be the top card of the face-down packet, the 8-spot the bottom card. The performer may either memorize the position of these cards, or have them stacked on the bottom of the pack. It is suggested, for a better effect, that you memorize them.

When the spectator cuts the cards, the performer reverses (turns over) the *bottom card of the cut group*, excepting when the bottom card is an ace, 6, or 10. When an ace, 6, or 10 shows as the bottom card, the performer reverses (turns over) the top card of the group resting on the table (the bottom group). Should it happen that the upturned card is a 2-spot, the performer calls it a deuce, and spells out deuce when doing the trick. The performer will note that all the cards spell with either three, four, or five letters, and as described above, we have a method of eliminating all the three-letter words.

Therefore, if the card is a four-letter word, the performer spells out the number and turns the following card up. For example, the performer spells F-O-U-R (when the upturned card is a 4-spot) and turns up the next card on top of the packet (the fifth card in the original packet). This is the ace. The performer spells F-O-U-R again, turns up the next card (fifth); it is the 2-spot, etc.

Should the upturned card be a five-letter word, the performer turns up the card which is the last letter he spells. For example, if the upturned card was a queen, the performer spells out Q-U-E-E-N and turns over the card that was the N. This you will notice is also the fifth card in the original packet. Therefore, the performer has turned up the ace. If the directions are followed correctly, this trick cannot fail.

16. CARDINI'S MIND READING CARD TRICK

This trick was created by Cardini, the top-flight vaudeville magician.

PRESENTATION AND EFFECT

The performer removes a deck of cards from the card case, turns the deck face up on the table, and gives the deck a riffle shuffle. Then, turning the deck face down, the performer deals six cards face down into a pile on the table, dealing the cards singly and placing each card dealt on top of the card previously dealt. After this, six more cards are dealt in the same manner, forming a second pile.

The performer now says, "This is purely a mind reading effect, and requires considerable concentration on the part of the performer." He then instructs a spectator to select either one of the two piles.

A free choice is offered the spectator. When he decides on one of the piles, the performer says, "You can change your mind and take the other pile, if you so desire." The performer stresses this point. After the spectator has selected a pile, the performer replaces the remaining pile on top of the deck.

He then instructs the spectator to think of any one of the six cards in his chosen pile; the spectator looks through the six cards and decides on one, taking pains not to let the performer see the faces of any of the cards. The performer now cuts the deck in half and hands the bottom half to the spectator, instructing him to shuffle the six cards into this part of the deck, but to keep concentrating on his chosen card at all times. The performer then takes the shuffled cards from the spectator, and places the top half of the deck he (the performer) is holding on top of the spectator's shuffled half.

The performer now places the entire deck behind his back for a few moments. Then he brings the deck forward and hands it to the spectator, reminding the spectator to concentrate on his card. The spectator is instructed to mentally (silently) spell out the name of his card, taking one card off the top of the deck and dealing it onto the table face down for each letter he spells. When he arrives at the last letter of his card, he is to place this card on the table face down to one side.

The performer takes the deck and all the dealt cards, and pockets them, saying, "Would it be a miracle if the face-down card on the table is the card you are thinking of?" The spectator is asked to name his card, and told to turn up the card on the table. A card miracle has happened. It is the card the spectator originally thought of.

THE SECRET

To perform this mind reading card trick, the performer must use six duplicate cards. These can be taken out of another pack having the same color and design. The performer removes the 7 of diamonds, 5 of diamonds, queen of hearts, 4 of hearts, 6 of spades, ace of spades from one pack of cards; the remainder of that pack is not to be used. He adds this sequence of six cards to another deck of the same color design, puts the same six cards belonging to the deck in the sequence named above. He removes any six indifferent cards from the deck, so that the deck will contain only fifty-two cards.

These two groups of six cards are placed on top of each other and then placed on top of the remainder of the deck. The 7

32

of diamonds is the top card of the deck, and the other 7 of diamonds is the seventh card in the deck. The other cards are arranged as described above. The performer riffle shuffles the deck face up, making certain not to disturb the twelve setup cards which are on the bottom of the face-up deck. At the same time this gives the spectator a chance to see the faces of the cards.

The performer then turns the deck face down on the table and, from the top of the deck, deals six cards singly into a pile face down on the table; then six more cards are dealt in the same manner to form the second pile. Because of the way the cards were set up on top of the deck, when the two groups were dealt onto the table—beginning with the top card of each face-down group, each group will be arranged; ace of spades (top card), 6 of spades, 4 of hearts, queen of hearts, 5 of diamonds, 7 of diamonds (bottom card of each group).

The performer places the pile rejected by the spectator on top

S-E-V-E-N O-F
D-I-A-M-O-N-D-S

of the deck, making certain not to disturb the position of these cards. He must keep them on top of the deck. That is why when the remainder of the cards is returned to him by the spectator he places them at the bottom of the setup group which he holds.

The performer, with this setup on top of the deck, places the deck behind his back, silently counts nine cards from the bottom of the deck, and places them on top of the deck.

All that remains now is to hand the deck to the spectator and have him mentally spell out the card he is thinking of. He will always end up at the right card. If he is thinking of the 7 of diamonds, he must spell all three words: "Seven of diamonds." Since this totals fifteen letters, his card will be the fifteenth card in the deck. Be sure the spectator understands that he must spell all three words, for example: "Ace of spades."

The performer cannot hand the deck out at the completion of the trick for fear of having the spectator find the duplicate cards, so it is best to put the cards away in the pocket immediately upon completion of this trick.

17. SENSITIVE FINGERTIPS

A combined creation of magician Bob Hummer and the author.

PRESENTATION AND EFFECT

The performer produces a group of cards with a rubber band around them. He announces that some of the cards in the group are face up and some are face down. While talking, he removes the rubber band from the group of cards. The performer fans the cards out rapidly, proving to the spectators that some are face up and some are face down. At no time, however, does he mention the number of cards in the group. He now places the cards on the table, and asks a spectator to cut the cards, placing the bottom group on top of the cut group. After the cards are cut several times, the performer takes the group of cards and hides them under the table or behind his back. He announces that he is going to attempt to adjust the cards so that they will all be faced the same (either all face up, or all face down).

A little bit of "patter" by the performer, to the effect that this trick requires extra sensitive fingertips, helps to "sell" this effect. Lo and behold, when the performer brings the cards into full view, all the cards are facing the same way, just as he said they would! The performer now places the cards in his coat pocket. Naturally, a spectator will ask the performer how many cards were used in the trick, so the performer removes the cards from his pocket, or allows the spectator to remove them, and upon counting, we find a total of twenty-one cards was used.

THE SECRET

Before the start of the trick, the performer takes one card from the deck and places it in his coat pocket. He then counts twenty cards off the deck and reverses every other card. For example the first card is face down, the second is face up, the third face down, the fourth face up, etc., until there are ten cards face up and ten cards face down, each card faced opposite to the card next to it. A rubber band is now placed around the group of cards to hold them in their proper order.

When the performer invites a spectator to cut the cards, this procedure, regardless of the number of cuts, will not affect the success of the trick.

When the cards are taken by the performer and placed under the table or behind his back, he merely separates the cards in the following manner. Holding the cards in his left hand, he deals the top card into his right hand, holding it between his thumb and index finger. He then deals the second card into his right hand between his index finger and middle finger. He deals the third card into his right hand between his thumb and index finger just as he did the first card. The fourth card is dealt between his index finger and middle finger just as the second card was dealt. This dealing, described above—alternating between the thumb and index finger, and the index finger and third finger —is continued until all the cards have been dealt out and there are ten cards between the thumb and index finger and ten cards

between the index finger and third finger of the right hand. The performer now takes the ten cards which are held between the thumb and index finger into his empty left hand, and reverses the group (turns them over). He then places this group on top of the ten cards still held between the index finger and third finger of his right hand, forming one group. He now brings forward this one group containing all twenty cards, and spreads it on the table. It will be found that when the cards are spread out, all of them are faced in the same direction.

Picking the cards up before any person can count them, the performer places the twenty cards into his pocket, which contains the one card he placed there before the start of the trick. When he or the spectator takes the cards from the pocket, there will be a total of twenty-one cards instead of twenty. The reason for this little "dodge" is that it is impossible to do this trick with an odd number of cards, so if a spectator suspects the method used in this trick, this little ruse will certainly make it more difficult for him to discover it.

18. SEPARATING RED AND BLACK CARDS

This cute trick, sometimes called "Red and Black," is a variation of the previous one, but the effect derived is somewhat different and probably more dramatic, merely because it allows more freedom in the showing of the cards at the start of the trick.

PRESENTATION AND EFFECT

The performer produces a group of twenty cards—some are face up, some are face down, some of the face-up cards are red and some are black. The cards appear to be all mixed up. He asks a spectator to cut the cards several times. The performer announces that his fingertips are so sensitive he can feel the difference between red and black cards. To prove this, he is going to separate the red from the black behind his back, and the fact that some are face up and some face down only makes the trick harder. Then, just as he said, he puts the cards behind his back or under a table, separates the red from the black, and hands the two groups of separated cards to the spectator to examine.

THE SECRET

The performer must arrange the cards before the start of the trick. They must be arranged: red, black, red, black, red, black, from beginning to end. In other words, every other card will be red, the balance will be black. He turns six or seven of these cards face up, making sure not to disturb their positions in the group. This gives the group the appearance of being selected haphazardly, and makes it harder to spot the red and black sequence. The spectator may cut the cards as much as he wants, as this will not change the arrangement in the least. When the performer puts the cards behind his back to separate the red from the black, he knows that the first is red, the second black, the third red, etc. One way to separate them is to deal out two groups. Holding the cards in the left hand, deal one card between the thumb and index finger of the right hand, deal the second card between the index finger and middle finger of the right hand, deal the third card between the thumb and index finger of the right hand again, the fourth card between the index finger and third finger of the right hand, and continue in this fashion until all cards have been dealt out. Then take one of the groups into your left hand, leaving the other one in the right. Bring both hands in front of you and hand the groups to the spectator to be examined. The red cards will be in one group, the black in the other.

19. SYMPATHETIC ACES

PRESENTATION AND EFFECT

The performer requests a spectator to think of a number between 10 and 20. Holding the pack in his hand, he asks the spectator to call out the number he has in mind. The spectator will call one of the following numbers: 11, 12, 13, 14, 15, 16, 17, 18, 19—the numbers between 10 and 20. Example: If the spectator calls out 15, the performer deals the cards onto the table one at a time on top of each other, counting as he goes along. When he arrives at number 15, he stops dealing, and places the remainder of the pack which is in his hand to one side. He now picks up the fifteen cards (still face down) and places

4 ACES ON TOP OF DECK

them in his hand. He states that the number the spectator was thinking of is 15, so he will add the first and second digits of the number, getting a total of 6 (5 plus 1 equals 6). He then deals off five cards one at a time onto the table, one on top of the other, from the group of fifteen he is holding in his hand, counting them aloud as he goes along. The sixth card he deals off the pack, and places it to one side, face down, away from all other cards. That finishes the trick with spectator No. 1.

Note: The following is very important. The performer places the nine cards remaining in his hand on top of the five cards he had dealt onto the table. He picks up this group of fourteen cards and places the group on top of the deck that had been put to one side.

He now picks up the pack which is comprised of fifty-one cards, and asks spectator No. 2 to think of a number between 10 and 20. He follows exactly the same procedure as he used for spectator No. 1. After the spectator calls out his number, the performer uses the formula described above to determine the card to be put aside near the first spectator's.

Then the performer has spectator No. 3 call a number, and repeats the procedure detailed above. Then spectator No. 4 calls a number, and the performer again goes through his act. He now has four cards placed to one side of the table.

These four cards (after the performer utters a few magic words) are turned over, and to the amazement of all, we see the four aces.

THE SECRET

To do this trick, the performer must make the following preparations, which the spectators must be unaware of. The performer has the four aces together, and places them in the deck as the tenth, eleventh, twelfth, and thirteenth cards from the top. In other words, there are nine cards on top of the four aces. If the performer desires to shuffle the cards at the start of the trick, he may do so, provided the top fourteen cards are not disturbed. Therefore, if the performer cannot shuffle without disturbing the top fourteen cards, he should not shuffle at all.

No matter what the number called, the net result is the same —nine cards will be left, and the last card dealt off will be the tenth card, one of the "planted" ones. Subtract from any number between 11 and 19 the sum of its digits and you will always get 9. When you count off from the deck the number mentioned by the spectator, you automatically reverse the position of the cards, so that the nine cards on top of the key cards are now under them.

Variation

Should the performer desire to find a Royal Flush in the same manner, he merely places the nine cards above the Royal Flush (ace, king, queen, jack, 10 of any suit), and repeats the procedure five times instead of four, as described in the "Sympathetic Aces." Any hand the performer desires to find can be located in this manner. It is suggested that the performer change to a different hand now and then when doing this trick.

20. THE FOUR PACKS

PRESENTATION AND EFFECT

The performer hands a pack of cards to a spectator, with the request that he deal off the top of the pack four cards one at a time, and that he separate these cards one from another. Performer then informs the spectator that he now must continue dealing cards on top of these four cards in any manner desired (one at a time, two or three at a time, etc.), putting cards on the four heaps until the pack is exhausted.

The performer then instructs the spectator to look at the top card of each pack, making sure the performer doesn't see any of them, and to remember the four cards he has looked at. If there are four persons watching the trick, the performer requests each one to look at the top card of a pack. The spectator is then told to place the four packs of cards one on top of the other, and then to cut the deck. The performer requests each person that has selected a card to concentrate on his card, and he proceeds to find the four selected cards.

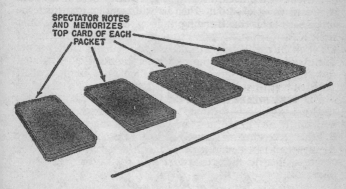

SPECTATOR NOTES
AND MEMORIZES
TOP CARD OF EACH
PACKET

THE SECRET

Without letting anyone know about it, the performer took the four deuces out of the deck and placed them face down on top of the deck before the start of the trick. Therefore, the four deuces are the first four cards on top of the deck. When the spectator deals out four cards onto the table, he doesn't know it but he is dealing out the four deuces. He continues to deal cards on each pack. The spectator places each group on top of the other to form one group, and then cuts the cards. It is now very easy for the performer to find the cards the spectator looked at. Cutting the cards does not change their sequence: each deuce is now on top of a selected card—a top card of a group. All he has to do is run through the pack and take out the card that is under each deuce. He tosses each card onto the table, face down, until he has located the four selected cards. Then he dramatically holds the four cards in his hands, asks each spectator the name of his card, and then turns that card over.

21. THE WIZARD

A favorite of Steffi Storm's, the female trickster.

PRESENTATION AND EFFECT

The performer tells the spectators about an amazing man called the Wizard. The Wizard has great mental powers. Nobody knows who the Wizard is. He only speaks to people on the phone. He spends most of his time at home concentrating. He doesn't like to be bothered by the outside world; but to show that he's no fake, and really knows all that's going on, if you pick a card out of the deck, then call the Wizard, he will tell you what card you picked out. Then he will hang up immediately, and go back to his concentrating.

Needless to say, this story is scoffed at by the spectators, and championed by the performer. Finally, to prove there is a Wizard, the performer asks one of the spectators to pick out a card from the deck, after taking particular pains to shuffle the cards thoroughly before making his selection. Then the spectator is told to show the chosen card to all in the room. The per-

40

former now dials the Wizard's number, asks to speak to the Wizard, and hands the phone to the spectator—who hears a voice saying, "This is the Wizard, you are thinking of the three of diamonds." Then the Wizard hangs up.

Now everyone in the room believes in the Wizard. Each tells how many times he saw, with his own eyes, a successful demonstration by this fabulous character.

THE SECRET

The performer works with a confederate who poses as the Wizard. After a card has been selected and shown around to all, including the performer, the performer calls his confederate, the Wizard, informs him of the card in some secret way, and turns the phone over to the spectator, who hears the Wizard tell him the name of the selected card.

Here is how the Wizard is informed what card has been selected. When the performer calls, he says, "Is the Wizard there?" If someone else should answer the phone, the performer hangs up, saying the Wizard is not there now, so we will have to try again later. But if the confederate answers the phone, as soon as he hears the question, "Is the Wizard there?" he says slowly, pausing between each number, "One, two, three, four, five, six, seven, eight, nine, ten, jack, queen, king."

The performer who knows what card has been selected stops the Wizard when he names the correct number. Example: If the card selected is the 6 of diamonds, as soon as the Wizard says, "Six," the performer says, "Hello, Wizard?" This gives the spectators the impression that the Wizard just answered the phone, but the Wizard already has learned the rank of the selected card.

As soon as the performer says, "Hello, Wizard?" the confederate (the Wizard) says slowly, "Clubs, diamonds, hearts, spades." Since the card is the 6 of diamonds (example above), the performer stops the Wizard when he calls "diamonds," by saying, "One moment, please"—and he hands the phone to the spectator. The Wizard now knows the suit of the card as well as the rank; in this example, the 6 of diamonds.

When the spectator says, "Hello," the Wizard in answering uses a very mysterious voice, and says, "This is the Wizard, you are thinking of the six of diamonds." Then the Wizard hangs up, before any questions can be asked.

22. REVERSO

PRESENTATION AND EFFECT

The performer spreads out a pack of playing cards in his

41

hands, and asks a spectator to pick out two cards from any part of the deck. He tells the spectator to look at the cards and remember them. The performer squares up the deck and asks the spectator to insert the cards one at a time into the pack. He then announces that behind his back he will riffle the deck, and the cards selected by the spectator will be found upside down in the deck.

The Secret

Before the start of this trick the performer must have the bottom card of the deck face up. All the other cards are face down. Then the performer fans out the deck, making sure that he does not expose the bottom card. After the spectator selects two cards, the performer squares up the deck. While the spectator is looking at the selected cards, the performer, who is

holding the deck in his hand palm up, turns his hand over, holding the deck palm down. This means that the bottom card will now be on top. Now this top card is face down, but all the rest of the deck is face up. When the spectator pushes his two selected cards back into the deck, they will be the only face-down cards in a face-up deck except for the top card. The performer now puts the deck behind his back and riffles the cards as he said he would. But he also turns the top card over, so that it is face up like the rest of the deck. Then he turns the entire deck over. When he fans the deck out in front of the spectator, we find all the cards are face down except the two selected by the spectator, which are face up in the deck.

23. THE DEAN'S POKER DEAL

PRESENTATION AND EFFECT

This trick comes from "The Dean," a very colorful gambling man from New Jersey. And I must say that he won quite a few dollars with it. It came in handy for The Dean, particularly when it came time to pay a restaurant or night club check. Then he would say to a person in the party, "How about dealing a hand of Poker? The losing hand pays the check." He would produce a pack of cards from his pocket, count the top ten cards off the pack, and remark that it was less conspicuous to use ten cards rather than the entire pack, especially in a place where gambling is prohibited. "Tell me when to stop shuffling." When the opponent called, "Stop," The Dean would hand him the cards and ask him to deal two Poker hands. Naturally, The Dean got the winning hand each time.

THE SECRET

The Dean always had his deck prepared. He would always have three of a kind, and one odd card on top of the deck. (For example, three kings, three 4's, three 10's, and an odd card, such as the deuce of any suit. These ten cards may be arranged in any sequence, but the odd card *must* be the top card of the pack.) The Dean would then place the fixed deck of cards in the card box and place the box in his pocket. When the opportunity presented itself, out came the deck. He would then count off ten cards from the top of the deck, without exposing the faces but making sure that the odd card was still on top of the ten cards after they were taken from the pack. The remainder of the cards were put into the box and back into his pocket. Now The Dean would shuffle the cards, making certain that the odd card remained on the bottom of the group when the shuffling was completed.

This move requires no skill whatever, if you can do the overhand shuffle. You merely shuffle the top card of the group by itself into your left hand, and then shuffle the remaining cards on top of the odd card. If you think that you are now a sleight of hand expert, you may continue to shuffle these cards several more times, and still leave the odd card on the bottom merely by pulling off the top and bottom cards for your first part of the shuffle, although one shuffle will do the trick.

When the shuffle has been completed, hand your opponent the cards and ask him to deal you and himself a Poker hand. Your opponent will hold the odd card because he will deal it to himself at the last of his five cards, and thereby hold the losing hand. With the above setup, it is impossible for the opponent to have a higher-ranking hand than the performer, since the opponent will hold the odd card.

If you want to repeat this trick, arrange the pack so that you will have four stacks of ten cards each; take the remainder of the pack and deal off the next ten cards, etc., always putting the previously used ten cards on the bottom of the pack. This way it is almost impossible for anyone to ever figure out the secret because they don't know the cards used, and never give the odd card a thought.

If you want to lose a hand, *you* deal the cards out, and of course you will hold the losing hand, since you will be dealt the odd card.

24. THE MEMORY TEST

A favorite of Charles Jordon's, the magician.

PRESENTATION AND EFFECT

The performer states that he has developed his memory, particularly with a pack of playing cards, to such an extent that he can memorize at least half a pack of cards. To prove this he has a spectator shuffle the pack and cut the cards into two equal groups, or as close to that as possible. He tells the spectator to pick the group he would like to have memorized and hand the selected group of cards to him. The performer looks carefully through the cards. Then he returns the cards to the spectator. He tells the spectator that he is going to turn his back, and while his back is turned he wants the spectator to select one card from the group, look at it, and place it in his pocket. Then the spectator is instructed to shuffle the cards thoroughly. When this is done, the performer turns around to face the spectator again, asks to be handed the group of cards being used in this experiment, carefully looks through the cards again, then names the card the spectator has removed from the pack and put into his pocket. The spectator removes the card from his pocket, and we find the performer has called the card correctly.

THE SECRET

The spectator shuffles and cuts the cards into two groups. He hands the performer the group he wants him to memorize. The performer looks through the cards, apparently memorizing them but actually adding together all the pips (values of the cards). This is quite simple, because each time your total exceeds 10,

44

you drop the 10. For example: The first card is a 7, the next a 9. The total being 16, you merely carry 6 in your mind. Do not count the court cards till last, adding them to your previous total. The value of court cards are as follows: jack, 1½; queen, 2½; king, 3½. If the halves confuse you, do not count them until the end. Merely count 1 for jack, 2 for queen, 3 for king. Then count the number of court cards, adding ½ for each court card. The performer must remember the total of the card count. Running through the cards again, the performer adds the value of the suits together. He counts as follows: club, 1; diamond, 2; heart, 3; spades, 0. The spades are not counted at all. The performer must only carry the excess of 10 in his mind, the same as the pip-adding principle. The performer now has two totals to remember: card count and suit count. Let's use, for example, the totals 6½ and 5.

Upon completion of the above, the performer hands the spectator the cards, requesting him to select a card and place it in his pocket. The spectator now thoroughly shuffles the cards while the performer's back is turned. When this is done, the performer once again faces the spectator and is handed the group of cards being used in this experiment.

As before, the performer looks through the cards and counts the pip value. For example, let's say his total is 4. He subtracts the 4 from the first pip total, which was 6½, and gets an answer of 2½, which signifies the chosen card was a queen.

He now looks through the cards again and counts the suit value. For example, he gets a total of 3. He subtracts the 3 from his previous suit total, which was 5, and gets the answer of 2, which is listed above as signifying diamonds. Therefore, the card selected was the queen of diamonds.

In other words, he must always subtract the last pip total from the first to find the denomination of the selected card. Then subtract the second suit total from the first to arrive at the suit of the selected card.

Should the number to be deducted be larger than the first number, you add 10 to the smaller number. Then deduct and you have the name of the missing card.

If the performer has difficulty using half the deck, he may have the spectator cut the cards into three groups. In this way he will be using approximately eighteen cards for this experiment.

25. SPECTATORS' MAGIC COUNT

PRESENTATION AND EFFECT

The performer after doing one or more card tricks turns to

the spectator and says, "You, too, can do a card trick if you concentrate hard enough. I am going to think of a card, and to prove I'm telling the truth, I will write the name of the card I am thinking of on a piece of paper and hide it from view." Then he continues, "Here's what I want you to do. Think of any number from 1 to 52, then take the deck, count down to that number, and if you are successful, you will be at the card I am thinking of."

The performer then goes on to say, "So that you will understand, I will illustrate what you are to do. Supposing the number you are thinking of is seven, all you do is this." The performer deals the cards face down one at a time onto the table. When he reaches the seventh card, he holds it in his hand and says, "This is supposed to be the card that *I* am thinking of. Now, have you got it straight? Okay, let's go." The performer can also add laughingly, "This will be a sensational trick if it works." The performer replaces the seven cards on top of the deck.

Now the performer thinks of a card and writes it down on a piece of paper which he folds so that the writing cannot be seen. He hands the deck to the spectator, tells him to think of a number, and deal down to that number. When the spectator reaches the number he is thinking of, he turns the card over, and alas, it is not the performer's card.

The performer tells him, "That's not my card. Try it again, but be sure to concentrate very hard. What number were you thinking of? Tell me and I will concentrate on it, too; then we can't go wrong." The performer picks up the cards dealt onto the table and replaces them on top of the deck, and says, "Okay, try it again."

The spectator counts down to the number he's thinking of (the same number as before), turns the card over, and says, "That's it." Then they open the folded paper on which the performer had written the card he was thinking of, and we find that the spectator is psychic, otherwise what made him stop at just the right card?

THE SECRET

The performer proceeds as described above. When he illustrates how the trick is to be done, he deals off seven cards. He does not put the seventh card down, neither does he show it to the spectator, but the performer himself makes sure to get a good peek at it. This he does when he explains, "This is supposed to be the card I am thinking of." Now he puts this card down on top of those he dealt, and places the entire group (seven cards) on top of the deck.

Now the performer thinks of a card and writes it down. He writes down the name of the card he has just peeked at, which is now on top of the deck. The spectator thinks of a number and deals down to it. When the card is turned over, he is found to be wrong. He couldn't be right because the card written down by the performer is at the bottom of the dealt group, since it was the first card dealt off the pack. The performer picks up the entire dealt group and places it on top of the deck. Then he instructs the spectator to do it again, thinking of the same number and concentrating harder. Naturally, he will stop at the right card this time. Looking at the paper, we find the card written down by the performer is the same the spectator dealt to.

Here's how it works. The card the performer writes down is on top of the deck, as explained above. If the spectator thinks of number 20, he deals down to that count, and is wrong, because the performer's card was the first one dealt. Picking up this dealt group and placing it on top of the pack, the spectator once again deals down to the same number. This time he's right because the performer's card is now twentieth in the pack. Dealing the cards out the first time reversed the order of the dealt cards.

26. TOPSY-TURVY DECK

Several tricks of this type have been created by the author, but credit for this one must be given to the author's good friend and brother magician, Bob Hummer. He was one of the first to make use of the subtle principle employed in this sort of trick.

PRESENTATION AND EFFECT

The performer produces a pack of cards that are all mixed up, some face up and some face down. The performer gives the pack several legitimate shuffles, either a riffle shuffle or an overhand shuffle. Then he hands the pack to the spectator to shuffle and cut.

He announces that he will place the cards under the table or behind his back, and cut the pack into two equal groups, twenty-six cards in each, in such a manner that he will have the same number of cards face up in each group. He states that while having the cards behind his back, he may have to reverse the position of some of the cards to do this trick.

Lo and behold, after a bit of counting and feeling, the performer places two groups of cards on the table. Upon examination it will be found that each group contains an equal number of face-up cards (and naturally an equal number of face-down cards).

THE SECRET

The deck is prepared by counting twenty-six cards from the

deck and reversing them. They are shuffled together with the twenty-six face-down cards. The performer does not inform the spectator that he has twenty-six face up and twenty-six face down. He just doesn't mention it at all. The shuffling by the performer or the spectator doesn't matter.

All the performer does behind his back is to count twenty-six cards into his left hand, turning these cards over in the hand.

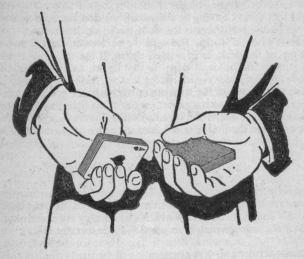

Putting the two groups on the table, it will be found that they contain an equal number of cards face up.

Note: This trick can be performed with any even number of cards, providing half are turned face up and the other half turned face down; but I would suggest that not less than twenty cards be used.

27. FINDING A SELECTED CARD

"All Red and All Black."

PRESENTATION AND EFFECT

The performer cuts a pack of playing cards into two groups. He fans, or spreads, each group face down on the table. He instructs a spectator to pick a card from one of the fanned groups. He instructs another spectator to pick a card from the other group. Both spectators are told to look at their cards and show them to each other. Spectator No. 1 is instructed to put his card into the group other than that from which it was selected. Spectator No. 2 is told to do likewise. The performer scoops up the two groups of cards, places one on top of the other, and squares the deck. He then announces that he has no way of knowing what cards were selected, but he will be able to find the two selected cards nevertheless. By intense concentration, while running slowly through the cards, he will be forced to stop at each of the selected cards. This the performer does. He runs through the pack, stops at a card, withdraws it, runs further through the pack, stops at another card, withdraws it: and when the cards are shown, they turn out to be the cards selected by the spectators.

THE SECRET

Before the start of the trick, the performer has his pack prepared: all the red cards together on top of the deck, and all the black cards together in the bottom half of the deck. Each spectator selects a card. One will have a red card, one will have a black card, because one of the groups fanned out by the performer is all red cards, and the other is all black cards. When spectator No. 1 returns his card to the opposite group, he is putting his red card in the middle of all the black cards. Likewise, spectator No. 2 is putting his black card among all the red cards. When the performer runs through the deck, he can't miss finding the selected cards. He withdraws the only red card in the black group and the only black card in the red group. While the spectators are talking over the effect, it is best for the performer to shuffle the deck so that examination of the cards will not give away the secret.

28. THOUGHT CONTROL

This trick is a favorite of Howard Wurst's, the New Jersey magician.

PRESENTATION AND EFFECT

The spectator holds a piece of paper on which is written the name of a card. The performer calls out the name of this card, also telling the position in the deck at which the card will be found.

The performer must have ten pieces of paper, about one inch square each, plus a pencil and an ash tray. The performer spreads a deck of cards face up on the table and requests a spectator to select a card. This the spectator does by pulling it out of the deck. Since the cards are face up, the selected card is known to both performer and spectator.

49

The performer states that he is going to write the name of this card plus a number on one of the slips of paper, but he is not going to let the spectator see what he is writing. After the performer writes the name of the card and a number on a piece of paper, he folds it up so no one may know what was written on it, and places it in the ash tray.

The spectator is requested to select another card, and the performer writes the name of that card plus a number on the second piece of paper, folds up the paper, and puts it in the ash tray.

The same procedure is followed until the spectator has selected ten cards, and the performer has written the name plus a number on each piece of paper. The selected cards are now placed in a group, then placed on top of the pack.

The performer requests the spectator to mix the ten pieces of paper thoroughly, then to select one and hold it in his closed fist.

The performer burns the remaining nine pieces of paper, and while spreading the ashes with the pencil, concentrates. He then predicts what name will be found written on the paper held by the spectator. Upon opening the folded paper, the spectator finds the performer's prediction to be correct. The paper also has a number written on it. The performer asks the spectator to count down from the top of the deck to that number, and behold! the spectator finds the predicted card at that number.

THE SECRET

The performer writes the name of the first card selected on all ten pieces of paper. Below this he writes the number 5. For example, the spectator selects the 2 of diamonds for his first card. The performer writes down 2 of diamonds and, below that, number 5. The performer writes the same thing on the other nine pieces of paper instead of writing the names of the other cards selected.

As the cards are being picked, the performer puts them to one side, face down, one on top of the other until six cards have been chosen. The first card selected will be the bottom card of this group. Then he asks the spectator, "How many cards were selected?" He picks the cards up and counts them face up, so that the first selected will now be the top card of the group.

Thereafter, the remaining four cards to be selected are put on top of the group. This leaves the first card selected the fifth card from the top of the group. The entire group is now placed on top of the deck.

The spectator selects one of the pieces of paper. The performer burns the rest. The purpose of this procedure is to dispose of the evidence. The performer announces that the spectator holds a piece of paper on which "2 of diamonds" is marked. This proves to be true. He also says, "The paper has the number five written on it, and I predict if you count down five cards in the deck, you will find the two of diamonds." This also proves to be true, and the trick is a success.

29. MAGIC IN YOUR OWN HANDS

This is a real baffler with several different conclusions, and is a favorite of Cliff Green's, the clever vaudeville card manipulator.

PRESENTATION AND EFFECT

The performer while spreading the cards face down from hand to hand requests a spectator to select a card, and to memorize it. The performer cuts the deck, and has the spectator return the card to the pack at the cut position. Squaring up the

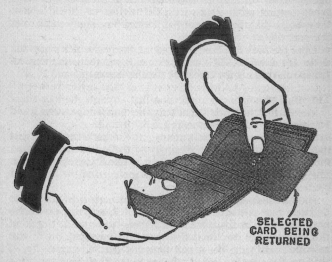

SELECTED
CARD BEING
RETURNED

deck, the performer states that from now on the magic will happen in "the spectator's own hands." The performer will never touch the deck again. After this remark, he instructs the spectator to place his hand palm up, and the performer puts the deck of cards on the spectator's outstretched palm. The performer now requests the spectator to call out a low number, preferably between 5 and 10, and to count down to that number in the deck. Behold! the spectator finds his selected card at the right count.

THE SECRET

The pack is prearranged as follows. A 7-spot is placed on top of the deck and an 8-spot is placed at the bottom of the deck. Above the 8-spot is placed a 9-spot, turned face up in the deck (this is the second card from the bottom). With this setup the performer is ready to do the trick.

While spreading the cards from hand to hand—and at the same time requesting the spectator to pick a card—the performer secretly counts six cards from the top of the deck. Holding these six cards with his right hand, he spreads the remaining cards with his left hand. After the spectator has selected and memorized his card, the performer cuts off these six cards with his right hand and requests the spectator to return the selected card back to the top of the lower portion. The performer places the six cards on top of the selected card, squaring the deck. When cutting off the six cards, the performer should square them up so that the spectator has no idea how many cards have been cut off.

After the deck has been squared up, the performer places the deck face down on the spectator's hand, and requests the spectator to call out a low number, preferably between 5 and 10. The reason for stating a low number at first, then saying between 5 and 10, is to create the impression that any low number could be called. But the truth is that only the numbers *between* 5 and 10 can be used. These numbers are 6,7,8, and 9.

Should the spectator call number 6, the performer instructs the spectator to deal six cards singly off the top of the deck onto the table, and then asks the spectator to name his selected card. The spectator is told to turn over the top card of the deck, and there is the spectator's selected card.

Should the spectator call number 7, the performer states that he knew the spectator was going to call 7, and turns over the top card of the deck—which is a 7-spot—to prove it. Counting this card as number one, the spectator counts down to the seventh card in the deck, and finds his selected cards.

Should the spectator call number 8, the performer turns the deck over and exhibits the bottom card, which proves to be an 8-spot. This proves he knew the spectator was going to call out number 8. The performer puts the 8-spot on top of the deck, requests the spectator to count down eight cards, and the spectator finds his selected card at that number.

Should the spectator call number 9, the performer requests the spectator to cut the deck. Then the spectator is told to deal the cards one at a time onto the table until he arrives at a face-up card. The spectator finds a 9-spot face up in the deck. Counting the 9-spot as number one, the performer instructs the spectator to count down to 9 (which is the number he called) and his selected card is found at that count.

30. MATHEMATICAL FINDER

This is a very novel method whereby the spectator finds his own selected card. Totaling the value of one or more face-up cards, the spectator counts down to that number in the deck, and arrives at the exact location of his selected card.

PRESENTATION AND EFFECT

The spectator is requested to shuffle the deck thoroughly. He then returns the cards to the performer. The performer fans the deck and has the spectator select a card. The spectator is told to hold the card in front of himself, to concentrate on it a few moments, and to remember it. The performer cuts the cards, and has the spectator place the selected card on top of the bottom group, places the top group on top of the selected card, and perfectly squares up the deck. The performer riffle shuffles the deck, then hands it to the spectator. The spectator is instructed to deal the cards off the top of the deck one at a time. turning each card face up as he deals it. Dealing the first card onto the table, the spectator says, "Ten"; dealing the second card, he says, "Nine"; and so on, counting down from 10 to 1. Every time the card he deals corresponds with the number he calls, he is to take that card and place it to one side face up.

For example: Let's assume the cards were dealt off the deck, as follows: ace, 7, 3, 5, 6. Dealing off the ace, the spectator calls out, "Ten," then, "Nine, eight, seven, six." You can see that when he called, "Six," he dealt a 6. Therefore, the 6 is placed to one side face up. The spectator now starts all over. The next card dealt, he calls out, "Ten," again, and continues down to 1. If none of the cards correspond with the number called, the spectator, after he has gone down to 1, takes the top card of the deck and places it on the table to one side face down. He repeats this until he has four cards placed to one side. They may be all face up, all face down, or some face up and some face down. The performer explains that since the deck was shuffled, any value could have been turned up. He instructs the spectator to add the pips of the face-up cards, and when he arrives at the total, he is instructed to count down from the top of the deck (cards remaining in his hand) until he reaches the number of the total. When he turns up the card falling at the total, he will be surprised to find his selected card.

If it should happen that none of the four cards placed to one side are face up on the spectator's fourth count, the performer says, "Stop. Name your selected card." After the spectator names his card, the performer says, "The top card of the deck is your selected card." The performer is always right.

THE SECRET

After the spectator has shuffled and handed the deck to the performer, the performer must count off eight cards from the bottom. He pushes the rest of the deck forward so that the eight cards will be in a group that can easily be distinguished by the performer. When he fans the cards, he leaves these bottom eight intact, and has the spectator select a card. While the spectator is looking and concentrating on his card, the performer cuts the cards, leaving only the bottom eight cards as the group. He has the spectator place his selected card on top of this group. Then he places the rest of the deck on top of the selected card.

If the performer does not think he can separate the eight bottom cards without being detected, he should shuffle the deck himself, and in the act of shuffling he can separate the cards. He says nothing about the trick he is going to do as yet, so he will not be watched as closely as if the spectator had shuffled. After he has his cards set, he can fan the pack and say, "Pick a card," as though he just got the idea for the trick.

After the spectator has replaced his selected card and the performer has squared the deck, the performer riffle shuffles the deck. But he must make sure not to disturb the position of the spectator's card, which is ninth from the bottom. This is easy to do. Just let twelve or fifteen bottom cards fall before you riffle the top half into the cards. Following these instructions, the spectator will always locate his own card.

31. SWIMMERS

This ingenious trick has been used by card trick enthusiasts for many years, but I have added an additional surprise that makes it doubly effective. Not only does the spectator locate the four aces, but after all kinds of mix-ups, he locates the four kings as well.

PRESENTATION AND EFFECT

The performer places a pack of cards on the table, and pointing to the pack, requests the spectator to cut the pack in half, putting the top half to his (spectator's) right about six inches from the bottom half. Pointing to the bottom half at the left, the performer asks the spectator to cut this group, putting the top half to the right (between the two cut groups on the table). Pointing to the top half of the deck, which is at the spectator's far right, the spectator is instructed to cut this group, placing the top half further to the right. This group is now at the extreme right. The deck is now cut into four groups.

For the purpose of clarity, we shall number the four groups: 1, at the spectator's extreme *left*; 2, next group to the right of group 1; 3 next group to the right of group 2; 4, the following group at the spectator's extreme right.

The performer now requests the spectator to do as follows:

a) take a card from top of group 1 and place it on group 2
b) take a card from top of group 3 and place it on group 1
c) take a card from top of group 4 and place it on group 3
d) take a card from top of group 2 and place it on group 1
e) take a card from top of group 3 and place it on group 1
f) take a card from top of group 4 and place it on group 2
g) take a card from top of group 4 and place it on group 3

Turning over the top card of each group, we will find we have turned over the four aces. Putting the aces to one side, the same procedure is followed, as described above, for moving a card from one group to the other. After going through the steps

outlined from a through g, the top card of each group is turned over, and we find we have uncovered the four kings.

THE SECRET

The performer must prepare the deck secretly before the start of the trick. The four top cards of the deck must be the four aces, and the four cards below the aces must be the four kings. Follow the instructions as described above under Presentation and Effect, and the trick will work out as shown. If the performer is capable of remembering where the critical cards are as he goes along, he does not have to follow the exact steps, i.e., a through g, but may use his own.

32. THE WEIGLE ACES

This trick was originated by Oscar Weigle of New York, and that is the reason for calling it "The Weigle Aces."

PRESENTATION AND EFFECT

The performer places the deck of cards on the table and instructs the spectator to cut it into four packets from left to right. The bottom cards of the deck are left at the spectator's left, the top cards of the deck form the packet at his extreme right. The spectator is then told to pick up the packet at his extreme left, deal off the three top cards one at a time onto the space left vacant by picking up the packet, then deal one card on top of each of the remaining three packets, then place the cards remaining in his hand on top of the first three cards dealt off. In other words, he places the packet back where it was.

The procedure is repeated with the second packet (packet to the right of the first packet)—three cards dealt to the vacant space, one card dealt on top of each of the other three packets, and the balance of the cards on top of the first three dealt (putting the remainder of the packet where it belongs).

The spectator does the same with the third and fourth packets. After all this has been done, the performer instructs the spectator to turn over the top card on the first packet (at extreme left). The spectator discovers an ace. He turns over the top card of the second packet, also an ace; turns over the top card of the third packet, which is also an ace. The spectator turns over the top card of the last packet (at extreme right), and instead of an ace, as he now expects to find, he finds a 3-spot.

What happened? Did something go wrong? The performer says, "Since this is not the missing ace, maybe this card is telling us where to find the ace. Since it's a three, count down to the third card in this packet."

Counting down to the third card, the spectator not only finds the missing ace, but finds it face up as well.

THE SECRET

The cards must be prepared in the following order. The three aces must be on top of the deck. Below the three aces must be placed a 3-spot of any suit (this is fourth card from top). Below the 3-spot must be placed two indifferent cards (fifth and sixth cards from top). Below these indifferent cards must be placed

56

the last ace, face up. This face-up ace will be the seventh card from the top of the deck.

Before performing this trick, the performer may shuffle the cards if he desires, but he must be sure he doesn't disturb the top seven cards of the deck which he has arranged.

Following the instructions—detailed above under Presentation and Effect—for the cutting of the groups and the redistribution of the top-most cards of each packet, the trick will always work out perfectly.

It is perhaps unnecessary to state that a card of a value other than a 3-spot may be used as an indicator card, so long as an appropriate number of cards is placed between the indicator card and the last ace. But experience has shown that three is about right. It is also noteworthy that there is actually little likelihood of the face-up ace being exposed before its time—at the climax. Of course, a deck with an over-all back design is not practical, since a reversed card will be noticed at the edges. With such a deck in use, the trick may be done as usual except that the ace will not face up, but the effect still remains a good one.

33. THE MATHEMATICAL CARD TRICK

This trick, although not of the sensational effect type, is one of the most baffling of card tricks. The author always uses it on a mathematically minded person, and not once has the secret or solution ever been discovered. Also favored by that clever card expert, Dr. Jacob Daly.

PRESENTATION AND EFFECT

The spectator is instructed to shuffle and cut the deck as much as he desires. He is then told to deal the cards face down from the top of the deck one at a time onto the table, and to stop whenever he desires. When he stops, the performer instructs him to look at the card he stopped at (which is pointed at by the performer), and to remember it. The spectator places the card on top of the dealt cards on the table and places the remainder of the deck on top of all the cards, then squares the pack.

A second spectator is now asked to pick up the pack and follow the same procedure as the first spectator for the free selection of his card. He deals off as many cards as he desires, looks at the card when he stops (the same instructions that the first spectator received), places the selected card on top of the dealt cards on the table, places the remainder of the deck on top of all the cards, and squares the deck. While the second spectator is selecting his card, the performer pays no attention to him at all. He may, in fact, turn his back on the procedure if he cares to.

After the second spectator has selected his card, he is instructed to square up the deck, cut it one or more times, and hand it to the performer.

The performer deals the cards into two equal groups. The performer spreads each group from hand to hand (faces to the

spectator, backs to the performer) for the spectators' verification that the two cards chosen have fallen into separate halves.

Now the performer replaces each group face down on the table, and deals one card from the top of each group simultaneously, turning them face up as he deals them. Before he starts this dealing, however, he has each spectator call out the name of his chosen card. The performer then starts the simultaneous dealing from the two groups, and repeating the names of the chosen cards, they suddenly show up at the same time and place.

THE SECRET

This trick must be done with a fifty-two card deck.

This effect is remarkable because a shuffled, unprepared deck is used and the performer never knows the position of a single card in the deck. The first spectator shuffles, then deals as many cards as he desires onto the table. The performer, pretending not to pay attention to the deal, nevertheless watches and remembers the number of cards dealt. If the number is *even*, he is asked to look at the *next card* on top of the deck in his hand, remember it, place it on top of the dealt cards on the table, place the remainder of the pack on top of all, and square the deck. If the number is *odd*, he is asked to look at the last card dealt onto the table, remember it, place it back on top of the dealt cards, and place the remainder of the pack on top of all.

The second spectator picks up the pack (does not shuffle but keeps it just as is), deals off as many cards as he desires, looks at the indicated card where he stopped—just as the first spectator did, places the selected card on top of the dealt cards, places the remainder of the pack on top of all the cards, squares and cuts the pack.

The performer pays no attention to the second spectator, but instead mentally divides the number the first spectator dealt (which the performer had counted) in half. The result is the performer's key number. For example: The first spectator dealt ten cards, then he selected one from the top of the deck because his number was even, placed the selected card on top of the dealt cards, and placed the pack on top of all. The performer divides 10 by 2. His key number is 5. If the first spectator dealt nine cards, he looks at the last card dealt, replaces it, places deck on top of all. The performer divides 9 by 2. His answer is 4½. His key number is 4 because fractions are dropped.

After each spectator has selected a card, and the deck has been cut, the performer deals out the cards into two equal groups, dealing from left to right. Picking up the group at the *left*, he holds the cards up in front of the spectator (faces toward the spectator) and spreads the cards from hand to hand, and asks the spectator to see if his card is in this group. While the spectator is looking, the performer counts the cards as they are spread (counting the top card of the group as one), and holds a break * below the key number. If the first spectator says his card is in the group, the performer cuts the key number of cards (above the break) from the top to the bottom of the packet. Then he places the group face down on the table, all squared up.

He picks up the second group (the one dealt to the right), fans it out (as he did with the other group) for the second spectator to see. After the second spectator affirms that his card is in the group, the performer squares up the group and places it on the table. He does not change the position of the cards at all when the second spectator looks at them.

When the performer shows the group of cards dealt on the left to the first spectator, it might happen that the spectator will say, "No, my card is not there." If that is the case, pick up the second group (dealt to the right), and fan them out for the *first* spectator to see. Count off the key number of cards *plus one more*. When the spectator says, "Yes, my card is there," cut to the

---

* A group of cards, held by the right hand, separated from the remaining cards.

break you are holding, bringing the key cards from the top to the bottom.

Then pick up the other group and show it to the second spectator. Do not change the position of any of the cards in this case.

Since there happens to be one selected card in each group (this must be the case, because of the handling at the beginning), the performer asks the names of the selected cards, deals one card at a time off the top of each group simultaneously, turning the cards face up as he deals them, and the chosen cards appear at the same time at the same location.

Re-examine the handling of the cards and you will see that the number of cards dealt by the first spectator is always the number of cards between the two spectators' cards. Then, later, since the deck is divided into two groups, this number must be divided by 2. When ten cards are dealt, the key number is 5. Let us assume that when the performer deals out the two equal groups, the second card dealt is the second spectator's card. That then becomes the top card of the right group. Meanwhile, the performer has taken five cards off the top of the left group, and therefore the top card of the left group will be the first spectator's card. (The other five cards of the original separating ten are in the right-hand groups, under the second spectator's card.)

34. NOMENCLATURE

This effect was created by Joseph Dunninger, the famous mentalist. It has the personal touch, using names of the people known to the spectators, and seems to dispel any doubt in the spectators' minds that the trick may not be self-working.

PRESENTATION AND EFFECT

The performer hands the deck to the spectator, then turns his back, requesting the spectator to shuffle the cards thoroughly, count off a small number of cards—not more than twelve, and place them in his pocket.

This being done, the performer instructs the spectator to count off the same number, note the bottom card of the group he counts off, and replace them on top of the pack in their original position. Taking the deck from the spectator, the performer asks three other persons to give him a name each. (If there is only one spectator present, have him call out three names. For example: William, Joseph, Margaret.)

Each person is to spell his own name (or names called) by dealing a card from the top of the deck onto the table for each letter. The performer illustrates this by casually spelling out the names in the order called, dealing a card off the deck onto the table for each letter spelled, letting each card fall upon the card dealt before it. The performer continues this until he has spelled out the three selected names. The performer replaces the group of cards on top of the deck and hands the deck to the spectator who has the cards in his pocket. He is instructed to place them on top of the pack, then to hand the deck to the person who called out the first name. This person spells his name by dealing a card off the deck for each letter spelled. The deck is then passed to the person who called the second name, who does likewise; then to the person who called name number three, who deals out his name as the others did.

At this point the performer reminds the spectators that: 1) the pack had been shuffled before the trick; 2) he does not know the chosen number; 3) he has no way of learning the selected card; 4) spectators chose names of their own personal friends, or at random, and spelled them individually. The performer then lifts the top card off the deck and asks for the name of the selected card. He turns over this top card, and it is the chosen card.

THE SECRET

When the performer deals off the cards from the deck and spells out the selected names he is actually reversing the dealt cards. With the addition of the cards in the pocket, the trick will always work. It cannot fail if done as described above.

35. HANDS-OFF MIRACLE

Recently, at a magicians' luncheon in the Dixie Hotel in New York City, Joseph Barnett, the lawyer magician, performed an old trick with a new twist that completely baffled most of the magicians present. This is it.

PRESENTATION AND EFFECT

The performer states that he is going to perform a card miracle without touching the pack of cards at any time during the selection and return of the card to the deck. The performer hands the spectator a deck of cards and instructs the spectator to shuffle and cut the deck to his heart's content. Upon completion of the shuffles and cuts, the performer tells the spectator to place the pack face down on the table, and states that it is impossible for him to know the position of any cards in the deck. He then asks the spectator to cut the pack at any position he desires and to note and remember the bottom card of the cut group. The performer now makes a gesture by flipping his forefinger about three or four inches from the top card of the group, which is still resting on the table, and tells the spectator to replace the cut portion of cards back on top of the packet on the table, thereby putting the cards back in their original positions. The spectator is then instructed by the performer to square the cards and to cut the deck several times. Up to this moment the performer states, "I have never touched the cards, and you have done everything yourself."

The performer instructs the spectator to place the deck face down on the table. The performer now for the first time cuts the deck and turns over the bottom card of the cut portion. It is found to be the spectator's selected card. A truly great trick has been completed.

The Secret

The directions are followed exactly as explained in the Presentation and Effect except that the secret lies in the fact that the performer must have some salt in his pocket—or some salt can be sprinkled on the table should salt be handy. The performer

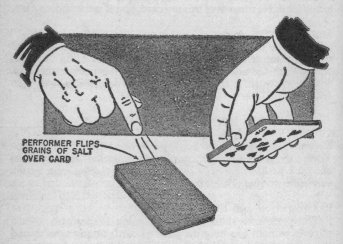

PERFORMER FLIPS
GRAINS OF SALT
OVER CARD

merely has to touch the salt with his forefinger and some grains will stick to his forefinger. When the performer requests the spectator to cut the cards and note the bottom card of the cut group, he merely points to the bottom portion which is resting on the table, and flips his thumb on his forefinger. This causes one or more grains of salt to fall on the packet of cards on the table. When the cut group is returned on top of this packet, regardless of the number of times cut, the performer merely cuts the pack and the pack breaks exactly at the position where the salt was dropped. Some performers place the deck on the floor and lightly kick the side of the deck with one foot.

It is suggested that the performer practice this trick several times before attempting it. It is also suggested that the performer refrain from urging the spectator to cut the deck too often when learning this trick, because if the performer knows approximately how far down in the deck the selected card is, it will be much easier to cut the selected card.

If the performer desires another method of finding the selected card, he can place the deck behind his back and cut the cards. The deck will also break at the spot where the salt is, or the performer may merely tap the deck on one side while the cards are resting on the table, and the cards will break at the exact position where the salt was placed.

A little practice, and the performer will have a real great trick.

Joseph Barnett cuts the deck behind his back, removes the bottom card of the cut portion, brings this card forward, and it is the noted card!

36. THE PHOTOGRAPHIC MATCH

This is a cute trick, and leaves the spectators more puzzled than mystified by the effect. This is from Russell Swan, the top-flight night-club magician.

PRESENTATION AND EFFECT

The performer requests the spectator to call out a number from 1 to 10. Spectator, for example, calls out number 6. Performer deals five cards off the top of the deck onto the table face down, and turns over the sixth card. This proves to be a 5-spot. The performer states that he will now count down five more cards. This he does, putting the next card on the table face down to one side. The performer states that the spectator had a free choice in selecting a card.

The performer removes a match box from his pocket and takes out a match. He states that he has made a new discovery in the field of photography. No film, camera, or developing process is necessary. To prove his theory, he turns the selected card face up on the table, strikes a match, and while it is burning waves it about an inch or less above the marking of the card. He announces, while doing this, that if he is successful, the number of the card will photograph itself on the head (tip) of the match. After the tip of the match has been burned, the performer examines its head, and on the burnt head, a number identical with the marking (plus the suit) on the playing card is seen. The performer remarks that with a little more experimenting, he will some day eliminate the camera entirely.

THE SECRET

The performer forces the spectator's card in the following manner. The performer, beforehand, arranges the top ten cards of the deck, as follows: On top of the deck is placed a 10-spot, following below, 9, 8, 7, 6, 5, 4, 3, 2, ace. Below the ace (eleventh card from the top of the deck) the performer places the card that he desires to force. For example, a 3-spot of diamonds.

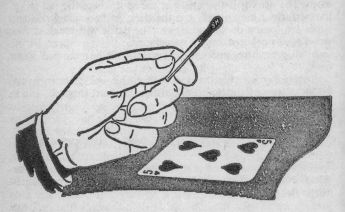

Then the performer takes a sharp, pointed lead pencil and a packet of matches and writes the number 3 plus the ♦ (diamond) on the match head of one of the matches in the packet. Naturally, it should be written on the side of the match that is hidden from view when tearing the match from the packet.

Only the two above preparations are necessary. The performer has the spectator call a number from 1 to 10. For instance, the spectator calls number 3. The performer deals the first two cards from the top of the deck onto the table face down. The third card from the top he turns face up. This card proves to be an 8-spot. The performer counts down eight cards, counting the 8-spot as number 1. After the eight cards have been counted off, he deals the next card on top of the table face down. This is the spectator's selected card. It proves to be the eleventh card from the top of the deck (which the performer had prearranged). Regardless of what number the spectator calls, the eleventh card will always be forced.

The performer turns the selected card face up on the table, he then tears the prepared match from the packet, keeping the side of the head which is marked facing the table, so that the "mark" is out of sight. He strikes the match and waves it over the indicia of the card. When the tip of the match has been burned, he blows out the match. He then turns the match around and shows the number photographed on the head of the match.

37. PERPLEXITY

This is a favorite of George Delaney's, the magician.

PRESENTATION AND EFFECT

The performer spreads a pack of cards from hand to hand and requests a spectator to select a card and memorize it. The performer turns away from the spectator stating, "Don't let me see the card." Turning back to face the spectator, the performer says, "On second thought, let me see the card."

Taking the card from the spectator, the performer turns the card face up and places it on the bottom of the pack, letting half of the card protrude. The performer then turns the deck over and shows that the selected card is face to face with the bottom card of the pack. He then turns the deck over again so that the selected card is once again the bottom card of the deck. The performer squares up the deck in this position, and turns the deck over several times. The performer cuts the deck, completes the cut, but does not square the pack. The performer again turns the deck over, proving that the selected card is still face to face with the original bottom card of the deck and both are in the center of the deck. The performer turns the deck over again to its former position and squares up the deck.

Placing the deck face down on the palm of the left hand, the performer states that the selected card is face up in the deck, that he is going to reverse the selected card so that it will be face down, and is going to compel the two black aces to reverse themselves in the pack—the selected card will then be found face down between the two face-up black aces.

The performer taps the pack, utters a few magic words, spreads out the deck, and all the cards are found face down with the exception of the two black aces. They are found face up, and in between them is a face-down card. It is the spectator's selected card.

THE SECRET

The performer places the two black aces face up on the bottom of the deck. Spreading the deck to permit the spectator to select a card, the performer takes care not to allow the spectator to see the two face-up aces on the bottom of the deck. As the spectator removes a card from the deck, the performer turns away, saying, "Don't let me see the card." At the same time the performer slips the bottom ace onto the top of the pack and turns the entire deck over, so that the bottom of the pack appears to be the top, and vice versa. Turning back to the spectator, the performer says it doesn't matter if he does see the card. Taking the card from the spectator, he places it face up on the bottom of the deck (this places it face to face with an ace which apparently is the bottom card of the deck). The performer stresses the fact that the selected card is actually reversed in relation to the rest of the deck. To bear this remark out, he turns the pack over and the spectator sees the selected card face to face with the bottom ace. (That is why he lets the bottom selected card protrude, so that it can be seen to be reversed.) Turning the deck over again the performer cuts the cards and the selected card (reversed) is seen in the center of the pack.

To complete the trick it is necessary to turn the deck over again so that the deck when spread out will be face down. To do this deceptively, here is a subtle move for accomplishing it. Place the right thumb underneath the deck, fingers on top of the deck. Hold the deck firmly, and turn the deck over and back several times (while talking) and stop with the thumb on top and the fingers underneath, then you have the pack turned over. This is very simple to do; it is accomplished just by turning the wrist. This reverses the pack very deceptively, and the spectator never notices the change. The performer then spreads the deck out, and the selected card is found face down between the two face-up black aces.

38. THE INITIALS WILL TELL

This unusual card trick, performed as described below, is attributed to all the following magicians, who at one time or another added a little something of their own: Cardini, Dai Vernon, Nate Leipzig, Francis Carlyle, and Martin Gardner. A few subterfuges have been added by the author.

PRESENTATION AND EFFECT

The performer removes a deck of cards from the card case, places them face down on the table, then riffle shuffles them once. He asks a spectator to cut the deck, and the performer completes the cut.

The performer then picks up the deck from the table and places it face down in his left hand. He then slides the top card into his right hand and says, "I am going to insert this card into the deck face up, and so that I don't know where I am going to insert the card, I will do it under the table." The performer now puts his left hand under the table; he also puts his right hand under the table, still holding the card face down. While both hands are under the table the performer remarks that he has turned the card face up and inserted it near the center of the deck.

He now brings the deck forward and spreads the face-down deck from his left hand into his right, looking for the face-up card that he inserted into the deck under the table. He finds this card face up in the deck and cuts the deck at the spot where the face-up card was found, bringing the face-up card to the top of the deck. For example, let us say the face-up card is an 8-spot. The performer places this card on the table to one side. He places the deck on the table in front of the spectator. He says, "The face-up card was an 8-spot, so will you take the deck, count down to the eighth card from the top of the deck, and note and remember that eighth card. Replace the cards in their original positions. Then return the 8-spot which is on the table to the deck, and thoroughly shuffle the deck."

After this has been done, the performer takes the deck and spreads it face up on the table in ribbon fashion. The performer tells the spectator to place his right hand about six inches above the cards and to move his hand from left to right the entire length of the spread cards.

The performer takes hold of the spectator's right hand and places it in the above-described position to illustrate what he wants the spectator to do. The spectator moves his hand back and forth several times, and the performer remarks that he does not seem to be getting any impression whatsoever, so will he (spectator) close his right hand into a fist and place it up to his forehead and concentrate real hard on the name of his selected card.

A moment of this, and the performer asks the spectator to open his clenched fist and to look at his palm. The spectator is surprised to see the initials of his selected card printed on the palm of his hand.

THE SECRET

A little secret preparation is required before the performer starts this trick.

The performer requires a cube of sugar. On one side of this cube he prints the initials of a card. For example, should the performer desire the selected card to be the ace of spades, he takes a pencil and prints the initials A. S. on one side of the sugar cube. It is advisable to print over the initials several times with a heavy pencil to get the best results. This being accomplished, the performer places the sugar cube in his small change pocket (which is inside his right-hand coat pocket). The initialed side is placed facing toward his body.

Now he arranges the deck of cards in the following manner. Take the desired selected card, the ace of spades in this instance, and place seven cards on top of it. Then place an 8-spot of any suit face up on top of this face-down group. Then place four or five indifferent cards face down on the table. The group of nine cards—ace plus seven indifferent cards, plus the face-up 8-spot —are placed on top of the four or five indifferent cards. The remainder of the deck is placed on top of the face-up 8-spot, which is the top card of the group now resting on the table. The deck, thus arranged, is placed in the card case.

At the start of the trick the performer removes the deck from the card case, riffle shuffles the deck once, taking pains not to disturb the bottom thirteen-card arrangement.

The spectator cuts the deck and the performer completes the cut himself. Then he takes the top card into his right hand and says that he is going to insert it into the deck face up, and so that he can't know at what position he inserts it, he is going to do it under the table. This business with the top card is purely psychological, because what the performer does under the table is merely to put this card back on top of the deck, face down. Then when he brings the cards into full view and the cards are spread, the spectator sees the face-up 8-spot, and is led to believe that it was the top card the performer inserted face up into the deck under the table. The selection of the ace of spades is now obvious.

The performer gets the initials of the ace of spades on the palm of the spectator's hand in the following manner. Before the performer tells the spectator to place his hand about six inches above the spread-out deck and move his hand back and forth, the performer dampens his right thumb with his tongue. Then he presses his dampened thumb on the cube of sugar where the initials have been printed. This procedure transfers the initials, A.S. in this instance, to the thumb. With the thumb still damp, the performer takes the spectator's hand to illustrate how high he should hold it. While this is being done, the performer presses his dampened thumb against the fleshy palm of the spectator's hand. This in turn transfers part of the initials from the performer's thumb onto the spectator's palm.

The conclusion of the trick is described under Presentation and Effect.

Note: Some performers may prefer the following variation to the above trick. The initials are transferred to the spectator's forehead. It is a great comedy trick. All other spectators look at the spectator's forehead and name the selected card. Finally a mirror is produced for the spectator and he sees the initials on his forehead.

This trick is done exactly as described under the preceding trick, "The Initials Will Tell," except that the performer pretends to read the spectator's mind through his eyes, and presses his thumb on the spectator's forehead to transfer the initials.

39. DOUBLE DUTY

PRESENTATION AND EFFECT

The performer produces a deck of cards and asks the spectator to cut the cards into two groups, taking the bottom half for himself, leaving the top half for the performer. The performer instructs the spectator to take as many cards as he desires, from one to ten, from his group, and to place them on top of the performer's group while the performer turns his back. The performer announces that he will fan out the cards, select one without looking at the faces of the cards, will show the selected card to the spectator, and it will be found that the denomination of the card will equal the number of cards the spectator put on top of the group. The performer can do this repeatedly, and no matter how many cards the spectator puts on top of the group, the performer will always pick a card equal to that number.

THE SECRET

Before the start of the trick the performer must arrange a group of thirteen cards, starting with ace, 2, 3, 4, 5, up to and including 10. It is best to use different suits, some cards from each to form this group. On top of these ten cards he adds three indifferent cards, which makes the group total of thirteen cards.

These cards are placed on top of the deck, the ace being the thirteenth card down, the 10 being the fourth card down, and the three indifferent cards being the first three on top of the deck. When the deck is cut, the spectator must pick his cards from the bottom half and place them on the top half. After this, the performer may square up the entire deck, making one group but keeping the arranged cards on top, or he may use just his top half of the deck to continue the trick, whichever he prefers. When he fans out the cards, he must be certain always to pick the fourteenth card from the top of the deck. This card will always equal the number of cards the spectator used in this experiment. If he wants to repeat the trick, the performer must get rid of the cards the spectator put on top of the prepared group. These can be taken from the top and put on the bottom of the deck, and he must be sure to return the card he pulled from the arranged group back to its proper place before attempting the trick again. This can be done while the spectators are discussing the effect of the trick.

40. THE LOVE BIRDS

PRESENTATION AND EFFECT

The performer shuffles a pack of cards and requests the spectator to cut off the top half of the deck for himself, leaving the bottom half for the performer. The performer and spectator each selects a card from his own group, looks at it and remembers it, and places it back on top of his group of cards. The performer places his half of the deck on top of the spectator's group of cards, requests the spectator to cut the deck several times, and announces, "We have each selected a card and placed it in different portions of the deck. With a mere snap of the fingers, those two cards will join each other in the deck. Upon looking through the cards, we will find them together. Call your card."

The spectator names the card he selected. The performer names the card he selected. The performer snaps his fingers and says, "Go." Then, looking through the cards, they find both selected cards together.

THE SECRET

While the performer shuffles the cards, he makes sure to see the bottom card of the deck and to remember it. The spectator cuts the top half for himself, leaves the bottom half for the performer. Each selects a card from his own group and returns it to the top of his own group. The performer places his half of the deck on top of the spectator's. The spectator names the card he selected, but the performer names the card he was remembering from the bottom of the deck. When the performer placed his half of the deck on top of the spectator's, he was placing the bottom card he was remembering on top of the spectator's selected card. That is how the two cards will be found together in the deck. You can see, therefore, that the card the performer really selected does not have to be remembered, as it does not play any part in this trick.

41. HIT THE DECK

PRESENTATION AND EFFECT

The performer requests a spectator to select a card from the deck while he is spreading them face down from one hand to the other. The spectator is told to look at the card and remember it. The spectator places the card back into the deck, and the performer cuts the pack several times.

Then, looking through the pack (face up), the performer states that he is having a little difficulty finding the card, but says, "Don't tell me what it is, I'll get it yet." The performer thinks for a little while, smiles, and says, "I think we can find this card by using magnetism. What I mean by that is, your fingers might just be magnetic enough to draw the selected card from the pack."

After saying this, the performer takes the top card from the pack and asks the spectator, "Is this your card?" To this the spectator will reply, "No."

Still holding the top card, the performer turns the deck so that the bottom card can be seen and asks, "Is this your card?" Once again the spectator will say, "No."

To this the performer replies, "Good. Your card is neither on the top nor bottom of the deck, so it must be some place else." Now he places the top card he's been holding on top of the bottom card, and leaves the deck face up.

"Here is what I want you to do," the performer says. "While I hold the pack with my fingertips, I want you to hit the deck hard, not my fingers though, so try to hit the deck about two inches from my fingers."

The spectator does as instructed, and is amazed to see when he hits the deck that all the cards fall to the floor except the card he had selected.

THE SECRET

The performer peeks and memorizes the bottom card of the deck when in the act of shuffling at the beginning of the trick. The spectator picks a card and looks at it. In the meantime the performer separates the cards he holds into groups, holding one group in each hand. The performer pushes forward the group containing the top half of the deck, and the spectator replaces his selected card on top of this group. The performer places the other group, which contains the bottom half of the deck, on top. This means the bottom card which the performer memorized is on top of the spectator's selected card. The performer cuts the cards several times. Cuts do not disturb the setup.

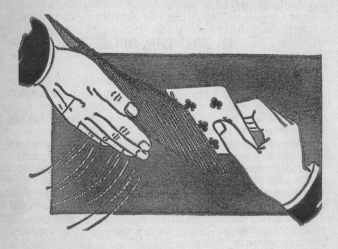

Looking through the cards the performer finds the spectator's card, and in the act of being confused he places this card second from the top of the deck.

After hesitating awhile, as if still looking for the card, the performer removes the top card of the deck and shows it to the spectator, who denies this is his selected card. The performer turns the deck over and exposes the bottom card, and the spectator again says it is not his selected card. The performer leaves the pack in this face-up position and replaces the top card, which he is still holding, on top of the face-up pack. (This means he is really placing the top card of the deck on top of the bottom card of the deck.) Therefore, the second card from the top of the deck, which is the spectator's selected card, is now the bottom card of the deck, since the deck has been turned face up.

The performer holds the deck, as follows: The tip of the index finger and middle finger on the bottom of the narrow edge of the deck, and the thumb on top. When the spectator strikes the deck, the performer should hold the deck fairly tightly. The blow will knock all the cards out of the performer's hand—except the bottom card which naturally is the spectator's selected card.

42. THE BETTING CARD TRICK

PRESENTATION AND EFFECT

The performer shuffles the pack and places it on the table. He remarks that he will do a card trick without once handling the cards himself until after the selected card has been returned to the deck.

A spectator is asked to cut the deck into three piles and then requested to remove a card from the deck. The spectator is told to look at the card and memorize it, then place it on top of any one of the three piles. Then he is instructed to reassemble the pack, placing one pile on top of the other till he has formed one deck.

The spectator is requested to cut the cards several times, then to hand the deck to the performer, who deals the cards from the top of the deck face up onto the table.

After dealing a number of cards, the performer stops dealing and remarks that he will make a bet that the next card he turns over will be the spectator's card. The spectator, who noticed that his has already been dealt face up, accepts the bet. Nevertheless, the performer always wins the bet.

THE SECRET

The method of finding the selected card is simplicity itself, but as in any card trick, the manner of presentation is important.

After the performer has shuffled the cards, he secretly notes and memorizes the bottom card of the deck. The spectator is requested to cut the deck into three piles. As the cards are being cut, the performer must keep his eye on the pile which contains his *key card*. The spectator is now requested to select a card from any one of the piles, memorize it, and place it on top of any one of the three piles. The performer requests the spectator to place each pile on top of the other, making certain that the pile containing the key card is placed on top of the selected card, and to cut the deck several times.

The above procedure is followed all the time except when the spectator places the selected card on top of the pile containing the key card. Should this happen, the performer requests the spectator to cut that pile "to lose your card in the middle." Then the spectator squares up the deck and proceeds as described above.

It is suggested that the performer point to the piles when informing the spectator to cut the cards, or to place one pile on top of the other.

When the above instructions are followed, the selected card will be below the key card.

Now the performer takes the pack and starts dealing the cards face up, onto the table, looking for the key card as the cards are dealt, knowing that the card dealt after the key card is the selected card. When he has seen the selected card, he forgets his key card and memorizes the selected card instead. He continues dealing several cards more from the deck onto the table, but always making sure part of the selected card is visible in the upturned pile.

He now stops dealing the cards, but holds the last card in his hand as if to turn it over, and says, "I'll bet you the next card I turn over will be your card."

The spectator having seen his card passed believes the performer means that the card in his hand is the one he is going to turn over next. When the spectator says, "Bet," the performer replaces the card that he holds on top of the deck, reaches into the pile for the selected card, and turns it face down on the table.

This trick not only fools the spectator but also is good for a laugh—and possibly for a little argument if the wager is more than a nickel.

43. THE CARD THAT TELLS

My acknowledgements to Jack Spalding, the hypnotist, for this odd effect.

PRESENTATION AND EFFECT

The performer deals five cards face up in a row, then changes his mind and turns them face down. The performer continues to deal one card on each face-down card until fifteen cards have been dealt and we have five piles containing three cards each.

The performer then hands the rest of the deck to a spectator, who is instructed by the performer to place secretly any number of cards (from one to ten) in his pocket and to hold the remainder of the cards out of sight so the performer can't get any clue as to the number of cards remaining.

The performer now instructs the spectator to bring forth a card from his pocket and place it face down on the table. The performer at the same time removes a card from one of the five piles and places it face down to one side on the table.

The performer instructs the spectator to continue this procedure, taking one card at a time out of his pocket, and the performer removes a card from the five piles and places it face down to one side. The spectator is instructed, "When you have removed the last card from your pocket, I want you to announce that it is your last card." The performer at this time will turn over the card he is holding, and the number of spots or pips on

74

the card will equal the number of cards secretly pocketed by the spectator.

THE SECRET

The performer arranges ten cards in sequence from ace to 10 and places them on top of the deck. Then he places five indifferent cards on top of them. The performer, with this setup, starts the trick by dealing the five indifferent cards face up in a row with about two inches separating each card. He then changes his mind and turns them face down, leaving them in the same position. This move is purely psychological and is done to impress the spectator with the fact that the cards were not prearranged.

The performer continues to deal a card face down on each card on the table, dealing the top card of the deck onto the card at the extreme left and continuing the deal to the right. Another card is dealt on each pile, starting from left to right and making five piles of three cards each. The ten setup cards are so dealt that the ace is the top card of the pile to the extreme right, and below the ace is the 6-spot. The top card of the pile at the extreme left is the 5-spot, and below the 5 is the 10-spot. Naturally, when the ten cards are set up for this trick, they must be arranged with 10 as the top card of the setup and the ace as the bottom card, so that the ace will be the last card dealt.

When the spectator removes the first card from his pocket, the performer removes the ace from the pile at the extreme right. The spectator removes his second card, the performer removes the 2-spot from the next pile, etc. This is continued until the spectator announces that he has removed his last card. Then the performer holds his card in his hand without showing it, and asks the spectator how many cards he pocketed, stating that for the trick to be a success the card that he is holding must be a card of the same number that the spectator pocketed. Upon turning over the card he holds, the performer proves the trick to be a success.

44. MIND CONTROL

This card trick was much favored by my good friend Max Holden, the Magical Dealer.

PRESENTATION AND EFFECT

The performer turns his back while the spectator is shuffling the cards. Turning around, he takes the deck from the spectator and explains what the spectator is to do when the performer turns his back the second time. The performer illustrates, "Think of any number, say 6, for example, and count off that number of cards from the top of the deck, remembering the last card (sixth card) you deal off." To show how this is done, the performer counts the cards out loud as he deals them one at a time into a pile on the table. "You thought of six, so you note and remember the sixth card, and place it on the pile on the table." The performer does not expose the face of the sixth card to the spectator. The performer now drops the remainder of the pack on top of the pile on the table. Picking up the entire deck, he hands it to the spectator. He instructs the spectator to deal off, in the same manner as illustrated, to any number he chooses or thinks of. The spectator must note and memorize the card dealt

off at the mentally selected number. Placing the balance of the pack on top of the pile resting on the table (balance of the deck goes on top of the selected card), the spectator is instructed to cut and square the pack several times. The chosen card is now hopelessly lost. All this is done while the performer has his back turned to the spectator.

The performer now turns, facing the spectator, takes the cards and spreads them face up on the table (sort of ribbonwise). The performer now slowly passes his hand back and forth over the cards, and finally his hand drops and pushes one card forward, out of the deck. It is the chosen card.

THE SECRET

When the performer is illustrating what the spectator should do when he arrives at number 6 (example given above), he does not expose the sixth card to the spectator, but does turn it up enough so that he can quickly get a glimpse of the card himself. He remembers that card as his key card. When the performer is slowly passing his hand over the cards, he is actually looking for his key card. When he locates it, he secretly counts six cards to the left of the key card, and the sixth card will be the spectator's chosen card. This is the card the performer pushes forward.

If the performer desires to make this a mind reading feature, it is suggested that he have the spectator hold his hand while it is passing over the cards, and state that he is trying to get a mental vibration from the spectator's mind.

45. THE WHISPERING CARD

This trick is credited to Ladson Butler, the New York magician.

PRESENTATION AND EFFECT

The performer riffle shuffles a deck of cards on the table, then requests a spectator to cut to as near the center as he can. The performer picks up the half that was originally at the top of the deck and asks the spectator to count off the other half, dealing one card at a time onto the table, dealing each card on top of the card previously dealt. The performer does the same with his half.

The performer asks the spectator, "How many cards have you got?" Regardless of the spectator's answer, the performer says, "Swell."

The performer now turns up the top card of his deck face up on the table and calls it a "whispering" card. For instance, if the card is the ace of spades, the performer calls it the "whispering" ace of spades, etc. The spectator is now asked to take the top card of his packet and insert it into the center of the packet he holds, then to do the same with the bottom card of the packet.

The performer then requests the spectator to note the top card of the packet (spectator's), to place it face down next to the "whispering" ace of spades, and to make sure that he does not reveal its identity to the performer. A second spectator is requested to remove the next card (top card of spectator's group), note and memorize it, and place it face down next to the "whispering" ace of spades. Likewise, a third spectator removes the next card (top card of spectator's group), looks at it, and places it face down adjacent to the "whispering" ace of spades.

The performer now takes the "whispering" ace of spades, puts one end on top of one of the selected cards, and bends his head so that his ear reaches the other end of the ace of spades. He pretends to listen, and states that the "whispering" ace of spades is telling him the name of the selected card. The performer names a card, and upon turning over the selected card, the performer's announcement is found to be correct. The same procedure holds true for the other two selected cards.

THE SECRET

The performer places three memorized cards face down on the table, then places one card below (at the bottom) the three memorized cards, and places the remainder of the deck on top of all. In other words, the performer has placed the three memorized cards in the deck at the following positions: the first memorized card, fifty-first card down in the deck; the second memorized card, fiftieth card down in the deck, and the third memorized card, the forty-ninth card down in the deck.

The performer riffle shuffles the deck, making sure not to disturb the bottom four cards. He asks the spectator to cut the deck, taking the top cut half for himself, giving the lower cut half to the spectator.

Now the performer requests the spectator to deal his cards face down one on top of each other (performer illustrates with his group), and to count the entire packet in this manner. The performer does likewise. The performer asks the spectator how many cards he is holding, and regardless of the answer, the performer says, "Swell." This question is only a subterfuge to cover up the real purpose of the count, which is to reverse the entire packet held by the spectator. The spectator's packet now contains the three memorized cards in the following positions: first memorized card is second from top, second memorized card is third from the top, and the third memorized card is fourth from the top.

Now all the performer has to do is turn his "whispering" card face up in the center of the table. Having the spectator bury the top and bottom cards of his packet into the center of the packet brings the three memorized cards on top. The rest is merely the noting of these cards by the spectator and the performer's noting where each memorized (selected) card is placed so that he can call it in its proper order.

46. THE STUBBORN CARD

This cute trick was created by my friend Bob Hummer, the clever Midwestern magician.

PRESENTATION AND EFFECT

A group of cards is freely shown, some cards of which are face up and some face down. After a considerable amount of cutting and turning over cards, the performer hands the packet to the spectator requesting him to cut the cards one or more times. The spectator is then instructed to look at the top card of the pack, and to remember it. If the top card happens to be face down, the spectator is told to reverse it and leave it face up on top of the pack. If the card happens to be face up, the spectator is told to reverse it and leave it face down on top of the pack. This reversing is done after the spectator has looked at the card and memorized it. Now the spectator is told he may cut the cards as often as he desires.

After the cut the performer takes the cards and, without looking at them, places them under a table or behind his back. He states that he is going to arrange the cards so that all but the card looked at by the spectator will face one way. The performer asks the spectator to name his card (although this is not necessary), and when the performer brings the cards into full view, they are all facing the same way except the card named by the spectator, which is the only reversed card in the group.

THE SECRET

Arrange twenty cards so that every other card is reversed (one face up, one face down, one face up, etc.). Keep the packet closed so that the spectator cannot discover the setup.

The performer cuts the pack, turns over the two top cards, cuts the pack, turns over the two top cards, cuts the pack, etc. The performer does this as many times as he desires. This little bit of cutting and turning over of two cards has not altered the setup of the cards at all.

Bob Hummer suggests that the performer hand the deck to the spectator and allow him to turn over the two top cards and cut the pack behind his back; but doing this gives the spectator

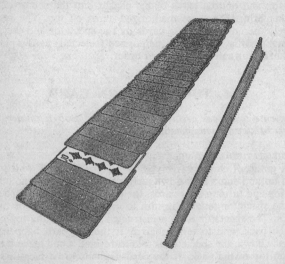

the impression that the trick is self-working, and this usually leads to the discovery of the solution. Also, since you might have a smart alec for a spectator, who will try to cross you up, or a spectator who will unwittingly do something wrong, it is better for the performer to do all the turning over of cards. After this he can hand the deck to the spectator, allowing him to cut as much as he desires.

The spectator is told to look at the top card of the deck, and to reverse it. Then he is instructed to cut the cards and hand the pack to the performer under the table or behind the performer's back.

Holding the cards out of sight, the performer deals the cards from one hand to the other. The first card is dealt in the regular way, the second card is turned over and then dealt, the third card is dealt in the regular way, the fourth card is turned over and then dealt. This method of dealing is continued until all the cards have been dealt from one hand to the other. On returning the cards to full view, it will be found that all the cards face the same way except the card named by the spectator, which will be reversed in the group. If the performer prefers, he may separate the cards as described in "Separating the Red and Black Cards," page 36.

47. COLOR SCHEME

This trick was created by Oscar Weigle, the clever New York magician.

PRESENTATION AND EFFECT

The performer removes a deck of cards from the card case and counts off twenty cards face down onto the table. While doing this he remarks that he is going to attempt a very difficult feat in color separation. The performer mixes the group of cards so that some are face up and some face down, all intermingled, in the following manner. The performer cuts the packet at any point, reverses the top two cards (so that they are face up), cuts the packet again, reverses the top two cards again, and continues in this fashion until he has repeated the procedure four or five times.

The performer now hands the pack to the spectator and requests him to cut the pack either under the table or behind his back, whichever is more convenient. After he has cut the cards, the spectator is instructed to take the top card of the pack and place it on the bottom of the deck. The next card which is on top of the deck he is instructed to reverse (turn over) and place on the table. The following card from the top is placed on the bottom of the deck as was the original top card. The next card on top of the deck is reversed and placed on the table. The spectator does this a few times, and is then told he may cut the pack. After cutting, he continues as described above. He places the top card of the deck on the bottom, places the next card on the table after he has reversed it, etc. He is to form two piles on the table, one for the face-up cards and one for the faced-down cards.

After ten cards have been placed on the table the spectator is told to reverse the entire packet, shuffle and then cut the cards. After this has been done, the spectator once again proceeds as described above. He places the top card of the deck on the bottom, reverses the next card and places it on the table.

Even though the spectator continues to mix the cards to his satisfaction before placing them on the table, the end result—when the packet has been exhausted—will be that all the red cards will be face up and all the black cards will be face down (or vice versa). The surprising part of this trick is that not only has the spectator succeeded in separating the face-up from the face-down cards, but he has made all the red cards face one way and the black cards face the other.

THE SECRET

The performer arranges the twenty top cards of the deck so that the colors alternate (first red, then black, then red, etc.). If the performer desires to repeat the trick, it is advisable that he arrange the top forty cards in the deck in the manner described above.

The cards are placed back into the card case, and at the proper moment the performer removes the cards and counts twenty cards face down onto the table without exposing their faces. He does not mention at this time what he is going to do or anything about the arrangement of the cards.

The performer, holding the group of twenty cards in his hand, takes off the top two cards of the deck, reverses them (turns them over), and places them face up on top of the deck. This means that since he took off the top two cards and turned them over together, the card which was second in the deck is now face up on top, and the card which was on top of the deck is now face up in second place.

The performer now cuts the deck, using a regulation square cut (taking a group off the top and putting it on the bottom). The performer takes the two top cards from the top of the deck, reverses them together, and places them on top of the deck. He cuts the deck again, and proceeds as described above until he has done this (reverses two top cards and replaces them on top and cuts the deck) four or five times.

There is a related arrangement to the cards at all times—no matter how often the performer continues to reverse two cards at a time or where he cuts the packet. The performer then shows the cards. They are found to be all mixed up: some face up, some face down, some red showing, some black. Now he hands the cards to the spectator and instructs him to hold them under the table out of sight.

The spectator is next directed to transfer the top card of the packet to the bottom. He is then to reverse the next card, bring it forward as it is then, and place it on the table. The next card goes to the bottom (as did the original top card) without reversal, while the following card is turned over, brought forward, and dropped on the table. The spectator starts two piles on the table, one for face-down cards and one for face-up cards.

The performer counts the cards as they are placed on the table. When ten cards are on the table, the performer says, "Stop. So you won't think anything has been arranged, and to give you a good chance to fool me, reverse the entire pack,

82

shuffle the cards again, and cut the pack. Now they must really be mixed up."

After reversing the pack, shuffling and cutting, the spectator is instructed to continue as before: place the top card on the bottom of the deck, reverse the next card and place it on the table in its proper pile.

When the entire packet has been exhausted, it will be found that the spectator succeeded in separating the red from the black cards. All red cards face one way, all black cards the other.

48. MAGIC NUMBERS

The following effect combines the magic of numbers with the magic of cards. It is positively a baffler and if performed properly will mystify the most skeptical spectators. This effect was created by the author and by Clayton Rawson, co-author of Scarne on Dice.

PRESENTATION AND EFFECT

The performer removes a pack of cards from the card box and gives the deck a thorough riffle shuffle. He states that he is going to deal cards onto the table face up until he has dealt five cards whose rank is 8 or less. If any court cards or 10's are dealt, they are to be put to one side and are not usable. The performer holds the deck face down and deals cards one at a time onto the table, turning each card face up as he deals it. When five cards have been dealt of the rank of 8 or less, the spectator is requested to arrange them in a row (horizontally) across the table in any order he desires.

The performer produces a pencil and piece of paper and states that he is going to write a "number prediction" on the paper. This he does, but does not allow the spectator to see what he writes. He folds the paper, gives it to the spectator to keep in his pocket.

The performer states that he is going to continue dealing from the top of the deck one card at a time face up, until five rows of five cards each have been dealt, all having the rank of 8 or less.

Example: If the spectator arranged the first five cards in a row so that they read 86542 from left to right, the performer deals off the next card and instructs the spectator to place it under the 8, the next card under the 6, and to continue across the row until five rows as described have been formed, each directly under the one above. After this has been done, the spectator is instructed to add the cards, starting with the card in the first row at the extreme right (in example above spectator would start with the 2), and to add down (vertically) just as though he were doing an arithmetic addition problem. The performer may add along with the spectator to see that the addition is done correctly.

The spectator records his total on a piece of paper. The performer scoops up all the cards and squares up the pack. The spectator takes out of his pocket the paper on which is written the performer's prediction. We find the performer's prediction and the total reached by adding up the cards to be exactly the same. The performer has correctly prognosticated the final result.

THE SECRET

The performer must secretly arrange the deck in the following order from the top of the face-down pack. The suit value of the cards does not count. The top card of the deck must be a *deuce*, directly below 4, 5, 6, 8, 3, 7, 8, 4, 2, 6, 2, ace, 5, 7, 2, 8, 3, 5, 4, 7, ace, 6, 4, 5, a total of twenty-five cards. After the performer has arranged this setup, he removes the seven remaining cards that have a rank of 8 or less from the pack (two 3's, two aces, one 6, one 7, one 8). These seven cards he places in his pocket. Now he places his setup group of twenty-five cards on top of the remainder of the pack. The pack comprises forty-five cards. Seldom will any notice be taken of the difference. The pack is placed in the card box, and the performer is ready to do the trick.

While the spectator is writing down the total of the addition, the performer scoops up all the cards on the table, squares up the deck and places it in the pocket where he has the seven cards he removed. Now, if a spectator wants to try to figure out how the trick is done the performer hands him the pack comprised of fifty-two cards, and he'll never be able to figure it out.

When the deck is removed from the card box, properly arranged, the performer places the deck on the table face up, cutting a group of cards from the top. The performer must make sure that the top card of the bottom half of the deck (which he can see, since the cards are face up) is a higher-ranking card than 8. This he can be sure of if he is careful not to cut more than twenty cards from the top of the deck. The performer then riffle shuffles together both halves of the deck. This he does only once. Then the deck is squared up and turned over face down on the table. This riffle shuffle does not disarrange the stacked cards, but merely inserts higher-ranking cards in between the setup. Since cards ranking higher than 8 are removed, the cards will be back in their exact original setup.

THE SECRET PREDICTION

The seemingly magical prediction is accomplished very easily. The performer merely looks at the five digit numbers represented by the first row, and subtracts 2 from the number at the extreme right, then places a 2 in front (extreme left) of his answer, making a six-digit number, which will be the correct prediction.

Example: Under Presentation and Effect we gave the example in which the first row of five cards arranged by the spectator would read 86542 from left to right. This being the case, the performer subtracts 2 from the figure on the extreme right, which in this case is also a 2. His answer would be 86540. Now he places a 2 to the extreme left of this answer, and the correct prediction which he writes down is 286540.

Another example: If the first row read 24856, from left to right, the secret prediction would be 224854.

49. THE ACROBATIC CARD

On one of my visits to the Torch Club in Union City, New Jersey, the owner of the club, Larry Klunck, described this fine effect to me.

PRESENTATION AND EFFECT

Larry said, "A fellow was sitting at the bar the other night, and he spread a pack of cards across the bar (ribbonwise). He asked me to pick a card from anywhere in the pack, concentrate on the card, and after I looked at it, push it back anywhere in the deck I liked. This man then squared the deck and had me cut it several times. He ran the cards from hand to hand with the cards facing him, and stated he might be able to find it if he shuffled the cards. He gave the pack a few riffle shuffles. Then he decided to throw the pack about five feet down the bar. He did this with a sort of sliding effect. And, John, what do you think? The 5 of clubs that I had picked out turned itself over on the deck, and it was the only face-up card in the entire deck."

Here is the solution.

THE SECRET

The performer has all the suits arranged from ace through king. On top of the deck are all the diamonds, below these he places all the clubs, then all the hearts, and at the bottom of the deck are all the spades. The cards are put into the card case after this arrangement until the performer decides to do the trick. He then takes the cards out of the card case and spreads the cards face down horizontally across the table. After the

85

spectator has selected a card and looked at it, he is instructed to push it back anywhere in the deck. All the performer has to do to find the selected card is to find the stranger card in any group. Or, if the card is returned to its proper group, he can easily find it because it will be the only card in the group not in sequence.

The only way the performer can fail to find the selected card is if it should be replaced exactly where it came from, but this very rarely ever happens.

By running through the cards without letting the spectators see their faces, the performer locates the selected card. He withdraws it and places it face down on top of the deck, then riffle shuffles the pack several times, making sure not to disturb the top card. This shuffling is done to mix the cards up so that the spectator cannot find any trace of preparation.

The performer takes the deck, holds it in his hand face down, and pushes the top card forward about three-fourths of an inch. The cards are gripped by the narrow edges. He releases the cards with a pushing motion so that the deck will slide over the

table, bar, or floor. But the pack must be held about ten inches above the surface on which it is to be dropped. A little practice will give you the right hold and the right angle at which to throw (slide) the deck.

When successful, all the cards remain face down except the top card, which will be turned over by the resistance of the air. Of course, this will be the spectator's selected card.

If you do not desire to slide the cards along the floor or table, you may drop the cards from the hand, holding the deck about one foot from the table, and the top card which is about three-fourths of an inch over the edge of the deck will turn itself over because of the resistance of the air.

50. FLIGHTY ACES

This trick is a "wow," according to that popular magician from Camden, New Jersey, Lu-Brent.

PRESENTATION AND EFFECT

The performer removes a pack of cards from the card case, looks through them, finds the four aces and withdraws them from the pack. They are placed face up on the table in full view of the audience. The performer deals from left to right one card face down on top of each ace, rotating the deal in poker fashion until he has dealt three cards face down on top of each ace, but he does not cover the aces completely. The aces should be seen at all times. The performer has a spectator name one of the four aces, whichever one he prefers. For example, the spectator may name the ace of hearts. This being done, the performer produces two ordinary envelopes and passes them around for inspection. When the audience is satisfied that the envelopes are perfectly plain, and empty, the performer takes the ace called by the spectator plus the three cards on top of it (in this case the ace of hearts plus three face-down cards), and places them just as they are into one of the envelopes. The envelope is sealed, the performer marks a large 1 on it, gives it to the spectator to initial, and instructs the spectator to place it in his pocket.

The performer scoops up the remaining cards on the table (the three remaining aces each with three cards on top of them) and places the twelve cards in the other envelope. This envelope he marks with a 2, and places in his own pocket.

The performer announces, "The spectator has an envelope in his pocket containing the ace of hearts" (example above) "and three indifferent cards. I have an envelope in my pocket containing the three remaining aces and nine indifferent cards. When I snap my fingers and say, 'Travel,' the three aces will leave my envelope and travel into the spectator's sealed envelope. The three indifferent cards in the spectator's envelope will travel and find themselves in my sealed envelope. In other words, if this trick is successful, the spectator will end up with the four aces, and I will have twelve indifferent cards."

The performer says, "Travel," and snaps his fingers. The spectator is instructed to tear open his envelope. Upon doing so he finds the four aces, and he holds them up for the audience to see. The performer then tears open his envelope, and it is found to contain twelve indifferent cards.

THE SECRET

The requirements for this trick are one regular pack of playing cards consisting of fifty-two cards, twelve additional aces (three of each suit) all having the same color and design as the deck of cards being used in this trick, one pencil, and three ordinary envelopes.

Before the start of the trick the performer places twelve indifferent cards from the deck into an envelope, marks the envelope with the number 2, seals it, and places it in his pocket. The cards should be placed in the envelope in the following manner: one face-up card, three face-down cards on top of it, one face-up card, three face down on top of it, one face-up card, three face down, one face up, three face down.

The twelve additional aces being used in this trick are placed face down on top of the deck in the following suit order from the top of the deck down: diamond, heart, spade, club, heart, spade, club, diamond, spade, club, diamond and heart (this being the twelfth card from top of deck).

The four aces that belong to the deck are placed as follows: the ace of clubs is placed about five cards from the bottom of the deck; the ace of diamonds, about ten cards from the bottom of the deck; the ace of hearts, about fifteen cards from the bottom of the deck; the ace of spades, about twenty cards from the bottom of the deck. Each of these aces should be about five cards apart. The pack of cards is then returned to the card case.

When the performer begins the trick, he removes the cards from the card case and turns the deck face up, deals the cards one by one (from the bottom of the deck) face up onto the table. When he arrives at the first ace, which will be the ace of clubs, he puts it face up on the table to the extreme left. The ace of diamonds will be dealt next. He puts this to the right of the ace of clubs (to form a row). Next he deals the ace of hearts, which is placed to the right of the ace of diamonds. The last ace dealt will be the ace of spades, which will be placed next to the ace of hearts at the extreme right of the row. The four aces are all placed face up. The performer picks up the cards he had dealt onto the table when looking for the aces, and returns them to the bottom of the deck (their original position).

The performer now turns the pack face down and deals from the top of the deck one card face down on each ace, dealing from left to right, and continues the deal until he has dealt three face-down cards on top of each ace (dealing Poker style). Dealing as directed, the performer deals the first card on top of the ace of clubs, and the twelfth card from the top of the deck he deals onto the ace of spades.

Each of the piles contain four aces, one of each suit, so no matter which ace the spectator calls out, the pile selected will contain four aces.

The spectator calls the name of one of the aces, and the performer puts that ace with the three face-down cards on top of it into one of the envelopes, without exposing the value of the three face-down cards. This is sealed and initialed by the spectator, and placed in his pocket.

The performer picks up the remaining cards, puts the three groups together without changing the position of the cards, and leaves the ace face up with three face-down cards on top, etc. He puts these twelve cards into the second envelope, seals it and marks it 2. He places it in his inside breast pocket, then immediately pulls it out again, saying he would like to have the spectator initial it also. Actually, he places the envelope in his pocket and leaves it there, and removes the envelope he placed there before the start of the trick (the one containing twelve indifferent cards).

After the performer's envelope is initialed, he places it in his outside breast pocket, and if the spectator does not already have his envelope there, he is instructed to put it in his own outside breast pocket so that the audience will have a chance to see the cards travel, if they can.

Needless to say, when the spectator opens his envelope he will find four aces, one face up and three face down. When the performer opens his envelope, he will find twelve indifferent cards, one face up, three face down, etc.

After the trick is finished the performer takes the spectator's four aces and his own twelve indifferent cards and returns them to the top of the deck. The cards can be passed around for examination, if desired, and it will be found to be a regulation fifty-two card deck with all cards accounted for. The twelve extra aces are safely out of sight in the performer's inside breast pocket, where it's a good place to leave them.

51. BRAUDE'S MENTAL CARD TRICK

The following effect was developed by Dr. Ben Braude, the clever amateur magician of New York City. Following is the good doctor's routine and patter.

PRESENTATION AND EFFECT

"Often during the course of doing some card tricks, I am challenged to read someone's mind. Without being fazed by the request, and with an attitude of 'bravado' (this is psychologically important), I challenge the spectator to think of any card in the deck he desires, and stressing the point by action, I hand him the deck to be shuffled. After he has shuffled to his heart's content, I ask him to hand me the deck. I then ask him to concentrate on the card he is thinking of, and I begin looking through the deck as if I were trying to find his card. I appear a bit disappointed, since I do not seem to get a clear impression because of disturbing influences. Then I square up the deck and place it face down on the table, explaining that I seem to have gotten one impression that is not very clear. I emphasize that I will mention a card, but if I am wrong, the spectator should just say, 'No,' and not mention his card. I then call out a card—if the spectator was thinking of that card it would be a miracle and the trick would be over.

"If the spectator says, 'No, that is not my card,' I place the deck face down on the table, and tell him that it might help to relax our minds and put us in a more receptive condition if he were to handle the deck and see his card. This is to be done fairly and squarely, under my supervision. I then proceed with the following instructions.

" 'Take about one-third of the deck from the top and shuffle as thoroughly as you wish. Place this back on top of the deck, and square up the cards. Take your card out of the deck now, and concentrate on it for a few moments, then place it square on top of the deck.

" 'Now, in order to hide that card so that I do not know where it is, take about one-third of the deck from the bottom, shuffle this packet well, and place it squarely on top of the deck. Now, you will admit that your card is lost among the cards and I have no idea or clue as to which it is. In order to make sure, please cut the deck, complete the cut, and if you care to you may cut them again, as often as you please. When you have finished, please hand me the deck.'

"I hold the deck faces toward me, backs toward the spectator, and start looking through the cards. I find the card the spectator has been thinking of, then I place the deck face down on the table. I ask the spectator to name his card, and then turn the deck over, exposing the bottom card (if I happen to have his card there), or turn over the top card of the deck (if I had placed his card there). Whichever way I do the trick, I always find the card the spectator is thinking of, proving that I really can read his mind."

THE SECRET

"The spectator thinks of a card, and shuffles the deck. When finished, he hands the deck to me. I look through the cards pretending I am trying to find his card while he concentrates on it. But actually I am counting the cards, starting from the top and counting down, without disturbing the order of the deck. I count down till I reach the twenty-sixth card, which I remember. This becomes my key card. After locating the key card, I fan through the rest of the deck, and place the deck face down on the table. I say that I've gotten an impression but it is not too clear. The card I call is the key card. You can see that if this happens to be the spectator's card, it would be a miracle. Since this is very unlikely, this is how I continue.

"The spectator cuts off the top third of the deck and shuffles it, then replaces it on top again. He looks through the cards, finds his card, and places it on top of the deck. He takes the bottom third of the deck, shuffles it, and places it on top of the deck. Then he cuts the cards. The spectator hands the deck back to me. I again look through the cards as if trying to find the spectator's card. What I am doing, however, is looking for my key card, which I have been remembering (the same card I called before). When I find it, counting the key card as number 1, I count upward through the deck to the twenty-sixth and twenty-seventh card. I place the twenty-sixth card on the bottom of the deck and the twenty-seventh face down on top of the deck. The spectator's card is either one of these two. I have him name his card, and then I show the bottom or the top card, depending on which card the spectator names.

"The spectator's card may be either twenty-sixth or twenty-seventh, depending on where in the deck it was originally. If it was in the lower part of the deck, my key card, which had been twenty-sixth from the top, becomes twenty-seventh from the top as a result of the transfer of the one card from the bottom to the top. If the card was in the upper part of the deck, the key card remains twenty-sixth."

Note: To find the spectator's card, the performer counts upward from the key card. When he reaches 26 he stops. If the key card should be the tenth card from the top of the deck, for example, counting the key card as number 1, when the performer reaches number 10, he would be at the end of the deck. He then starts counting the first card at the opposite end of the deck as number 11, and continues counting upward until he reaches 26.

52. THE MAGIC NUMBER TRICK

This trick is a pet effect of Jack Miller's, the professional magician, who has been doing it for over thirty years—which proves its effectiveness.

The performer hands a spectator a pencil and a piece of paper and asks him to write down a four-digit number of his own choice (this is done while the performer's back is turned). For example, the spectator may write down 1950. Then the spectator is told to total the numbers across: 1 plus 9 plus 5 plus 0—total, 15. Now he is to subtract this number from his four-digit number:

$$\begin{array}{r} 1950 \\ -15 \\ \hline 1935 \end{array}$$

The spectator is then requested to remove from a deck of cards four cards whose pip value corresponds to the final total. In this instance, he would remove an ace, 9, 3, and a 5. If a zero is part of the answer a queen is used. The spectator is told that each card he removes must be of a different suit. So he might have the ace of clubs, 9 of diamonds, 3 of hearts, and 5 of spades. This being done, the spectator is requested to place one of these four cards in his pocket and to hand the performer the other three cards in any order desired. The performer now names the card in the spectator's pocket.

THE SECRET

The trick is based on a mathematical principle. All the performer has to do is to add the pip value of the three cards, then subtract the total from the nearest figure of 18, 27, or 36, whichever is closest to his total. The difference will be the pip value of the other selected card, which is in the spectator's pocket. The suit naturally will be the missing suit. Since the spectator was instructed to select cards of four different suits, holding three cards, it is easy to determine the missing suit. Let us suppose the spectator placed the ace of clubs in his pocket. The performer adds the 9, 5, and 3, for a total of 17. He subtracts 17 from 18, and we know the spectator holds an ace. Since the club suit is missing, we know the spectator holds the ace of clubs.

53. INSTANTO

Cliff Green, the clever vaudeville magician, says this is one of the fastest effects possible with cards.

PRESENTATION AND EFFECT

The performer shuffles a deck of cards, then hands the deck to a spectator to shuffle also. Turning his back, the performer requests the spectator to take any number of cards, up to about one-third of the deck, from any part of the shuffled deck, and to put the remainder of the deck aside. The performer then requests the spectator:

1. To shuffle the cards he selected.
2. To note and memorize the bottom card of the group. This will be the spectator's selected card.
3. To think of a number smaller than the total amount of cards he is using. Then to deal this number (that he is thinking of) off the top of the packet and place them on the bottom of the packet.

The performer then turns around and faces the spectator. Taking the packet of cards from the spectator, he remarks, "This is the first time I have ever seen these cards. Concentrate on your card." The performer then studies the cards in the packet, attempting to find the spectator's card (looking at the bottom card first, next to bottom second, etc.). The performer then returns the cards to the spectator and turns his back again; he instructs the spectator to take off the top of the packet and place on the bottom of the packet a card or a number of cards equal to the number he originally thought of. This being done, the performer faces the spectator and requests him to empty his inner coat pocket, and the performer places the entire packet of cards into the spectator's inner (breast) coat pocket. Withdrawing his hand, the performer requests the spectator to concentrate on the name of his selected card. Putting his hand into the spectator's pocket, the performer instantly removes a card, without showing its face value. He asks the spectator to call the name of his chosen card, then the performer turns over the card he removed from the pocket, and it is found to be the spectator's card.

THE SECRET

The trick is actually self-working, but the performer has to do two things.

While he is attempting to find the card the spectator is thinking of, he actually reverses the position of all the cards, merely by dealing the cards face up from one hand to the other. For example, the card that was originally on the top of the packet is now on the bottom, and the bottom card is on the top, etc.

When the spectator deals off the top of the packet the number of cards equal to the number he was thinking of and places them on the bottom of the deck, the spectator has actually done the trick himself, because the spectator's card is now on top of the deck. Then, when the cards are in the spectator's pocket, the performer merely takes the top card of the packet and it is the spectator's chosen card.

If the performer desires, he can do this trick with more than one spectator, although the trick is sufficiently effective with only the one.

54. SWITCHEROO

An unusual effect whereby two selected cards change places in a packet. Credit this one to the famous mystery writer-magician, Walter Gibson.

PRESENTATION AND EFFECT

The performer requests a spectator to shuffle a deck of cards, then to count off twenty cards from the top of the deck in any manner he desires. The remainder of the cards are put to one side. The spectator is then instructed to look through the twenty cards and note any card he desires, and also to note its number from the top. For example, the spectator notes the ace of spades. It is ninth from the top.

The performer instructs another spectator to do the same, nothing, for example, the 4 of diamonds, fifteenth card from the top.

The performer now takes the twenty cards and places them behind his back for a few seconds, stating that he is rearranging the cards into a magical sequence. He then places the cards face down on the table and asks the two spectators at what number from the top each had selected his card. One spectator says, "Nine," and the other says, "Fifteen." The performer remarks that 9 and 15 make a total of 24, and there are only twenty cards in the group. So, he must deal four more cards onto the twenty-card group from the remainder of the pack, which had been placed to one side.

Now the performer counts down nine cards. He turns up the ninth card. It is the 4 of diamonds, the card selected by the second spectator and which was originally fifteenth card from the top. The performer continues counting until he reaches fifteen. He turns up that card. It is the ace of spades, the card noted by the first spectator, which was originally ninth from the top.

THE SECRET

The performer places the cards behind his back after the spectators have noted the cards and their positions in the packet. The performer simply counts the cards from hand to hand, placing each card upon the card before, thereby reversing the order of the twenty cards. But, when the twenty cards have been reversed, he takes the top card of the group and places it on the bottom of the group. In other words, he's really reversing the top nineteen cards, and leaving the twentieth card on the bottom where it was before the reversal.

When the performer asks for the two numbers denoting the position in the pack of the spectators' cards—if the two numbers total over 20, the performer adds cards from the deck to make the group total that number. If the two numbers total less than 20—such as 8 and 9: total, 17—the performer removes that many cards from the top of the group (in this case three cards are removed from the top of the packet).

If the two numbers total exactly 20, the performer does not add or subtract any cards, but continues with the trick, using the twenty-card group.

Should both spectators select the same card, the trick works anyway, although this occurrence is not desirable. For example, each spectator takes a card at position number 8. The performer adds 8 and 8 for a total of 16. The performer removes four cards from the top and deals down to the eighth card. And there is the selected card.

55. QUADRUPLE COINCIDENCE

This card trick may sound long and complicated, but actually it is a very easy trick to perform. It is a favorite of George Starke's, the magician-lawyer.

PRESENTATION AND EFFECT

The performer produces two packs of cards, retains one and hands the other to the spectator. The performer now instructs the spectator that success or failure of this experiment depends upon being able to follow out orders, and should the spectator fail to follow orders, the trick cannot possibly work.

The performer states that he is going to shuffle his deck, and instructs the spectator to shuffle the deck he holds.

The performer instructs the spectator merely to think of a card, and the performer does likewise.

The performer and spectator now exchange packs.

The performer requests the spectator to remove the card he thought of from the pack, and the performer does the same. The spectator is now instructed to place the selected card on top of the pack he holds; the performer does the same. The performer instructs the spectator to cut the cards under the table so that there will be no possibility of knowing the whereabouts of the selected card; the performer does likewise.

Packs are now brought into full view again, and the performer and spectator exchange packs.

The performer instructs the spectator to look through the pack he is now holding and remove his mentally selected card. The performer does the same with the pack he holds.

The performer instructs the spectator to turn over the selected card, and he does the same. Both cards are found to be identical.

The performer now instructs the spectator to place his deck of cards on the table, to cut off about three-quarters of his deck, and to place the cut portion to one side. The performer does likewise with the pack he is holding.

The performer instructs the spectator to pick up the smaller packet and to count the cards one at a time face down onto the table. The performer does the same with his own smaller packet. At the end of the count the performer calls out the number of cards he counted, and asks the spectator for his total. To the spectator's surprise, both counts are identical.

The performer instructs the spectator to pick up his smaller packet of cards and place them criss-cross on top of the larger packet of cards. The performer does the same with his cards.

The performer now requests the spectator to turn over the top card of the smaller packet, and he does likewise with his own deck. Another surprise, both cards are identical.

The performer now requests the spectator to lift off the smaller packet of cards from the remainder of the deck and put it to one side. The performer does likewise. The spectator is instructed to remove the top card of the remaining cards (larger packet), and the performer does the same. Again the cards prove to be identical.

THE SECRET

The performer hands the spectator a pack and retains one pack himself, with the instructions that each is to shuffle his own deck. However, the performer, while the spectator is busy shuffling his cards, has stopped shuffling and is secretly noting and memorizing the top and bottom cards of the deck he holds. Often the performer has difficulty remembering the two cards, therefore it is suggested that he previously place certain cards on the top and bottom of the deck he is to retain. For example, he may place the ace of spades on top and the 2 of diamonds on the bottom. Then he should use a riffle shuffle and not disturb the position of the top and bottom cards. For better understanding of this trick, let's use the example above and assume that the performer has the ace of spades as top card and the 2 of diamonds as bottom card of his deck. Now the spectator and the performer each thinks of a card.

The performer and spectator now exchange packs.

The performer now instructs the spectator to do exactly as he does. The spectator is told to remove the card he thought of from the deck he now holds. While this is taking place the performer secretly places the 2 of diamonds on the bottom of his pack. The performer then removes the ace of spades, the same card that is the top card of the deck the spectator now holds.

The performer now requests the spectator to place his chosen card on top of the deck he is holding, and the performer does the same (performer puts ace of spades on top of his pack).

The performer requests—so that there be no possibility of either the spectator or himself knowing the whereabouts of the chosen cards in the deck—that each put his deck under the table, cut the deck, complete the cut, and square the pack. Actually, the performer goes through the gesture of cutting the cards under the table but leaves the pack exactly as it was before, with the ace of spades on top and the 2 of diamonds on the bottom.

Bringing the cards into full view again, the spectator and performer exchange decks.

The performer instructs the spectator to fan the cards out and remove his mentally selected card and put it face down on the table, and announces he will do the same. However, the performer removes the card that lies between the ace of spades and the 2 of diamonds, which is the spectator's card.* At the same time, the performer cuts the pack he is holding so that the ace of spades will be on top and the 2 of diamonds on the bottom of the deck.

The performer instructs the spectator to place his pack face down on the table, and he does likewise with the pack he holds. He now instructs the spectator to turn over both cards on the table. They are found to be identical.

The performer instructs the spectator to cut off about three-quarters of his deck and place the cut portion aside. He does the same. The performer tells the spectator to count the number of cards in the smaller packet onto the table one at a time, placing each dealt card on top of the previously dealt card. The performer does the same. Actually, while pretending to count his cards, the performer is counting the spectator's cards as they are being dealt. So when the performer states how many cards are in his smaller packet, he calls out the spectator's total instead. The spectator calls the same number. Quite a surprise!

The performer now requests the spectator to place his smaller packet criss-cross on top of the remainder of the deck, and he

---

* Ace of spades was top card and 2 of diamonds was bottom card when spectator was instructed to place his selected card on top of the deck. Then, when the deck was cut, the 2 of diamonds was placed on top of the spectator's card.

97

does likewise. Each turns over the top card of the smaller packet, and both have the same card. It will be the 2 of diamonds, originally on the bottom of each deck.

The performer requests the spectator to cut off his smaller packet from the rest of the deck and place it to one side. Then he is told to turn over the top card of the larger packet, and the performer does the same. Both cards again prove to be the same.

56. THE NEW DEAL POKER HAND

A favorite trick of Dr. Al Berndt's and Peter Musto's, two amateur card tricksters from New Jersey.

PRESENTATION AND EFFECT

The performer opens a new deck of cards by breaking the seal (tearing off the revenue stamp), takes the deck out of the card case, and removes the joker and the advertising cards that come with a new deck. The performer then relates a story of a Draw Poker game he witnessed in which he saw the dealer cheating. "Here is what this card cheater did," he says. The performer places the deck on the table to be cut, completes the cut, and has the cards cut one or more times.

The performer states that there were seven players in this Poker game, and with this remark he deals seven cards face down from the top of the deck (Draw Poker style), one to each of the seven players. The performer then says that the dealer he watched was crooked, so he illustrates by dealing each player's second card off the top of the deck, but when it comes time to deal his (the dealer's) second card, he deals it from the bottom of the deck. He remarks, "The guy I saw do this was naturally faster than I in dealing cards from the bottom."

The performer deals each player's third card, including his own, from the top of the deck. Each player's fourth card is dealt from the top of the deck, but the performer deals his own (dealer's) fourth card from the bottom of the deck. He does this very obviously, with the remark, "If the crooked dealer I saw dealt from the bottom as slow as I, I probably would have witnessed a shooting that night."

Each player's fifth (last) card, including the dealer's, is dealt from the top of the deck by the performer.

After the performer has dealt each player a five-card Poker hand, he remarks, "I took two cards from the bottom of the deck, and, according to Scarne, that's not fair, so I won't take this hand." Instead, the performer deals himself five cards from the top of the deck and discards the five cards previously dealt.

The performer now turns each of the six players' Poker hands face up on the table, and it is found that each holds a *Full House* (three of a kind and a pair).

The performer exposes his first dealt hand (the dealer's discarded five cards) and it is comprised of three of a kind. He remarks, "You see. It doesn't even pay to be dishonest when playing Poker, because I would have lost even though I dealt two cards from the bottom of the deck."

The performer then turns up his hand (hand dealt from top of the deck). It is a *Straight Flush* (five cards in a sequence of the same suit), and it beats all the Full Houses. "Proving again," says the performer, "that it pays to be honest."

THE SECRET

Every pack of cards prior to being sealed by the manufacturer is arranged in order from ace, 2, 3, up to king, in each suit. Therefore, when the performer opens a new deck, he merely removes the joker and the advertising cards, leaving the deck exactly as it was arranged when packed. When the performer removes the joker and advertising cards, he doesn't show the card arrangement to the spectators but faces the cards toward himself.

The cutting of the cards does not disturb the arrangement of the setup, although it must be understood by the performer—he must complete each cut before allowing the deck to be cut again, and no center cut is to be permitted. Only the simple standard cut of taking a group off the top of the deck is to be used.

Now, all the performer has to remember is—when dealing out seven Poker hands he must deal himself (the dealer) the second and fourth cards from the bottom of the deck. All the remaining cards are dealt from the top in regular Draw Poker fashion. Following the instructions given in the Presentation and Effect, this trick cannot fail.

Note: The performer does not have to use a new deck of cards every time he desires to do this trick. The performer can use any deck of cards by arranging the deck beforehand from ace through king in each suit.

57. HOUDINI'S DOUBLE-TALK CARD TRICK

This is one of the best old-time card tricks performed by such magicians as Houdini and Herman the Great. It appears to be a miracle when performed by Dr. Jacob Daly or Sam Horowitz, two top-flight card manipulators.

PRESENTATION AND EFFECT

The performer hands a spectator a deck of cards and requests him to shuffle the deck thoroughly, then to count off twenty cards from the top of the deck and hand them to the performer.

The performer then requests ten or less persons to select two cards each from this group of twenty cards. Each person is instructed to remember his two selected cards.

The performer now gathers the cards by having each person place his two selected cards on top of the previously gathered cards until all the twenty cards have been collected.

Should the number of persons who selected cards number less than ten, each person is requested to place his cards on top of the remainder of the group held by the performer. Each two selected cards are placed on top of the previously collected cards. After all the selected cards have been returned to the top of the group, the performer cuts the cards.

The performer now turns the deck face up, looks through the cards and cuts them again. The performer turns the cards face down in his left hand and then slowly proceeds to deal the cards face up onto the table one at a time, placing the cards on the table in a sort of irregular fashion. For example, he places the first dealt card near the top left-hand corner of the table, the second dealt card near the bottom right-hand corner, the third dealt card next to the first dealt card; the next dealt card he places to the right of the last dealt card, leaving a vacant space between the cards so that a card may be dealt into that space later. This irregular method of placing cards on the table continues until all the twenty cards have been placed face up on the table, forming four rows of five cards each.

The performer now says that any person who selected two cards may step forward, look at the cards, and inform the performer in which row or rows (rows read horizontally) his two selected cards appear. Upon being told, the performer instantly names the two selected cards that were selected. Another person steps up and is requested to do the same, name the rows in which his two selected cards appear; and the performer names his cards. This procedure is continued until all the selected cards have been named by the performer.

THE SECRET

This trick requires quite a bit of practice before it can be presented properly.

After being handed the twenty cards by the spectator who has shuffled the deck, have ten or less persons each select two cards. If there are ten persons who selected cards, the performer may pick up the selected cards here and there. The order in which they are replaced doesn't matter, provided none of the pairs (two cards each person selected) is separated. When all the cards have been placed on top of each other, the performer secretly takes a glimpse at the bottom card, and then cuts the group (twenty cards). The performer may cut the deck as often as desired, provided he places the bottom half on top of the top half after each cut. This procedure does not disturb the position of the pairs (two selected cards of each person).

The performer now turns the cards face up and looks for the card he glimpsed on bottom before the cutting took place. He separates the cards into two groups, putting one on top of the other, in such a manner that the glimpsed card is again at the bottom of the group.

Should less than ten persons select cards, their selected cards are placed two at a time on top of the remainder of the cards the performer holds, in the same manner as described above. Twenty cards must always be used regardless of the number of cards selected.

Now for the part of the secret that requires considerable practice on the performer's part in order to do this trick successfully. The performer must imagine that there are four words printed on his table, each letter of each word large enough for a card to rest on when placed face up on the table. The twenty cards which are held face down in the performer's hand are now dealt onto the table in the following system. The first word, which is the imaginary top row, reading horizontally is MATAS. The row below is PEPIT; the third row ROMER; and the bottom row LOLIS.

The performer deals the top card of the twenty-card group face up and places it on the spot on the table where the imaginary M of MATAS would be. The second card dealt goes on the imaginary M in ROMER. The third and fourth dealt cards are dealt on the imaginary spots occupied by the two A's in MATAS. This procedure is followed until the twenty cards have been placed into four rows of five cards each. It will be noted that the four words used consist of ten letters only, M-A-T-S-P-E-I-R-O-L, each of these letters repeated twice.

The principle of this trick is to put each pair of cards dealt on two similar imaginary letters. Following is a chart showing the dealt cards, which are numbered from 1 to 20, as they are dealt. For example, the first dealt card, number 1, is under the M in MATAS. Number 2 is under the M in ROMER. The last two dealt cards are numbers 19 and 20 under the two L's in LOLIS.

M	A	T	A	S		R	O	M	E	R
1	3	5	4	7		15	17	2	12	16

P	E	P	I	T		L	O	L	I	S
9	11	10	13	6		19	18	20	14	8

After the cards have been arranged as shown in the above chart, it is easy for the performer to name the two selected cards after the person has told him in which row or rows his selected cards are. Should he say both are in the top row, the performer knows that they are the second and fourth cards in that row represented by the letter A.

Should the person say that one of his cards is in the first row and the other in the third row, the performer instantly knows that these two cards are represented by the letter M. This system is followed until all the selected cards have been named by the performer.

58. LOCATRIX

This card trick was nominated by that clever mentalist and magician, Ted Anneman.

PRESENTATION AND EFFECT

The performer hands a deck to a spectator and then turns his back. The performer requests the spectator to deal the cards face down into a pile, singly and silently onto the table, and to stop dealing at any time he desires.

At such time the performer instructs the spectator that he may look at and memorize the top card of either pile (the pile he has dealt onto the table, or the pile he still holds in his hand). Then he is instructed to place the two piles together and cut the assembled deck one or more times.

The performer turns around to face the spectator for the first time, takes the deck and passes some cards from hand to hand, glancing at each card as it passes, and finally the performer says, "I think it is much easier to locate the card while the deck is behind my back." Putting the deck behind his back for a few seconds, he says, "I have it." He brings the deck into full view and places it face down on the table. The spectator is requested to name his chosen card. Without a bit of hesitation the performer discloses it correctly.

THE SECRET

While this is not the greatest trick in this book, the performer will find that it is one of those nice impromptu tricks that can be done at a moment's notice and requires little or no preparation.

Before the cards are handed to the spectator, the performer notes and remembers the top and bottom cards of the deck. These are the key cards.

The deck is given to the spectator very, very carelessly, leaving the impression on the spectator's mind that he does everything he pleases. He stops dealing when he desires, selects the top card of either pile, assembles both piles into one, and cuts the deck several times. These things must be impressed on the spectator by the performer.

When the performer locates one of his key cards, he removes the card to the right and secretly slips it to the top of the deck. Locating the second key card, he removes the card to the right and secretly places it also on top of the deck. One of these two top cards is the spectator's selected card. The performer must remember the top card of the deck.

The performer states that it might be easier to locate the card behind his back. He places the deck behind him, and out of the spectator's sight, takes the top card of the deck, reverses it, and pushes it into the center of the pack, face up. The deck is brought into full view again and laid face down on the table.

The performer requests the spectator to name his chosen card. And the performer formally discloses it, either by turning over the top card of the deck or by spreading the deck on the table to reveal the face-up card in the center of the deck.

59. DOUBLE PREDICTION

This mental card effect was created by the author and Bill Simon, the New York magician.

The performer requests a spectator to shuffle the pack. Then he takes back the pack and asks for the loan of a pencil and a business card. If the spectator fails to have one, the performer uses his own. The pack is then spread face down on the table by the performer (sort of ribbonwise). The performer writes a message on the back of the business card and conceals the message from the spectator's view.

This being done, the spectator is handed the business card with the message part face down, and told to insert the card into any part of the pack, allowing part of the business card to stick out. This being done, the performer squares the pack together, pushing the business card into the pack, and places the pack on the palm of his left hand (cards face down).

Spreading the cards from the left hand into the right hand, the performer stops when he arrives at the business card, leaving it on top of the packet of cards in his left hand. He turns the business card over and states, "I don't think I'll let you see my prediction yet," and squares up the deck again.

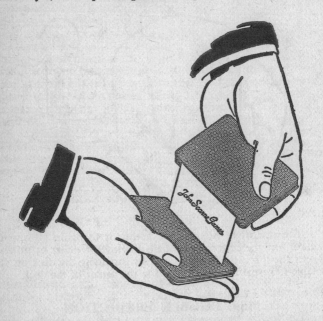

The business card is then taken from the pack along with the card above it and the card below it. The message reads, for example: "You have placed me between the ace of clubs and the 10 of diamonds." Upon turning over these two cards, the prediction is found to be correct.

THE SECRET

After the spectator has shuffled the pack, the performer asks the spectator for a pencil and business card. While the spectator is getting them, the performer secretly notes the top and bottom cards of the deck. These two cards he memorizes. If the spectator does not possess a business card, the performer requests the spectator to initial the performer's card on any side he desires. This gives the performer ample time to glimpse and memorize the top and bottom cards of the pack.

The performer now writes a message on the blank side of the business card: the names of the top and bottom cards of the pack. Handing the card with the message face down to the spectator, the spectator inserts the business card into the deck. The performer squares the deck and picks up the pack, pushing the cards face down from the left hand and into the right hand. The performer stops when he arrives at the business card. Here is where the trickery takes place. This move is very deceptive and easy to do. The performer drops his right hand (which holds all the cards that were above the business card) to a position about two inches lower than his left hand (which holds a packet of cards with the business card on top). In this position, the thumb of the left hand pushes the business card slightly off the edge of the packet held in the left hand, turning the business card over and letting it fall on top of the packet of cards held by the right hand. Then, with the remark, "I don't think I'll let you see my prediction yet," the performer immediately places the cards held in the left hand on top of the message and packet of cards held in the right hand. It is obvious now to the performer that the business card is now between the original top and bottom cards of the deck.

60. CARD COUNTING EXTRAORDINARY

From Bob Dunn, the famous cartoonist-magician.

PRESENTATION AND EFFECT

The performer removes a deck of cards from the card case, places the deck face down on the table, and requests a spectator to cut off as many cards as he desires.

The performer takes this cut group from the spectator, pretends to weigh the cards, and proceeds to name the exact number of cards cut by the spectator.

The performer prepares the deck before placing it into the card case as follows.

He divides the deck into four face-down packets of thirteen cards each, ranging in value from ace to king. Suits are best disregarded. Set each packet in this order: 4, 10, king, queen, 9, ace, 2, jack, 7, 3, 6, 5, 8, the 4 being the top card of the deck, the 8 being the thirteenth card in the deck. Collect packets one on top of the other.

This arrangement—which, incidentally, is not apparent, should the cards be spread face up on a table—has a direct relationship to one known to magicians as the "Eight Kings" arrangement. The latter incorporates all thirteen values in two simple lines of verse: "Eight (8) kings (K) threatened (3, 10) to (2) save (7) ninety-five (9, 5) queens (Q) for (4) one (A) sick (6) knave (J)."

To clarify the working, take only the top thirteen cards from the arranged deck. Cut this packet at any point, noting the card at which it is cut. Whatever its value, the performer runs over the "Eight Kings" ditty in his mind *and the number that follows that value in the verse is the number of cards held!*

Thus, by cutting to an ace, the performer discovers, in going over the verse, that this value is followed by "sick" or 6—signifying that six cards have been cut off. Again, the bottom card is an 8. In the verse, a king (13) follows the 8, signifying thirteen cards.

After the first thirteen cards, the arrangement repeats itself, as it also does after the twenty-sixth and thirty-ninth cards. These three numbers, 13, 26, and 39, are key numbers. When someone cuts off a packet of cards, the performer takes the cards and notes the bottom card. To the audience, he may now pretend to weigh the cards or thumb them rapidly in a pretense of rapid counting. Taking the value of the bottom card, a number is immediately arrived at by the method already outlined. Suppose the bottom card is a queen, giving the number 4. If the spectator has only a few cards, he has four. If, however, it appears that he has about a quarter of the deck, it couldn't be four cards, so the first key number, 13, is added for a total of 17, which indicates the number of cards. Similarly, if it appears that more than half of the deck was cut off, 4 would be added to 26 to make 30; and if more than three-quarters of the deck was cut, 4 would be added to the key number 39 to get 43. The performer can't go wrong because it is virtually impossible to miscalculate by 13, and he is therefore enabled to state the correct number every time.

The performer may repeat the trick as often as desired, provided he does not disarrange the cards on the count.

61. DOUBLE SURPRISE

This trick, called "Double Surprise," is the creation of Bill Simon. The effect is astonishing because the trick has an air of improvisation on the part of the performer. This always goes well with the audience because people always like to see a magician get himself in a "spot." If he can successfully get out of it, they concede he must be a very skillful magician.

PRESENTATION AND EFFECT

The performer removes a deck of cards from the card case and requests the spectator to call out a number between 1 and 10. This being done, the performer deals the cards face down one at a time onto the table until he reaches the number called. The card at this number he gives to the spectator to look at and remember. The performer is not allowed to look at the face of this card. After the spectator has seen the card, the performer takes it back and inserts it face down into the deck approximately in the center. The performer then states that he will turn over the top card of the deck, and this card will determine where the spectator's card will be found in the deck. For example, if the top card is a 5, the spectator's card will be the fifth card from the top of the pack. If the top card is a queen, the spectator's card will be the tenth card in the pack, as court cards count as 10. But to make the trick even better, the performer announces that not only will the spectator's card be found at the correct number, but it will be found reversed in the deck (face up in the face-down pack).

The performer turns over the top card of the deck, announces its value, counts it as number 1, and proceeds to count off cards until he reaches the number that equals the rank of the top card. Here he finds a card face up. Triumphantly he says to the spectator, "This must be your card." Much to the performer's sorrow, the spectator will tell him, "That is not my card." Now the performer is in a "spot." Hurriedly he fans through the pack. Both he and the spectator find that all the cards face the same way. The performer admits that something must have gone wrong. He squares up the deck and places it face down on the table. He asks the spectator to name his selected card. The performer says a few magic words, snaps his fingers over the deck, fans out the cards, and we find one card reversed (face up) in the deck. What card is it? The spectator's card, of course. It took real skill to get out of that one, didn't it?

THE SECRET

The performer arranged ten cards, from ace, 2, 3, 4, 5, 6, 7, 8, 9, 10, of mixed suits and placed them on top of the face-up pack. The 10 will be on top of the deck, the ace the tenth card from the top. This means all the cards are face up except the top ten, which are face down. The performer asks the spectator to call a number between 1 and 10 (this means any number from 1 through 9). The performer deals the cards onto the table from the top of the deck. The card at the number called he gives to the spectator to memorize. The performer takes this card back and inserts it face down in about the center of the deck (this means he has placed a face-down card in a face-up deck). The performer turns the top card of the deck over, and says the spectator's card will be found at that number, reversed in the deck. Inasmuch as the cards were arranged from 10 to ace, when he counts down to the number shown on the top card, the 10, he will always arrive at the first face-up card in the deck, since one of the top ten had been removed. Naturally this is not the spectator's card, as we know it was placed in about the center of the deck. The performer finds he is wrong and fans out the deck, not carefully but in bunches, so everyone can see that the entire deck is face up. The first face-up cards and the last few face-up cards can be spread carefully, but the middle cards should be bunched together because among them is the spectator's card face down, and the performer must not allow any of the audience to see it.

The performer states that in spite of his mistake he will still reverse the selected card. The deck is placed face down on the table. The spectator names his selected card, the performer says the magic words. Spreading out the deck we find all the cards face down except the spectator's card, which is face up.

62. THE STAPLED CARD

A fine and unusual card trick—which makes use of two cards stapled back to back to be used as an indicator card—with a very surprising finish. Created by the author based on a suggestion from Joseph Prieto, the very clever New Jersey magician.

PRESENTATION AND EFFECT

The performer removes a deck of cards from a card case. He riffle shuffles the cards once and has a spectator cut the deck and complete the cut. He now places the deck face down in his left hand and takes the top card off the deck with his right hand. He takes a quick look at the card and says, "It's the nine of spades," but does not show its face to the spectator. He immediately brings both of his hands holding the cards under the table. The performer says, "I am inserting the nine of spades face up in the deck."

He then brings the deck above the table, still holding the deck in his left hand, and spreads the deck face down from his left hand into his right. This spreading is continued until the faced-up 9 of spades is located.

The performer with his right hand removes all the cards above the 9 of spades. With his left hand he drops the 9 of spades onto the table to one side. All the cards remaining in his left hand (bottom half of deck) he places on top of the cards in his right hand (original top half of deck). Since a 9-spot was the faced-up card, he then deals nine cards face down from the top of the deck onto the table. These cards are dealt singly; each dealt card is placed on top of the previously dealt card. The performer asks the spectator to look at and remember the top card of the pile. The spectator is told by the performer to assemble all the cards on the table and shuffle them, and to remember the noted card.

The performer takes the deck from the spectator, faces the cards toward himself and looks through the cards, seemingly attempting to find the chosen card.

He then says, "I know how to find the chosen card." And with this remark he places the deck of cards into his left-hand coat pocket. The performer then reaches into his inside breast coat pocket and brings out two cards stapled together. This he calls his lucky locator.

This locator is comprised of two cards stapled together, with their backs facing inward and their faces facing outward. One card is the joker, the other a 4 of spades. The performer asks the spectator for his first name, and then writes it across the face of the 4 of spades.

The performer says that he is going to insert this locator into the deck while the deck is in his pocket, and he is sure that he will insert it on top of the spectator's chosen card.

The performer takes the locator card in his left hand and puts it into his left-hand coat pocket, remarking that he will insert it exactly on top of the chosen card.

The performer brings the deck out of his pocket and spreads it face down on the table. The locator card with the joker faced up is found. The deck is separated at the exact position where the stapled card is located.

The performer now asks the spectator to name his chosen card. For example, the spectator calls out, "Ten of diamonds." The performer then pushes out the locator card and the card below it, and very happily says, "My lucky locator never fails. This card below the locator card is the ten of diamonds." The card is turned over, and it is the 4 of spades, with the spectator's name written across the face of the card. Naturally the spectator turns over the locator card, and is surprised to find—stapled back to back with the joker—his chosen card: the 10 of diamonds.

The cards may be examined by the spectator, but no trace of another 10 of diamonds will be found.

The secret preparation is as follows: The performer prepares two lucky locator cards in the following manner.

The performer takes a joker and a 4 of spades, and glues them back to back. These cards can be taken from any deck; since they are glued together the color and design of the back of the cards cannot be seen. Then the performer staples the cards together. Four staples should be used, one near each corner. *This stapled card is placed in the performer's inside breast coat pocket.*

The performer takes a joker and a 10 of diamonds from any deck, and glues them together back to back. Then he staples these cards together exactly in the same spots as the other lucky locator card.

The performer then takes the pack of fifty-two cards which he intends to use in this trick and removes the 4 of spades. On the face of the 4 of spades he writes the first name of the spectator for whom he intends to do the trick. After this has been done, he places the 4 of spades with its back next to the face of the stapled 10 of diamonds. These cards are placed together

STAPLE

4 OF SPADES
ON OTHER
SIDE

into the performer's left-hand coat pocket, the face of the 4 of spades facing away from the performer's body.

The performer now takes the remainder of the deck he is going to use, removes the 10 of diamonds, and places it face down on the table. He places eight indifferent cards on top of this card, and a 9 of spades is turned face up and placed on top of all these nine cards. Then the remainder of the deck is placed face down on top of the upturned 9 of spades. The performer puts the deck thus arranged into the card case and is now ready to perform this trick.

When the performer removes the deck from the card case and riffle shuffles the deck, he must make sure not to disturb the position of the ten bottom cards. If the performer cannot do this, he may skip the riffle shuffle entirely. The cards are cut and the cut completed.

The performer peeks at the top card of the deck and says he is going to insert it into the deck under the table. What happens is he disregards the value of the top card and calls out the 9 of spades. What he does under the table when he says he is going to reverse the 9 of spades and insert it into the deck is merely to replace the card he took off the top of the deck in its original position. Following the directions as described in the Presentation and Effect, the spectator selects the 10 of diamonds. When the performer looks through the deck after the 10 of diamonds has been shuffled into it, he finds the 10 of diamonds and cuts it to the top of the deck.

The performer now places the deck face down in his left hand, and puts the deck into his left-hand coat pocket. As he does this, he lets the top half of the deck slide toward his body. Then he drops the lower half of the deck away from his body. This puts the two hidden cards (lucky locator card and 4 of spades) into the center of the deck. The performer now brings his hand out of his pocket, leaving all the cards there.

Now the performer produces the lucky locator card from his inside breast coat pocket, showing the joker and the 4 of spades stapled together. The performer asks the spectator for his first name, and proceeds to write it across the face of the 4 of spades. He must try to write the name as nearly in the same size and script as he wrote the name on the other 4 of spades before the start of the trick. However, the writing should be done quickly and casually. If it is not exactly the same, it does not matter, as the difference will never be noticed by the spectators. The writing should be done in pencil on both cards so that it can be erased later; the same indicator cards can be used again and again.

After the performer has written the spectator's name on the lucky locator card, he takes this card with his left hand, joker face up, and places it into his left-hand coat pocket. He pretends to be placing it into the center of the deck on top of the selected card, but he is really placing it on top of the 10 of diamonds, which is the top card of the deck. He grips the deck with his left hand and deals the two top cards off the top of the deck with his left thumb. The cards he deals off are the selected 10 of dia-

111

monds and the lucky card which was just shown to the spectators.

The performer removes the deck from his pocket, leaving these two cards behind, and with them all the evidence of trickery.

Note: If the performer does not know the spectator's name beforehand, he will find that he can easily obtain it merely by listening to a bit of conversation among the spectator's friends. Then, a little walk to the lavatory is in order, and there the name of the spectator can be written across the face of the lone 4 of spades and placed into the coat pocket with the hidden lucky locator.

63. ALLERCHRIST CARD TRICK

This trick is credited to two great performers: Bert Allerton, whose magic is known to all visitors to the famed Pump Room in Chicago; and Henry Christ, the New York magician, who developed the principle used in this trick and other tricks of a similar nature.

PRESENTATION AND EFFECT

The performer hands a deck of cards to a spectator to shuffle, stating that at no time will the performer touch the deck of cards. "As a matter of fact," he says, "this trick can be done over a telephone." (And that statement is correct.) "I will turn my back on the entire procedure," the performer then says.

The performer turns his back and instructs the specator to shuffle and cut the deck. The spectator is instructed to deal out two five-card Draw Poker hands face down. The performer tells the spectator to note the top card of either one of the two dealt Poker hands; to deal a few cards from the deck on top of this noted card; then to drop the remainder of the deck he is holding in his hand on top of this group (which contains the noted card). Then he is to pick up the entire deck and drop it on top of the remaining dealt Poker hand.

The performer turns to face the spectator and instructs him to pick up the entire deck and place it face down in his left hand. The following instructions are given to the spectator. All court cards (jack, queen, king) are valued at 10; all other cards, their numerical rank. Ace is 1; 2, 2; 3, 3, etc. The joker counts for anything the spectator desires to call it.

"I want you to deal four piles of cards in the following manner," the performer tells the spectator. "Deal the top card of the deck face up on the table, and call out, 'Ten.' " If the first card dealt is a 10-spot or a court card, whose value really is 10, the performer puts this first dealt card to one side. It will be the first of four cards whose total numerical value will indicate the exact position of the noted card in the deck. Then the spectator deals the next card onto the table face up to begin his second pile, and calls out, "Ten." If this card is not a 10 or a court card, he deals the next card from the top of the deck face up on top of the previously dealt card, and calls out, "Nine." If this card is not a 9-spot, he deals the next card face up on top of the previously dealt card, and calls out, "Eight." He continues to deal out the cards and continues counting. He counts one number for each card dealt. He counts from 10 down through 1. Any time the number he calls matches the card he turns up, he stops counting, takes the matched card and places it face up to one side. He then starts another pile by turning the top card of the deck face up on the table, calling out, "Ten," again. If none of the numbers he calls matches the card he turns up, and he has counted 10, 9, 8, 7, 6, 5, 4, 3, 2, 1, he takes the next card on top of the deck and places it face down on the table alongside the other cards he has put to one side. This is counted as one of the four cards whose total numerical value will indicate the exact position of the noted card in the deck. In this group of four cards, face-down cards carry no value. The spectator forms four piles only, and places four cards to one side.

For example, if two cards of the four were face down, and the two face-up cards were a 2-spot and a 4-spot, the performer would add the numerical values and say that 4 and 2 are 6. The spectator is then instructed by the performer to count down to the sixth card of the remaining cards he still holds in his hand, and it will be the card that the spectator noted at the start of the trick that is found at this location (sixth card from top of deck in above example). If none of the numbers called was matched, the fourth card to be put aside (after the fourth count of 10) is the selected card.

THE SECRET

The performer merely has the spectator follow the directions as given in Presentation and Effect, and the trick works by itself. The performer requires a fifty-two card deck plus the joker in order to do this trick. Should the joker appear in the spectator's count, the performer instructs the spectator that he can make the card a wild card, and can call it anything he likes (naturally, whatever value the spectator gives the joker must be used in the follow-up tabulation when locating the noted card). For example, the spectator calls number "eight," and turns over the joker. He can call the joker "eight" and use it as one of the four indicator cards, or he may pass it by, saying to himself or aloud that it is not an 8-spot. If he decides to give the value of

8 to the joker and use it as one of the indicator cards, he must remember, when counting the total value of the face-up indicator cards, to count the joker for 8 points.

When the spectator notes the top card of one of the dealt Poker hands, he places a few cards on top of this card, at the request of the performer, and then places the remainder of the deck on top of these. Then he places the entire deck on top of the remaining dealt Poker hand. All this is done solely for psychological reasons. Regardless of all these directions, the noted card will always be the tenth card from the bottom of the deck. This trick is purely mathematical and cannot fail if the directions are properly followed.

64. THE TRIPLE DEAL CARD TRICK

Credit this to magicians H. C. Cleveland, Carlton King, Sid Margulies, and Ira Zweifack.

PRESENTATION AND EFFECT

The performer removes a deck of cards from the card case, hands it to a spectator to shuffle, and patters along these lines: "Many years ago a wonder worker discovered a method of locating a mentally selected card, merely by letting the spectator see it several times while dealing some cards face up on the table. These wonder workers had an easy time reading people's minds, merely because the people were uneducated, superstitious, and gullible. I learned one of their tricks recently by reading an old book on witchcraft written in 1724."

The performer takes the deck from the spectator and places it face down in his left hand. He then deals three face-up piles of cards, nine cards in each, a card at a time dealt in each pile, dealing from left to right. While this dealing is going on, the performer requests the spectator to think of any one of these cards. The performer then hands the remainder of the deck, which he is still holding in his left hand, to the spectator, instructing him to shuffle them thoroughly. The performer takes the cards from the spectator after the shuffle and drops them into his right-hand side coat pocket.

The performer now asks the spectator which pile contains his mentally selected card. The performer, upon being told which pile contains the card, instructs the spectator to pick the piles up, putting one on top of the other in any order he desires. The performer takes the packet of twenty-seven face-down cards, and deals them into three face-up piles, as before.

The performer again inquires which pile contains the mentally selected card. After the spectator tells which pile contains his card, he is allowed to pick up the piles and place one on top of the other in any order he desires.

The performer takes the packet of twenty-seven face-down cards (cards are dealt face up after piles are assembled by spectator and handed to performer), and turns the entire group of twenty-seven cards over so that they are face down for dealing. He deals each face-down card from the top of the group, turning it face up as he places it on the table, and for the third time deals out three face-up piles the same as he did before. The performer again asks the spectator which pile contains his mentally selected card. Upon being told, the performer allows the spectator to assemble the piles, by placing one on top of the other, and then to place the entire group face down on the table.

The performer now goes over what has happened up to this point. "Now," says the performer to the spectator, "you thought of a card in one of the piles, shuffled the rest of the cards, which I placed in my right-hand coat pocket before any of the piles were assembled, then you picked up the piles to suit yourself."

The performer says, "I will now remove a number of cards from the shuffled group in my pocket, the numerical total of which will tell me the exact position of the mentally selected card in the twenty-seven card packet. For example," the performer goes on, "I will remove four cards from my pocket, and the numerical total will tell me the exact position of your selected card in the packet resting on the table."

The performer removes four cards one at a time from his pocket, putting each face down on the table. After four cards have been removed from the pocket, they are turned face up and their numerical value added. They are found to be: a 10-spot, an 8-spot, a 4-spot, and an ace. Their combined total is 23. The performer counts down twenty-three cards, counting the top card of the packet as number 1, the next card as number 2, etc. Turning over the twenty-third card, it is found to be the card the spectator selected.

THE SECRET

Before the start of the trick the performer secretly removes the ace, 2, 3, 8, 10, and another 10, paying no attention to the suits. These six cards are put into the right-hand side coat pocket with their backs facing outward. When the remainder of the pack is dropped into the pocket, the performer makes certain to put the pack in such a fashion that the six planted cards will be the top cards of this group. The performer must practice taking out the cards he desires before doing this trick for a spectator. With these six cards the performer can make any number from 1 to 27.

For example, should the desired number be 25, the performer says, "I will take four cards out of my pocket whose total numerical value will coincide with the position of the selected card in this packet of twenty-seven cards." The performer removes the two top cards, which are 10's, then skips the 8, takes out the 4, then takes out the ace (which is the third card from the top after the 10's and 4 have been removed). All numbers are formed in this manner. The performer removes one, two, three, or four cards, as many as are necessary.

The performer is now capable of taking out of his pocket one or more cards whose total numerical value can be from 1 to 27. Next, the performer must be able to ascertain the position of the selected card in the twenty-seven card packet after three deals have been completed.

This is quite easy when the following mathematical formula is used. The performer merely has to note the position in the twenty-seven card packet of the nine-card pile which contains the selected card. If it is on top of the other two piles when the packet is *face down*, it is called the *top*. If it is between the two other piles, it is the *middle*. If the other two piles are on top of it, it is the *bottom*. Each one of these positions is given a different number on each pick-up.

First Pick-Up

If the selected card is in the *top* pile, the performer remembers number 1.

In the *middle* pile, the performer remembers number 2.

In the *bottom* pile, the performer remembers number 3.

Second Pick-Up

If the selected card is in the top pile, the performer adds 0 to number remembered in first pick-up.

In the middle pile, the performer adds 3 to remembered number.

In the bottom pile, the performer adds 6 to the remembered number.

Third Pick-Up

If the selected card is in the top pile, performer adds 0 to previous total.

In the middle pile, performer adds 9 to previous total.

In the bottom pile, the performer adds 18 to previous total.

The total of the three figures gives the performer the location of the selected card by counting from the top of the face-down twenty-seven card packet. Example: In the first pick-up the spectator placed the pile containing the card in the middle. The performer's formula number is 2. In the second pick-up it went into the middle of the packet again. Adding 3 to our previous formula number 2, we get 5, and that is now our code number. In the third pick-up the pile containing the card goes to the bottom. Our formula number for that is 18. Add to that the 5 we are remembering, and we find that the selected card is the twenty-third card down in the packet.

65. THE SPELLING BEE

This trick is much favored by magicians John McArdle, Jack Chanin, John Weiss, and Al Flosso.

PRESENTATION AND EFFECT

The performer riffle shuffles the deck once, then turns the deck face up and removes the thirteen spade cards from ace through king. The performer places these cards face down on the table into a pile as each is removed from the pack. The thirteen spades are then placed face down in the performer's left hand, and the performer states that he is going to spell the name of each card correctly—and sometimes will spell a name incorrectly—and invites the spectators to watch what will happen.

The performer, holding the thirteen cards face down in his left hand, starts to spell, commencing with the ace. He spells A and removes a card from the top and adds it to the bottom of the packet; spells C and removes another card from the top and places it on the bottom; spells E and removes the top card and places it on the bottom of the packet. Then the performer removes the top card of the packet and places it on the table face up, and it is found to be the ace.

The performer does the same with the 2, 3, etc., until the thirteen cards have been spelled correctly and placed on the table in proper sequence. There is only one exception to this rule, the performer occasionally misspells a word. For example, he spells "three" *threi*. He turns up the next card; it is not a 3, just an indifferent card. The performer returns the wrong card face down on top of the packet, and spells "three" correctly this time. Sure enough, when spelled correctly, the 3-spot turns up. This method of spelling correctly and incorrectly continues until the entire packet is exhausted.

THE SECRET

The thirteen spade cards are placed on top of the deck in the following positions: queen, jack, 10, ace, 6, 9, 3, 2, king, 8,

7, 5, 4, the queen being the top card of the deck. The deck is then cut in half and riffle shuffled together. This does not disturb the arrangement of the thirteen spades. The performer now turns the deck face up and removes the 4 of spades first, putting it on the table face down; next, the 5 of spades, placing it face down on top of the 4. He continues to remove the spades from the deck, placing each on top of the previous one until the thirteen spades have been removed. The performer now has the original setup as described above.

The performer then places the thirteen cards face down into his left hand and spells out A-C-E for ace, taking a card from the top of the packet and placing it at the bottom, one card for each letter spelled. In this instance, three cards have been removed one at a time from the top and placed at the bottom of the packet. The next card (top card) is removed from the packet and placed face up on the table. It is the ace. The same holds true for the 2. But when spelling "three," the performer spells it incorrectly. For example, he spells *threi*, turns up the next card and it is not the 3-spot. He then returns the wrong card to the top of the packet and spells "three" correctly. The next card removed is the 3-spot.

Following is the entire spelling routine. In order to make it easy for the performer to remember when to misspell a word, starting with the 3-spot, all the odd cards are misspelled once.

The cards to be misspelled are the 3, 5, 7, 9, jack. When misspelling a word, spell the word correctly until the last letter, then spell the wrong last letter. In this manner you always spell the correct number of letters, which is very important, but the last letter is wrong. The second time you spell the word, spell it correctly, and the right card will be found. The performer must always spell the misspelled number correctly the second time.

66. DOUBLE REVELATION

This effect has been used by many card tricksters, but is especially favored by magicians Herb Rungie, George Pearce, and Ande Furlong.

PRESENTATION AND EFFECT

The performer hands the spectator a card case containing a deck of cards. The performer instructs the spectator to take out the deck and shuffle it.

The performer remarks that whenever a magician does a trick with a deck of cards behind his back, the average person believes it is based on the magic number 52, which is the number of cards in a deck. To dispel any such thought the performer instructs the spectator to put a few cards back in the card case while his back is turned.

Facing the spectator again, the performer takes the deck and illustrates what he wants the spectator to do. He deals two piles of cards face down onto the table, saying to the spectator, "I am going to turn my back, and I want you to do the same thing as I've just done. You must deal two packets of cards face down onto the table, each pile must contain the same number of cards, and each pile must not contain more than ten cards." The performer pushes aside the cards he dealt and says, "We don't need these."

Then he turns his back and instructs the spectator to deal out two piles, as directed before. This being done, the performer tells the spectator to place one of these packets in his (the spectator's) pocket. After this, the spectator is told to look at the top card of the deck, remember it and then replace it on top of the deck.

The spectator is told to put the remaining dealt packet on top of this card (top card of deck). The performer then faces the spectator, takes the deck and places it behind his back or under the table, whichever is easier for the performer, and patters along these lines. "If I found your card behind my back, that would be an excellent trick, wouldn't it?" The performer, after a bit of fumbling behind his back, brings the cards forward with the remark, "Do you know how many cards you have in your pocket?"

If the spectator has forgotten, the performer turns his back again, and requests the spectator to count them and then to place them on top of the deck. If he remembers the number, he is told to place them on top of the deck without counting them. The performer then takes the deck again and places it behind his back or under the table, and after a bit of fumbling, as if it's a difficult maneuver to find the selected card, he takes a card out of the deck and places it face down on the table in front of the spectator.

He then looks through the deck to make sure that it was the selected card, and then seems to remember something. He says to the spectator, "By the way, do you still remember the number of cards you placed in your pocket?" Putting the cards behind his back or under the table for a moment, he comes forward with a pile of cards in his hand. These he puts in front of the spectator, saying, "That is the number of cards you had in your pocket at the start of the trick." Both the selected card and the number of cards prove to be correct upon examination by the spectator.

THE SECRET

When the performer takes the shuffled deck from the spectator and illustrates what he desires the spectator to do while his back is turned, he catches a glimpse of the bottom card of the deck. This he does while pushing the dealt cards to one side and saying, "We don't need these cards."

The spectator is instructed as described under Presentation and Effect. Now, when the performer takes the deck and places it behind his back, he silently counts off fourteen cards from the top of the deck, reversing them in the process (counts the first card off into his right hand, the second card on top of this, etc., until fourteen cards have been counted off, and the original top card of the deck is now the bottom card of the fourteen). Then he returns the fourteen cards to the top of the deck; he then takes the bottom card of the deck (which he knows, having glimpsed it) and places it on top of the deck.

When the spectator is instructed to place the cards in his pocket on top of the deck, these cards will be placed on top of the glimpsed card.

The performer places the deck behind his back again, counts down to the fifteenth card, and removes it. (The performer does not reverse the cards this time, instead he keeps them in their exact positions.) The fifteenth card which the performer removes is the selected card. It will always be the fifteenth card, provided the spectator has not dealt more than ten cards in a pile by accident. Now the performer, after placing the selected card face down, makes a sort of check-up, saying, "I'm sure that is the correct card." But, in reality, he is looking through the cards attempting to spot the glimpsed card. He counts the number of cards above the glimpsed card, and that is the number of cards the spectator had in his pocket. The performer places the deck behind his back, counts off that number of cards and places them in front of the spectator.

Example: Spectator made five-card piles. Therefore, five cards were placed on top of the selected card, which makes the selected card sixth from the top. When the spectator reverses fourteen cards, the sixth becomes the ninth. Then, when the bottom card is placed on top of the deck, the ninth card becomes the tenth. The spectator puts the five cards from his pocket on top of the deck, making the tenth card the fifteenth.

67. WALSH'S LONG DISTANCE CARD TRICK

This one is identified with Audley Walsh, the exposer of rackets. It can be worked over a telephone or from one room to another.

PRESENTATION AND EFFECT

The performer calls up a person on the telephone, or stays in one room and has the person stay in another room. He instructs the person whom we shall call the spectator to do as follows:

The performer tells the spectator to get a deck of cards and shuffle them thoroughly, and to cut the cards so that at least twenty cards must be in each cut group. The performer then tells the spectator to select one of the piles and to discard the other by pushing it to one side. The spectator is then instructed by the performer to count the number of cards in this selected pile. Now he is told to add the two digits of that number and to discard that number of cards from the selected pile by pushing these cards to one side with the other discards. "For example," says the performer, "if you have counted twenty-one cards, the total of those two digits is 3. Therefore, you would discard three cards of that pile and retain the remainder."

The performer now instructs the spectator to think of a number from 1 to 9, remove that many cards and place them in one of his pockets. The spectator is then told to note and memorize the card at the position designated by that number in the remainder of the selected pile, counting the top face-down card as 1, the next as 2, etc. Then he is to replace the cards which have been counted off in their original position in the packet. The performer instructs the spectator to place the remaining cards in the selected pile face down in his left hand, to deal them slowly one at a time face up onto the table, and to call out the name of each card as it is dealt.

This being done, the performer asks the spectator to concentrate on the name of the selected card. The performer says, "I get an impression. Your card is the five of diamonds" (or whatever it may be). The performer's impression is correct.

The performer also says, "I received a mental impression when you were placing those cards in your pocket. You have x number of cards in your pocket." This number which the performer calls also proves to be correct.

THE SECRET

The performer requires a piece of paper with numbers from 1 to 26 written down in a column. As the spectator calls his cards, the performer notes the name of the card under or alongside each number. For example, if the spectator calls 10 of spades for his first card, the performer jots down 10S under or alongside number 1. Next the spectator calls 5 of hearts; the performer jots down 5H below or alongside number 2.

When the spectator has finished calling his cards, the performer notes the number alongside the last card called, and that gives him the key number in this mathematical trick.

If the number is 8 or less, subtract it from 9. The answer is the number of cards in the spectator's pocket, and the selected card will be found alongside that number on the performer's chart.

If this number is from 9 to 17, subtract it from 18.

If this number is from 18 to 26, subtract it from 27.

For example, the spectator has called twelve cards. Subtract 12 from 18. The spectator has six cards in his pocket, and the card the performer jotted alongside number 6 is the selected card.

68. SCARNE'S DRUNKEN POKER DEAL

This terrific Poker deal was created by the author. It is such a "socko" that after teaching it to one of his friends, he performed it at a club in New Jersey and won $100 from a couple of smart gamblers.

PRESENTATION AND EFFECT

The performer says, "Several years ago I was having a beer

in one of the local taverns. In wandered a drunk who was very loud and boisterous. It didn't take him long before he said that he could beat anyone at the bar, no matter what the sport—at a fist fight, wrestling, golfing, or you name it. The bartender was ready to throw him out, but before he had an opportunity to get on the outside of the bar, the drunk had taken a deck of cards from his pocket. He began mixing them by turning a group face up and a group face down."

At this point the performer takes a deck out of the card case and illustrates the manner in which the drunk was mixing the cards. The performer turns a group of cards face up, then part of this group face down, then another group face up, etc. He continues this until the cards are haphazardly mixed, some face down and some face up.

In this trick the performer takes the part of the drunk, so in the description of it, we will refer to the performer as the drunk.

With the cards mixed as described above, the drunk says that he will deal out two Draw Poker hands, one to himself and one to the spectator. The drunk now deals the top card of the deck face down on the table in front of the spectator. The second card, which is a faced-up jack, he deals to himself, but instantly turns it face down on the table in front of himself. This procedure is continued until he has dealt two Poker hands of five cards each. The drunk has dealt three face-up jacks as part of his hand, but he does not mention this fact at any time. Instead, he rapidly turns each face down when dealing to himself. This is purely psychological and creates the impression in the spectator's mind that the drunk does not want him to see these three jacks.

After the deal the drunk picks up his hand, looks at it, and places two cards face down on the table in front of himself, as if he intends to discard two cards.

Looking at the spectator, who is requested to pick up the other Poker hand, the drunk asks, "How many cards do you want to draw?" The spectator looks at his hand and finds that he holds four kings and an ace. He knows that the drunk has three jacks and will draw two cards, and the best that he can make is four jacks—which will not beat the four kings. The ace in his hand checks out any idea of four aces. With this thought in mind the spectator believes he has an unbeatable hand, and often will want to bet the drunk some money that his hand will beat that of the drunk. The spectator does not know if the drunk is aware of the fact that he holds four kings. Whether the spectator stands pat (does not draw cards) or draws one card, the drunk still draws two cards.

And on the showdown, the spectator is surprised no end to see that his four kings have been beaten by a Straight Flush in hearts.

THE SECRET

The fourteen cards are arranged in the following order from the top of the deck:

1. King of diamonds, face down.
2. Jack of hearts, face up.
3. King of clubs, face down.
4. Jack of spades, face up.
5. King of hearts, face down.
6. 10 of hearts, face down.
7. King of spades, face down.
8. 9 of hearts, face down.
9. Ace of diamonds, face down.
10. Jack of diamonds, face up.
11. Queen of hearts, face down.
12. 8 of hearts, face down.
13. 7 of hearts, face down.
14. Jack of clubs, face down.

The performer (drunk) has these cards arranged as described above. The king of diamonds on top of the deck, and the jack of clubs, the fourteenth card from the top.

The deck is then put into the card case in this prearranged manner, and the performer, when ready to do the "Drunken Poker Deal," tells the story about the drunk—as given under Presentation and Effect—and takes the deck out of the card case. He gives the deck what appears to be a thorough mixing,

but actually it is a false shuffle (a false shuffle is a shuffle that retains the same position of all or some of the cards in the deck). This shuffle was invented by the author particularly for the readers of this book, and it can be used to great advantage when doing other tricks. It is undoubtedly one of the best false shuffles ever created, and unlike other false shuffles, this one requires no manipulative skill. Just a little practice to acquaint oneself with its workings is all that is necessary.

Getting back to the "Drunken Poker Deal" and the shuffle. The performer holds the deck face down in his left hand. The thumb of the left hand pushes about forty-five cards into the right hand, which in turn takes them and flips them over, letting them fall face up on top of the remaining few cards in the left hand. The performer then turns over, by flipping, about ten cards from the top of the deck, then about five, then one or two, then about twenty, then one or two, then about fifteen, then one or two, then about twenty-five, then about two, then about ten. The one and two card turnover should be done before a larger group of cards is turned over. It makes the deck look thoroughly mixed, with cards face up and cards face down, and offers a logical reason for the three jacks being dealt face up during the dealing of the two Poker hands.

The performer must be careful not to turn over any cards in the setup, which is near the bottom of the deck. The performer for his last flip-over, turns over the same number of cards as he did for his first turnover. This can easily be duplicated because the king of diamonds, he knows, is the first face-up card from the bottom of the deck. The performer's left hand pushes the deck toward the right hand, at the same time holding the cards below the king of diamonds with his left hand. The right hand turns over all the cards on top of the king of diamonds, including the king of diamonds. In other words, with this last turnover, the king of diamonds will be the top card of the deck, and the fourteen-card setup will be back to its original position on top of the deck.

The performer then deals out two five-card Poker hands, one to the spectator and one to himself. Naturally, the performer is dealt three jacks face up. He doesn't say a word about them, but after laying the pack down, he casually turns his three jacks face down. Then he asks the spectator (who by this time has picked up his hand and is surprised to find he holds four kings and the ace of diamonds) how many cards he wishes to draw.

The spectator naturally will either draw one card or stay pat. The performer then discards the jack of diamonds and the jack of spades, and with his two-card draw makes a heart Straight Flush to beat the four kings held by the spectator.

Should a smart alec spectator draw two cards, the performer discards the 9 and 10 of hearts and makes four jacks.

Note: If the performer desires to shuffle the cards further, which heightens the effect, he can do so easily by turning the pack over and shuffling the top thirty cards in the same manner as described under Presentation and Effect and explained in The Secret. The performer stops shuffling when a card is face down on the top. Then he taps the pack on the table sideways to create the impression that he is squaring the cards, but actually he turns the deck over and deals the stacked cards from the top of the deck.

69. PERFECT PREDICTION

This nice prediction trick requires no setup. It is a favorite of Chester Morris', the magician and movie star.

PRESENTATION AND EFFECT

"I want you to take your own deck of cards and mix them thoroughly," says the performer to the spectator. That being done, the performer asks for the shuffled deck, and continues. "Before I tell you what to do, let's remove the joker, if it is here." Looking through the deck the performer says, "I see there is none, so we can proceed. First, I want to write a prediction on this slip of paper." The performer proceeds to write and hands the folded paper to a spectator to hold.

"Now," says the performer, "remove any ten cards from any part of the deck, not necessarily in one group, and please shuffle these ten cards without looking at them." After this, the spectator is instructed to retain any four cards of the ten and place them face up on the table. The other six are placed at the bottom of the deck.

"Look," says the performer, "ten cards were taken and four cards are shown. We will build up the value of each card to equal ten. Any picture card will count as ten, so nothing needs to be added to a picture card." (The face cards, for example, are 7 of diamonds, 6 of clubs, 8 of hearts, 4 of spades.)

"We will need three cards for the seven of diamonds, four for the six of clubs, two for the eight of hearts, and six for the four of spades, giving us a total of fifteen cards to be added." These fifteen cards are then dealt off from the top of the remainder of the deck, and are placed on the bottom of the deck.

"Now," says the performer, "let's take a total of the four cards that are shown. We find that they total twenty-five. Before anything happened, I wrote a prediction which the spectator now has in his hand." Giving the deck to the spectator, the performer requests him to deal off twenty-five cards and to turn the twenty-fifth card face up. "If you will open the piece of paper," says the performer, "you will find that my written prediction matches the twenty-fifth card which you turned up."—And it does.

THE SECRET

After the deck has been shuffled to the spectator's satisfaction, the performer takes it back, and on the pretext of looking for the joker, he mentally notes the third card from the bottom of the bottom of the deck. This third card from the bottom is the card which the performer notes on the piece of paper as his prediction. If the performer does find a joker in the deck, he removes it, since this trick will work only with a deck comprised of fifty-two cards, no more and no less. Regardless of what four cards are retained by the spectator, the performer merely follows this procedure: each card to total 10 except picture cards, which are counted as 10.

Important: The six cards that are handed back to the performer from the ten originally selected, as well as the number of cards needed to bring the value of each of the four cards retained up to 10, are all placed at the bottom of the remaining part of the deck. Regardless of what cards are built up, the total value of these four cards will always be the third card from the bottom of the deck before any cards were taken away.

70. THE PUZZLER

This trick gets a big hand from the New Jersey magician Bob Short.

PRESENTATION AND EFFECT

The performer hands a spectator a pack to shuffle. After thoroughly shuffling the pack, he is requested to cut the deck and complete the cut. The performer then turns his back and instructs the spectator to turn the deck face up in his left hand, and to note the top face-up card. The spectator is told to place this card face down on the table, to count off as many more cards as are required to make twelve, and to place these face down on top of the face-down card he already placed on the table. For example, if the top face-up card of the deck is a 2-spot, the spectator places it face down on the table. Counting the next card as 3, he counts up to 12, and places all the counted-off cards face down on top of the face-down 2-spot. In this case he would place ten cards on top of the 2-spot.

After he has formed a twelve-card packet on the table, he takes the top face-up card of the deck and again goes through the same procedure, forming another packet on the table. If this face-up card happens to be a 5-spot, the spectator places it face down on the table and adds seven cards to that packet, making the count reach 12. This is continued until the entire deck is exhausted. In case 12 cannot be counted when forming the last packet, these cards are placed to one side. Any court card, such as jack, queen, or king, is counted as 10.

When all the piles are completed, the performer faces the spectator and immediately gives the total (addition) of all the

pips of the bottom cards of each packet. When the piles are turned face up, and the pip values of the bottom cards are added together, the performer's announcement is found to be correct.

THE SECRET

After the performer faces the spectator he mentally notes how many piles are on the table. Suppose there are seven piles dealt on the table, with five cards left over. The performer first subtracts 4 from the number of piles on the table—4 from 7 leaves 3. He multiplies 3 by 13, which gives him a total of 39. Then the performer adds the leftover cards to this total. In this case, 39 plus 5, which gives us a total of 44. This answer proves to be correct.

Note: Should there be only five packets on the table, the performer subtracts 4 from 5, which leaves 1. He multiplies 1 times 13, for an answer of 13. To this he adds the number of cards left over. Again he will have the correct answer.

71. SELECTED CARD VANISHES INTO POCKET

This card trick, created by the author, was suggested by the magician Johnny Albenice, of Flushing, New York.

PRESENTATION AND EFFECT

The performer allows the spectator to shuffle and cut the deck. The performer then takes the deck and passes cards one at a time before the spectator's eyes. The performer passes the cards from his left hand to his right—without disturbing the position of the cards—from the top of the deck. He requests the spectator to note well one of the cards and also to remember its numerical position in the top of the deck as it is passed by. To make it easier for the spectator to remember the location from the top, the performer counts, out loud, the position of each card from the top. For example, when the performer pushes the first card from his left hand to his right he says, "One"; the second card, "Two"; the third card, "Three"; etc.

When the spectator has noted the card and its position in the top of the deck, he says, "I've got one," or "Okay." The performer returns the cards to the pack in their original positions.

The performer takes the pack and places it behind his back, stating that he is going to remove a card and place it in his left-hand coat pocket. This he does, and states that this is the chosen card.

The performer then brings the pack into view again, requests the spectator to call the number where his card is located. Dealing down to that number, the performer places that card face down on the table. The spectator is requested to name his card, and to turn the card face up on the table. This is not the spectator's card. The performer then reaches into his left-hand coat pocket and produces the chosen card.

THE SECRET

When the performer places the pack behind his back to find the chosen card, he moves the bottom card of the deck to the top, and then takes the next bottom card with his left hand and places it into his left-hand coat pocket.

Now the performer counts down to the spectator's number. Let us assume the number was 9. He counts down to the ninth card and places it face down on the table. The performer asks the spectator to name his chosen card. This being done, the performer asks the spectator to turn up the face-down card to see if it is correct. While this is being done, the performer pretends to go into his left-hand coat pocket for the selected card, but actually he has the deck in his left hand with the chosen

129

card on top. After he has placed the deck part way into the pocket, he deals the top card off the pack with his left thumb and lets it fall into his pocket. Coming out with his hand, he places the deck on the table and reaches into his pocket with

his left hand—he makes sure to remove the card he dropped into his pocket instead of the card previously placed there. The card he removes is found to be the chosen card, vanished from the deck and found in the coat pocket.

The performer still has that extra card in his pocket. A good way to get it out is to put the deck in the pocket before turning over the chosen card (card removed from the pocket), thereby eliminating all evidence that an extra card was in the pocket.

72. JAMES'S MIRACLE

This trick was created by Stewart James, the notable Canadian magician.

PRESENTATION AND EFFECT

The performer removes a deck of cards from the card case, and requests a spectator to think of a number from 1 to 10. He does the same with a second spectator. The performer requests each spectator to call out the number he is thinking of. For example, Spectator No. 1 calls out, "Five." Spectator No. 2 calls out, "Seven." The performer, counting out loud, deals five cards singly one on top of each other into the center of the table. Then he deals seven cards, forming another pile.

Stating that the total number of cards in each pile corresponds to the numbers selected by the spectators, the performer then places the larger packet of dealt cards on top of the smaller, forming one pile. These in turn are placed on top of the deck.

The performer then says that there is a sympathy existing between the two spectators and the numbers they are holding in mind. To prove this sympathy or relationship exists, the performer says, "A card whose pip total is the same as the number the first spectator thought of will be found at the number in the pack that corresponds to the number thought of by the second spectator. The same will hold true for the number thought of by the second spectator. A card equal to that number will be found at the number thought of by the first spectator." Using 5 and 7, the two numbers in the example given above, the performer first counts down to the smaller number. He counts down to 5, turns over the fifth card, and it is found to contain seven pips, which is the second spectator's number. Placing the five cards back on top of the deck, he now counts down to 7, turns over the seventh card, and it is found to contain five pips, the number called by the first spectator, proving that there is a corelation in numbers.

The performer replaces the seven dealt cards on top of the deck, and looking at both spectators, he says, "You thought of

number five, and you thought of number seven. Five and seven total twelve." He hands the deck to a spectator and instructs him to deal off eleven cards, to take the twelfth card from the deck for himself, and to note its face value.

The spectator is surprised to find a message written on this card, which reads, "Were you fooled?" Upon examination, this is the only card in the deck with a message written upon it.

THE SECRET

To perform this card trick, the following preparation is necessary. The performer takes from the pack two groups of ten cards, each comprised of ace, 2, 3, 4, 5, 6, 7, 8, 9, and 10. These two groups are arranged in sequence. The top ten cards run from ace to 10, the ace being the uppermost card; the next ten cards which are placed below the top ten are arranged in sequence running from 10 to ace. These twenty cards are placed on top of the remainder of the deck.

A card, preferably a 4-spot because it has more white space to write a message on, is taken from the deck, and the message, "Were you fooled?" or any message the performer prefers, is written on its face in pencil or ink. This card is placed on top of the twenty-card setup. In other words, this card will be the top card of the deck. The deck of cards is now placed into the card case with this arrangement, and the performer is ready to perform "James's Miracle," merely by following the instructions given under Presentation and Effect.

If the performer does not care to mutilate a card by writing on it, he may get an exceptionally strong prediction merely by writing the name of the top card of the deck on a piece of paper before the trick is started, and placing it in the spectator's pocket to be unfolded upon the completion of the trick. This predicted card must be placed on top of the twenty-card setup in the same manner as the card with the message written on it.

73. THE OBEDIENT CARDS

From Nat Bernstein and from Morty Zuckert, who is a New York City magician.

PRESENTATION AND EFFECT

The performer hands a pack of cards to the spectator to shuffle. The spectator is then told to think of a number from 1 to 10, and to count down to that number from the top of the deck. When the spectator reaches the number he is thinking of, he is told to note and memorize the card at that number, and to replace the cards so that they will be in their original positions in the deck.

The performer now takes the pack and requests a second spectator to name a number between 10 and 20. The performer then places the deck behind his back and states that he is arranging the cards in a magical sequence. This being done, the performer brings the pack forward and hands it to the second spectator.

The performer asks the first spectator to name the number which determines the position of his card in the deck. The second spectator is requested to count down to his number, but to start with the number called by the first spectator.

For example, first spectator's chosen card is located at number 5. The second spectator called number 15. Therefore, the second spectator starts counting by calling the top card "five," the next card "six," etc., and continuing until he has counted up to 15. Upon turning this last card over it is found to be the card chosen by the first spectator.

THE SECRET

The performer asks the second spectator to call a number between 10 and 20. Whatever number the second spectator calls, that is the number of cards the performer reverses when he has the deck behind his back. For example, the second spectator calls number 15. The performer takes the deck and places it behind his back and at once reverses the fifteen top cards of the deck. To do this silently, deal fifteen cards from the left hand into the right hand, one card on top of the other. (Top card is dealt into right hand, second card from top is dealt on top of the card in right hand, etc.) When fifteen cards have been reversed, they are then replaced on top of the deck. Then the deck is handed to the second spectator, the counting is started, and the trick is brought to a successful conclusion.

74. THE TRAVELING CARD

This card trick for finding a chosen card at an exact location in the deck has been a standby with Jack Miller, the New York professional magician, for over thirty years.

PRESENTATION AND EFFECT

The performer places a deck of cards face down on the table, and requests a spectator to cut approximately half the deck. The spectator is told to shuffle the cut portion (upper half of deck) several times and then note and remember the top card of that portion. He is then instructed to replace the group of cards he holds on top of the remaining half of the deck which is resting on the table. The performer then turns the pack over so the cards are face up. The spectator is now told to cut the deck and complete the cut (putting the two halves together after cutting); cutting continues until the performer tells the spectator to stop. Then the spectator is told to place the deck face down on the table and to place his finger on top of the deck.

The performer looks at the deck as if he were concentrating very hard, and says to the spectator, "Your card is now twentieth from the top of the deck. No, it is rising rapidly, it is now in fifteenth, twelfth, eighth, fifth position in the deck. I believe it is now coming up to the top. No, it has stopped traveling."

The performer looks at the spectator and says, "Sorry, I can't bring it to the top. You held your finger on the deck a bit too hard, therefore I could not bring it to the top of the deck. It is stuck at the fifth position from the top."

The performer has the spectator count the cards face down, stopping at the fifth card from the top of the deck. The spectator turns the card face up, and it is found to be the spectator's chosen card. The last number which the performer names determines the location of the selected card.

The Secret

The performer secretly arranges, on the bottom of the deck, thirteen cards of the same suit, such as thirteen clubs, although any other suit can be used. The clubs are arranged: ace, 2, 3, 4, 5, 6, 7, 8, 9, 10, jack, queen, king. The ace is the bottom card of the deck; and the king, the thirteenth card from the

bottom. The performer places the deck on the table, arranged as described above, and requests the spectator to cut approximately half of the deck, shuffle that group, note the top card, and replace the cut portion on top of the lower cut portion resting on the table. When the cards are cut, the selected card is next to the bottom card of the deck (the ace of clubs in the setup).

When the deck is turned face up on the table, the performer

instructs the spectator to cut the cards and complete the cut. This cutting procedure is continued until one of the cards of the setup group is the uppermost card of the faced-up deck. In other words, if the setup is clubs, whenever the spectator cuts to a club card, the cutting stops, and the value of the club card determines the position of the selected card in the top of the deck. For instance, if the ace of clubs is cut, the selected card is on top of the deck when the deck is turned face down. If the spectator cuts the 2 of clubs, the selected card is second from the top of the face-down deck, etc. Jack has a value of 11; queen, 12; and king, 13.

75. PERSONIFICATION

Here the performer uses a spectator's name for the discovery of a card. This trick was created by Oscar Weigle, the New York magician.

PRESENTATION AND EFFECT

The performer shuffles the deck and has the spectator cut the cards. Then the performer deals off cards singly from the top of

the deck, turning each dealt card face up on the table, and counting the cards aloud as they are dealt. The spectator is requested to remember any card dealt and also the number called out at the time the card was dealt.

After a reasonable number of cards have been dealt, they are gathered together and replaced on top of the deck in their original order. The performer places the deck behind his back for a moment, and then brings the deck into view again.

The spectator is requested to name the position of his card in the pack (the number called). The performer deals down to that number and the spectator's card is no longer at its original position.

Thereupon the remainder of the deck is given to the spectator and he is instructed by the performer to spell out his full name, letter for letter, dealing a card off the top of the deck for each letter. The card at the last letter spelled is turned face up, and it proves to be the card the spectator glimpsed and is remembering.

THE SECRET

When the performer places the deck behind his back he merely counts off the bottom of the deck and places on top of the deck a number of cards equal to the number of letters in the full name of the spectator who memorized the card. Thus, if the spectator's name is William Smith, the number of cards would be twelve. This trick is particularly effective if the performer apparently is not acquainted with the spectator's name but has learned it through another person or by some devious means unknown to the spectator.

76. MY LUCKY CARD

This quick and easy trick requires no preparation beforehand, and yet is really baffling. The following method was worked out by the author and by Bill Simon, the magician.

PRESENTATION AND EFFECT

The performer hands a deck of cards to a spectator to shuffle and cut. The deck is returned to the performer, who looks through the deck face up and say, "I am looking for my lucky card." He finds his lucky card and places it face down on the table, making certain that the spectator does not see it.

The performer places the deck face down on the palm of his hand, and requests the spectator to cut the deck and to retain the portion of the cards that he cut. The performer turns over the group of cards still on his palm, so that the group is face up, and places the *lucky card* (which was on the table) face down on top of this group, making certain that the spectator does not see the face of the lucky card. The performer takes the cut group from the spectator and places this group face up on top of the lucky card. The entire deck is now face up with the exception of the performer's lucky card, which is face down. The performer now turns the deck over so that it is face down, and spreads the cards, looking for his lucky card which is now face up in the deck. Removing the lucky card plus the card above it and the card below it, the performer places the three cards on the table in the same position as they were taken from the deck.

The performer states that the spectator shuffled the cards thoroughly, and then designated by cutting where the performer was to place his lucky card, but regardless of all these hazards, his lucky card will always be placed between two cards that will determine its value: one card will determine the suit, the other the rank.

The performer's lucky card, for example, is the 6 of spades. Upon turning over the two cards, one above it, the other below it, we find a 6-spot and a spade card, proving that the lucky card never fails.

THE SECRET

When the spectator returns the deck to the performer after

it has been shuffled, the performer secretly notes the top and bottom cards of the deck. For instance, the top and bottom

137

cards are the 6 of diamonds and the ace of spades. The performer notes these cards as he looks through the deck for his lucky card. The performer, when looking for the lucky card, finds either the 6 of spades or the ace of diamonds. Either one of these cards will do. In other words, the performer always has the choice of two cards in selecting his lucky card; therefore, the first one the performer sees, he takes out and places face down on the table.

From then on the trick is self-working. When the performer turns over the group of cards in his hand, the lucky card is placed on the original bottom card of the deck, and when the spectator's cut group is turned face up and placed on top of the lucky card, the card on top of the lucky card is the card that originally was on top of the deck. The spectator will be unaware of this ruse simply because he doesn't know what the performer is going to do.

Should two cards of the same rank, or two cards of the same suit, appear as top and bottom cards of the deck, have the deck cut by the spectator until this situation no longer exists.

77. THE POCKER-FACE CARD TRICK

This card trick requires no previous arrangements. It is much favored by Frank Garcia and George Schindler, both New York magicians.

PRESENTATION AND EFFECT

The performer, while standing up, approaches a spectator (who is seated) and has him shuffle the cards. The performer takes the deck from the spectator and places it in his left hand. He requests the spectator to cut the cards at any position he desires. This being done, and while the spectator is still holding the top portion of the deck, the performer moves forward, pushing the top card of the portion he is holding about a half inch to the right, so that the spectator can see the card. The spectator is told to memorize that card. The performer then hands the cards he is holding to the spectator and asks him to shuffle both portions of the deck together. The performer then says to the spectator that he wants him to deal the cards slowly off the top of the pack, one at a time, turning each dealt card face up on the table, placing each card on top of that previously dealt.

"But, before you do that," continues the performer, "I want you to know that I am going to conduct an experiment that I have been working often while playing Poker. It is my belief that no one—no one person can keep a so-called poker face. There are a number of ways to detect cards by looking at the facial expressions of the card player. Very often the shifting of the eyes gives you away, other times your smile, or the wrinkle of your forehead. Now, I want you to remember the card you selected a moment ago. As you deal those cards face up, you will see your card pass. I'm going to ask you to try as hard as you can to keep a straight face. I'll watch your face, and all I ask is that you watch the cards as they go by. Try not to laugh or crack a smile as you pass it. I want you to fight me. Now, here we go—you may now deal the cards."

The spectator deals the entire deck or part of the deck, which is discretionary with the performer. He is stopped by the performer, who says, "You had a twinkle in your eye, which I believe gave you away. It happened when you turned up the ——." The performer names a card, asks the spectator if that was the selected card—and the performer proves to be correct.

THE SECRET

When the performer holds the bottom portion of the deck, he and his left hand move forward, pushing the top card of that packet at a right angle, so the spectator can see its value. But the performer, since he is standing, can also see the indicia of the card by just leaning over a little. As soon as the performer

WRIST IS TURNED TOWARDS DIRECTION OF PERFORMER

does this, and sees the cards, he turns his head away, which gives the impression that he did not see it. Illustration shows this move more clearly.

The performer now knows the name of the selected card. After the spectator deals the selected card face up, or after he deals a few more cards on top of the selected card, the performer stops him from dealing, and tells him that the twinkle in his eye gave him away. Naturally, he names the correct card because he saw it at the same time the spectator did.

Note: Do not pass this trick by. A few trials and it will be one of your favorites.

78. WINNING POKER

In this Poker deal, as presented by Louis Zingone, the clever vaudeville magician, the performer permits each player to exchange hands and yet the performer always holds the winning hand.

PRESENTATION AND EFFECT

Seated at a table, the performer invites three friends to a friendly game of Poker. Taking off about half of the deck he requests that these cards be shuffled. Replacing this group on top of the remaining cards, he proceeds to deal out four hands of Closed Poker. "Now," says the performer, "you can have the choice of playing the cards dealt, or you can exchange your cards with any other player including myself." One of the players usually decides to exchange his five cards with the performer. Each player then discards and draws what he requires up to and including four cards. At this point the performer places the balance of the cards on the table, and now for the first time looks at his hand (that originally belonged to another player). He decides to draw four cards, and deals them from the deck. The friendly bets proceed, and when all hands are shown, the performer displays four aces—the winning hand.

"Now," says the performer, "that might be just a stroke of good luck, so let's play one more hand." Gathering the twenty cards along with the discards, once more he requests that the cards be shuffled. When this is done, these cards are again placed on the remainder of the deck and four more hands are dealt out. After the discards are made and the draw completed, even though another player has exchanged his hand with the performer, the performer wins again with four kings.

THE SECRET

Before starting the game, the performer secretly places face up on the table four aces, and on top of these four kings, followed by three or four indifferent cards. The balance of the deck is placed face down on this prearranged group. You now have a complete deck with about forty cards on top in a normal face-down position on the secret packet of the other cards, which are face up. When you remove about half of the deck to be shuffled this bottom group is not disturbed.

After the deal, discards, draw and any exchange of hands, all that is required before the performer looks at his own hand is merely to turn the deck over casually as he places it on the table. This turning of the deck brings the four aces on top, ready to be dealt to the performer. After he has dealt the four aces, the deck is again reversed casually, so that the four kings are now on the bottom of the deck. When the second deal has gone through, the performer merely repeats exactly what he did to obtain the four aces. The deck is again reversed, and the four kings are now on top. This is done before the performer looks at his hand. (The reason for the three or four indifferent cards is simply to avoid having any cards shown face up when the second round is completed.) Do not hurry the one move required in dealing this winning Poker hand. The other players will be too busy picking cards dealt them, and their attention will not be directed at the performer at all. Four or five hands, or even six, can be dealt. Remember in any case not to disturb the bottom twelve or thirteen cards when offering part of the deck to be shuffled.

79. SCARNE'S FOLLOW THE LEADER

This popular card effect has heretofore been duplicated only by skillful sleight of hand. Created by the author, with some help from Dr. Alan Barnett.

PRESENTATION AND EFFECT

The performer requests the spectator to remove six red-faced cards from the deck and place them face down on the table in a pile, then to remove six black cards from the deck and place them face down on top of the red pile. The performer picks up the group of cards to verify the count, to see if there are twelve in all. Then he divides the group into two equal packets; all this is done by the performer with the cards face down.

We now have two groups of cards on the table. The performer picks up one group and removes the bottom card, then places this bottom card face up on the table. The remainder of the group he places face down below this card. He does the same with the other group, places the bottom card face up on the table and the rest of the group below it face down. The face up cards are called the indicator cards, and are used to identify the colors of the five remaining cards which are placed below them.

The performer transposes the indicator cards (switches them by putting the red card where the black one is, and the black where the red card is. Then the performer turns the top card of each group face up, revealing a sympathetic color reaction, since the two turned-up cards match the indicator cards. Each turned-up card is removed and placed face up on the corresponding indicator card.

Once again the performer transposes the indicator cards, turning up the top card of each group, and again the cards show they match in color. Repeatedly, magical transposition follows physical transposition until all of the cards are exhausted.

The Secret

A spectator is asked to remove six red cards and six black cards of his own choice from the deck, assembling them into one packet with the colors separated (it does not matter which color is over the other). The performer takes the packet, holding it face down in his left hand, and asks of the spectator, "You removed twelve cards, is that right? Let's just check to be sure."

The cards are now counted off into the right hand, one at a time, the right thumb slipping off each card so that it goes on top of its predecessor, and the order of the cards is reversed. The performer counts: 1-2-3-4-5-6-7-8. And then, as if to save time, he turns over the remaining cards, spreading them face up on the table, saying, "And four makes twelve—that's right." The eight cards which have been counted onto the right hand are dropped face down on top of the four in the left hand.

It must be emphasized that casualness is the keynote in this count. Its only purpose, to the onlooker, is to verify the number of cards. With the handling suggested, no tangible change in the order of the cards will be apparent to the audience, but the performer has rearranged the cards in preparation for what follows.

The cards are spread and the top six cards separated from the bottom six, forming two packets of apparently contrasting colors, which are then placed on the table side by side. Each packet is picked up in turn, turned face up, and the bottom card removed (letting it be seen indirectly that the new bottom card is of the same color) and placed face up at a position in front of the packet it was taken from. This, it is explained, is to avoid confusion as to where the respective colors are.

The analogy of birds of a feather flocking together is suggested by the performer. So it is with the color of the cards, he explains. The indicator cards are transposed. Then the top card of each face-down packet is turned over, and it is seen that the colors match the cards which have been transposed! The turned-over cards are placed with the indicator cards.

Each packet of face-down cards is now taken and counted, to show four cards remaining, as follows: The top card is counted off (from left hand to right hand, by using the right thumb), counting, "One." The next card is slipped off the top of the first card, counting, "Two." The remaining two cards are spread apart slightly, counted as "Three-Four" without any change in their order, and placed below the two cards previously counted off. Each packet is then replaced in its respective position on the table.

The indicator cards (which are now two red and two black) are transposed en masse, after which the top card of each pack is again shown to be of a matching color. These are placed on the indicator cards, which have now expanded to three reds and three blacks.

Again the indicator cards change position. Again the topmost card of each packet is turned over, shown to be alike in color with the indicator cards that are face up in front of the packets, and added to them, so that there are now four red and four black indicator cards.

The final transposition of indicator cards is made, and the two cards remaining in each packet are turned over. They, too, have followed the colors of the indicator cards.

The utter simplicity of operation for such an immensely astonishing effect should make this a real favorite with many.

80. THE GREAT POKER DEMONSTRATION

This terrific Poker deal has lots of surprises and builds up its effect as it continues. The entire routine runs about five minutes, as performed by magicians Harry Lorayne of Brooklyn, Clayton Rawson, Norman Jensen, and many others.

PRESENTATION AND EFFECT

The performer tells a story something like this. "On one of my trips to Reno, Nevada, I ran into a big fellow who was demonstrating a trick to a little fellow. The big fellow was bragging about his cheating skill at cards." The performer then says to the spectator, "I will take the part of the big fellow, and you take the part of the little fellow."

The performer starts dealing two Poker hands, one to himself and one to the spectator, but stops dealing after each has been dealt three cards. The performer upon dealing himself the last (sixth) card places it very obviously underneath the two cards that have already been dealt to himself. Then he puts the three cards he has been dealt back on top of the deck without looking at them.

The performer then turns over the spectator's three cards and says, "Look, the little fellow was dealt three kings." The performer places the three kings back on top of the deck and deals another hand in the same manner as described above, and the spectator again is dealt three kings.

The performer always places the last card dealt under the two already dealt to himself, and places all three cards back on top of the deck.

While dealing these hands, the performer states that the big fellow was showing off for the little fellow. But after two or three deals, as described above, the little fellow piped up and said, "That's fine, but remember, when you play Poker you play with five cards not three." So the big fellow said, "That's right, and I can do the same thing with five cards."

At this point the performer deals two hands, five cards in each. This time the performer slides his last card (tenth card dealt) underneath his four previously dealt cards, and places all five back on top of the deck. The performer now turns up the spectator's hand, and it is a *Full House*.

Putting these cards back on top of the deck, the performer relates how the little fellow said, "Let's see you do it again." The big fellow did it again, and to convince the little fellow, he did it once more, dealing the little fellow a Full House each time, always sliding his own fifth card under his previously dealt four cards, and putting them back on top of the deck each time he repeated the performance.

After the performer has dealt a Full House three times to the spectator, the spectator says to him, "I think I know how it's done. Let me try it."

The performer hands the deck to the spectator, as did the big fellow to the little fellow, and requests the spectator to do exactly as he did before: deal out two Poker hands. And this time the spectator slides his last dealt card under his own four previously dealt cards and places the entire five back on top of the deck. But when the spectator turns over the performer's hand, it is not a Full House, but a hand containing an odd card.

The performer relates that the little fellow said, "How do you get rid of that odd card?" And the big fellow said, "That's easy." (The performer emulates the big fellow and takes the deck.) "All you have to do is deal the cards slowly and place your last dealt card underneath the previously dealt four and place all five back on top of the deck. Then you turn over the other hand, and sure enough, here's the Full House." The performer demonstrates this as he tells it.

The performer hands the deck back to the spectator, saying, "Oh, the little fellow said he wanted to try it again."

The spectator tries once more, and again instead of a Full House the odd card appears. He says, "Let me try it again." And when the spectator deals, once again the odd card appears.

"Let me try it once more, and if I don't get rid of the odd card this time, I quit."

Again, (for the third time) the spectator deals out the two hands, and again the odd card appears. In each deal the performer instructs the spectator to slide his last dealt card underneath his previously dealt four cards and place them on top of the deck (spectator's hand).

Now the spectator says, "Now tell me how do you get rid of that odd card."

The performer takes the deck from the spectator. "Well, you don't have to get rid of the odd card. In other words, if you do it correctly, like this"—here the performer deals out two hands of five cards each, leaving both on the table—"you'll find you have a *pat hand* even though I haven't gotten rid of the odd card." The performer turns over the spectator's hand, and it is found to contain the four kings, plus the odd card.

The spectator says, "If you deal a hand like that to your opponent, that's not so good, is it?"

"Well," says the performer, "if you think that four kings beat four aces, you're crazy!"

At this point the performer turns over the second dealt hand (his own), and sure enough, it contains four aces.

THE SECRET

The setup for this sensational Poker trick is quite simple and can be done in a minute's notice.

The setup from the top of the deck is as follows: three kings, any odd card, the fourth king, and finally the four aces.

The entire routine is mathematical and is self-working. The performer must be careful not to disturb the position of the cards in the Poker hand when returning the hand to the top of the deck. The performer must remember the order in which the performer and the spectator deal. Then you can't go wrong. Here, in short, is the dealing order.

Three kings. Performer deals as often as desired (preferably two or three times).

Full House. Performer deals three times.

Odd card. Spectator deals once.

Full House. Performer deals once.

Odd card. Spectator deals three times.

Four kings in one hand, four aces in the other. Performer deals once.

145

81. UP AND DOWN

When Dai Vernon, one of the really great card manipulators of our time, is requested to teach someone a self-working trick, the chances are this will be the one.

PRESENTATION AND EFFECT

The performer removes a joker from the pack and places it face up on the table. Handing the deck of fifty-two cards to a spectator, he requests him to shuffle them and deal twenty cards face down onto the table. The twenty cards are now shuffled by the spectator. The remainder of the deck is taken by the performer, who looks through this remainder, takes out two cards, and places the two cards face down on the table. (One card is placed face down in front of each of two spectators.) One of the spectators is now told to insert the joker anywhere in the packet of twenty cards.

Spectator No. 1 is requested to look through the cards and note and memorize the card in back or to the left of the joker.

Spectator No. 2 is now handed the packet of cards and is requested to look through the cards and note and memorize the card in front or to the right of the joker. (This should be done by fanning the cards so that the position of the cards is not disturbed.)

The performer places the packet in the center of the table and requests one of the spectators to cut the cards once or twice, each time completing the cut before cutting again.

Picking up the packet, the performer holds the cards with the faces toward spectator No. 1, who noted the first card, and says that he will run through the cards, putting one up and one down, and the spectator is to note whether his card goes into the top (up) group or the bottom (down) group.

The cards are held in the performer's left hand, with the backs toward the performer, faces toward the spectator, and are separated as follows.

The right hand takes the top face-down card of the packet and calls it "Up." The next card of the packet is taken by the right hand (placed in front of the first up card) but lowered more than halfway until it covers about one-third of the first card. This second card is called "Down."

The next card is an Up card, and it goes in front of the second card and squares with the first card. The fourth card is a Down card, placed in front of the third card but squared with the second card. This Up and Down maneuver is continued by the performer until all the cards in the packet have been handled.

At the finish, the performer merely pulls out the bottom

(Down) interlacing group and drops them on top of the face-down (Up) group. (It doesn't really matter whether the spectator remembers in which group his card was, as this will not affect the success of the trick at all.)

Now the performer repeats the same thing with spectator No. 2. He separates the cards into Up and Down groups while the spectator notes his card, then places the Down cards on top of the Up cards.

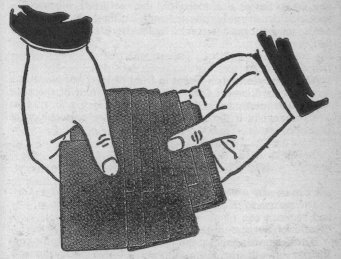

At the finish of the second run-through, the performer places the deck face down in the center of the table and has a spectator cut the packet once or twice.

The performer emphasizes that he has never once looked at the faces of the cards. Fanning the cards toward one of the spectators, he requests the spectator to remove the joker. The performer cuts the deck at this spot (where the joker was) but does not call the attention of the spectators to this.

The performer states that he is going to divide the packet into two equal groups, ten cards in each. He counts ten cards off the top of the packet (without disarranging their order), and places them face down on the table in front of spectator No. 1. The performer puts the remaining ten cards in front of spectator No. 2.

The performer now states that at the start of the trick, before a single card was selected, he placed a card in front of each spectator. These are "prophecy" cards and will indicate at what position in each group the selected card will be found.

The performer turns over spectator No. 1's card. It is a 5-spot. The performer counts down to five in the group before this spectator and holds the fifth card in his hand face down. The performer requests the spectator to call out his chosen card. The performer turns over the card he holds. It is the spectator's card.

The performer turns over spectator No. 2's prophecy card, and it is a 6-spot. Counting down and holding the sixth card of the group before this spectator, the performer requests the spectator to call out his selected card. Turning over the card he holds, the performer is correct again. He has found the spectator's card.

THE SECRET

The performer puts a 5-spot in front of spectator No. 1 as a prophecy card, and a 6-spot face down in front of spectator No. 2. The remainder of the trick is self-working, and will turn out successfully if the performer follows the presentation as described above.

82. THE MAGIC FOUR-SPOT

This trick gets a big hand from Paul Morris, the New York magician; and P. C. Sorcar, India's most famous magician.

PRESENTATION AND EFFECT

The performer hands a spectator a piece of paper and a pencil and states that he desires him to do a little card arithmetic. He then removes a deck of cards from the card case and deals approximately sixteen cards face down from the top of the deck onto the table in a sort of careless manner. The spectator is told to scramble these cards around face down on the table and then to select one of them and put it to one side, but not to look at its face value until told to by the performer. The performer picks up the remaining cards on the table, squares them up and places them on top of the remainder of the deck.

The spectator is told to look at his selected card and note the numerical value of it. Ace counts 1; 2, 2; 3, 3; etc.; jack, 11; queen, 12; and king, 13. After noting its value, he is instructed to square its value (that is to multiply the value by itself). For example, if the selected card is a 7, the spectator is told to multiply 7×7 which equals 49. To this total he is told to add 15, and then divide his total by 12, and to be sure to remember the remainder. For the spectator's convenience in doing this arithmetic, and in ascertaining the remainder, the pencil and paper are employed.

The spectator is then requested to think of a number *between* 20 and 30 (not including 30). The performer asks the spectator to call out the number he is thinking of. The performer then deals off the top of the deck face down onto the table, one card on top of the other. The total number of cards he deals equals the number called by the spectator.

The performer then adds the two digits of the called number and removes that many cards from the top of the cards just previously dealt onto the table.

The new top card of the group (top card of group dealt just after cards totaling the two digits were counted off) is handed to the spectator, who is asked to reveal the number of his remainder. He says, "Four." Turning over the card in his hand it is found to be a 4-spot.

THE SECRET

The performer removes all the 5's, 7's, jacks, and kings from the deck and places them into a pile face up on the table. He then adds two indifferent cards face up on top of these sixteen cards. Then he puts the important 4-spot face up on top of this pile. There is now a setup of nineteen cards in this pile. They are turned face down and placed on the remainder of the deck and put back into the card case in this arrangement.

After removing the cards from the card case at the start of the trick, the performer must make certain not to deal more than sixteen cards onto the table. The spectator is requested to select one of these cards and to retain it. This card must be a 5, 7, jack, or king, which are prime numbers. When one of these numbers is multiplied by itself and 15 is added, then divided by 12, the remainder will always be 4. (The remainder will always be 11 less than the number added. Should the performer desire the remainder to be 5, he tells the spectator to add 16, etc.)

When the spectator calls out a number from 20 to 29, and the first and second digits are added, and an equal number of cards are removed from the top, the spectator is actually only allowed one choice of numbers, and that number is 18.

The 4-spot was placed nineteenth card from the top, but the spectator holds his selected card. Therefore, we make use of only eighteen cards.

83. GARCIA'S CARD LOCATION

Another trick from Frank Garcia, the New York magician.

PRESENTATION AND EFFECT

The performer hands a spectator a deck of cards to be shuffled. The performer has a spectator select a card and then return the deck to him. The performer turns his back and has the spectator replace the card back into the deck which the performer holds behind his back. The spectator is then told to take the deck from the performer while his back is turned, and to shuffle the cards. The performer does exactly as described above with as many spectators as desired, although I would

ALL CARDS HAVE
PAINT SCRATCHED
OFF AS SHOWN
IN ILLUSTRATION

suggest having three cards selected by three different spectators.

After this has been done, the performer dramatically takes the deck, looks through it, and finds the selected cards.

THE SECRET

The performer requires one deck of cards with the following preparations. With a sharp needle scratch the index corner of only one end of each card, as shown in illustration. This is what is known as a one-way deck.

With this specially prepared deck, the performer arranges the deck so that the markings on the cards are all arranged one way (the prepared part of the cards all facing in the same direction).

When the performer hands the deck out for shuffling, he makes sure to hand it to a person who is standing up. This is done for the simple reason that the standing person will give the cards an overhand shuffle, and this shuffle does not disturb the order of the markings. If the performer prefers, he may shuffle the cards himself to avoid any shuffling hazards.

After the spectator selects a card and is still holding it, the performer places the deck behind his back and asks the spectator to insert the card into the deck any place he desires. This behind-the-back business automatically reverses the position of of the markings in the deck, and the selected card with its marked side will be reversed in the pack when returned.

The trick is now complete with the exception of finding the selected cards. The performer looks for the scratch marks among the unmarked corners of the cards in the deck. The cards with the scratch marks are the selected cards.

84. BREATH CONTROL

From magicians Larry Arcuri, Bill Pawson, Howard Wurst, Ken Krenzel, and Frank J. Kelly.

PRESENTATION AND EFFECT

The performer begins by saying, "Very few people believe this statement, but it is a fact that a person's breath leaves an imprint on an object in very much the same manner as a fingerprint. To prove that this statement is correct, I am going to find a selected card by looking for your breath imprint on its back."

He hands the spectator a pack of cards and says, "I want you to follow my instructions very carefully. While my back is turned, shuffle the cards thoroughly. Then deal two piles of cards face down on the table. Each of these piles must contain the same number of cards, and each pile must not contain more than thirteen cards; breath imprints are a little hard to see, and I don't want to have to look through too many cards or the trick will take too long."

After this has been done, the performer continues, "Now, select a card from any one of the two piles. Look at it and memorize it. Now place the back of the selected card near your mouth, and breathe on it. Now place the selected card face down on the other pile. Now place the pile from which you selected the card on top of the other pile."

After the spectator has completed this operation, the performer once again faces the spectator. Spreading the cards face down on the table, he looks at the cards for a moment, and says, "I am looking for your breath print on the back of your card. Ah yes, there it is." He pushes one of the cards forward from the face-down spread and says, "This card seems to have your breath print on it. What was your card?" As soon as the card is named, the performer turns the card face up to reveal the selected card.

THE SECRET

When the performer is apparently studying the backs of the cards for a breath print, he is secretly counting the cards. This will always be an even number. He then divides this number in half and counts that number (the number obtained as a result of division) from the top card to the center of the spread. Upon

reaching the number to which he counted, he pushes the card out of the deck, as it is the selected card.

For example, if the performer found that the spread contained twenty cards, he would divide this number in half. Half of 20 is 10. Counting the cards from the top of the spread, he pushes the tenth card forward. This is the selected card.

Note: Magician Bill Pawson suggests that in presenting this effect the performer should request the spectator to remove another card from the remainder of the deck and breathe on its back. This is done after the pile of cards has been spread face down on the table. The alleged purpose of this is so that the performer can "compare the breath prints." Holding this second card face down, the performer holds it momentarily next to each card. When he has counted down to the selected card, he pushes forward the selected card and holds the other card next to it as if comparing the breath prints very carefully.

The performer then definitely states that the card which he pushed forward is the selected card, and concludes the trick as above.

85. VERNON'S THREE-CARD ASSEMBLY

Much favored by Dai Vernon, one of the great card manipulators of today; and Carmen Da Mico, the clever Chicago magician.

PRESENTATION AND EFFECT

The performer hands the spectator a deck of cards to shuffle thoroughly and cut. The performer then takes the deck, looks through the deck, and removes either two black cards of the same rank or two red cards of the same rank. For example, the performer, after spreading the deck with the faces toward himself, says, "I will need for this trick two black queens." Thereupon he looks through the deck and takes out the queen of clubs and the queen of spades, placing them face up on the table. "I also need a red queen," continues the performer. He removes a red queen from the deck, shows the card casually, and slides it face up under the two black queens; then at the same time he flips over all three cards face down on the table, the red queen on top of the two black queens. Due to the calculated casual handling, however, the three cards are identified only as two black queens and one red queen.

The deck is now turned face down in the performer's left hand, and the top card is turned face up and shown to be an indifferent card. It is placed face down on the table about six inches away from the three face-down queens. Likewise for the next card on top of the deck, which is placed on top of the other (first dealt indifferent card). Another card is dealt (third card) off the top of the deck, but is not shown. This card is slid under the other two indifferent cards.

As it now stands, two packets, consisting of three cards each, are face down on the table. The deck is placed face down on the table as well, somewhat below, or above, or between the two small packets. Beginning with the "indifferent" card packet, and alternating with the other, the cards in the two packets are now replaced on top of the deck. That is, the top "indifferent" card is placed on the deck (still face down), then the top card from the "all of a kind" packet, then the top card from the "indifferent" packet again, etc. This action would seem to separate the "all of a kind" cards from each other, the "indifferent" cards between.

Then, slowly and deliberately, the top three cards are dealt off and turned face up. To all practical intents and purposes, the three cards first shown have reassembled in magical fashion.

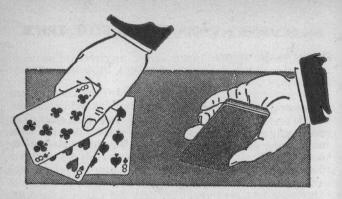

THE SECRET

After the spectator has shuffled and cut the deck, the performer takes the deck and spreads the cards in his hands with the faces toward himself and notes the *third* card from the back of the deck. The value of this card gives the cue for the cards that will be used. Assuming that it is the queen of hearts, the performer says, "I will need for this trick the two black queens." Thereupon he looks through the deck and removes the two black queens, and continues, "And one red queen." The queen of diamonds (in this case) is also removed, shown casually, and is then slid under the two black queens, which have been placed face up on the table. In a continuation of the same movement, all three cards are flipped over, face down, and the order of the three cards, from top down, is now queen of diamonds followed by the two black queens. Because of the calculated casual handling, however, the cards are identified only as two black queens and one red queen.

To make this clear, whatever the third card from the back of the deck happens to be, the performer always states that he will need two cards, naming the cards of the same value but of the *opposite* color. When these cards have been removed and placed face up on the table, the third card is introduced almost as an afterthought, and always shown rather casually, so as not to impress its exact suit on the minds of the spectators.

The deck is now turned face down; the top card is shown as an indifferent card, which is placed on top of the other. The third card (which is the value-duplicate of the first three cards) is merely taken off and slid under the other two cards. Again

154

the handling is such that no suspicion is aroused, and it is matter of factly assumed that the third card is just another indifferent card.

86. SCARNE'S TWENTY-TWO STOP TRICK

Created by the author.

PRESENTATION AND EFFECT

The performer removes a deck of cards from the card case and riffle shuffles it. The performer deals six cards onto the table from right to left, slightly overlapping each other. The performer then instructs the spectator, "When I turn my back, I should like to have you look at one of the cards spread before you. Merely lift up a corner. In other words, do not disturb the position of the cards more than you can help, so that I may not have any clue whatever as to what card you looked at. Be sure to remember the card—and when you have done this, let me know."

The performer, suiting action to words, shows exactly what he wants done by lifting a corner of one of the cards at the spectator's end, so that the procedure may be fully understood.

"Perhaps you may think that I have seen some of these cards," continues the performer. "Just to keep me honest, suppose we start off with a fresh batch of cards." So saying, the cards on the table are scooped up, placed on the bottom of the deck, and the ten cards on top are dealt off face down one at a time and slightly overlapping each other, just as in the case of the six cards which were used to illustrate the procedure.

When the spectator indicates that he has made a selection, the performer turns and scoops up the cards, replacing them on top of the deck. The performer cuts the deck and completes the cut. He then takes the deck, spreads it face up toward himself, and looks through the cards, saying, "Wouldn't it be a good trick if I could find your card." He then, as a sort of afterthought, cuts the cards and places the deck in his pocket, saying, "I'll find the selected card in a more novel manner."

The performer states that he will remove cards from his pocket, one at a time. As the cards are withdrawn, the spectator is to keep a mental count, starting with the number which is equal to the value of his card. For example, if the spectator selected an ace, his first count is 1; a deuce, his first count is 2; a 3, his first count is 3; a jack, his first count is 11; queen, 12; king, 13; etc.

He is to start with the number equal to the value of his card and to stop the performer when the number 22 is reached.

"Twenty-two," explains the performer, "is an ancient mystic number which has been found to hold much significance. Just how significant it is we will attempt to demonstrate."

The performer starts removing cards one at a time from his

pocket, putting each card face down on the table, keeping the value of each card hidden from view. In the meantime, the spectator is counting mentally. When he reaches a mental count of 22, and the performer has already removed a card from his pocket, the spectator calls out, "Twenty-two, stop."

The performer asks the spectator to name his selected card. The spectator names the card. The performer turns the card he is holding face up, and it proves to be the selected card.

THE SECRET

In this trick, before the cards are placed into the card case, a preliminary arrangement is required. Ten cards, ranging in value (but irrespective of suit) from ace to 10, are set in numerical sequence on top of the deck. The ace is on top. Over this ten-card setup are placed six indifferent cards. With this arrangement the deck is inserted into the card case.

The performer removes the deck from the card case, riffle shuffles it without disturbing the top sixteen cards, and deals six cards face down on the table. He tells the spectator what to do by illustration. This procedure is purely psychological and is done only to impress the spectator that no arrangement is used. These six cards, after the demonstration, are placed on the bottom of the deck and the ten crucial cards are dealt onto the table. A subtle psychological point may be brought into play here by dealing off six cards, pausing, and then, as if for extra

156

measure and to give the impression that the number of cards is immaterial, by dealing off four more cards. The spectators need not ever be aware of the actual number of cards laid out for them, as it is best not to emphasize this point.

Dealing off the cards one at a time has, of course, reversed their order, so that the 10-spot is now the uppermost, or right-hand, card on the table.

The spectator selects a card. The performer scoops up these cards and places them on top of the deck, and the deck is cut. The performer now looks through the cards pretending to find the selected card, but instead he is looking for the ten-card setup. When he reaches this setup, he cuts the cards so that the ten spot will be the top card of the deck, followed by the remainder of the setup.

The performer now instructs the spectator to start his count with a number equal to the value of his selected card. It is suggested that the performer, as a point of misdirection, should instruct the spectator that if the card he looked at was a jack, it is to count as 11; a queen, 12; and a king, as 13. Actually, because these cards are not present in the arrangement, such cards can not be selected, but if the cards were dealt out at random (which is apparently the case) such a contingency is possible.

To do this trick successfully, the first twelve cards that the performer removes from his pocket are taken from the bottom of the deck; thereafter the cards removed are from the top of the deck. In other words, the thirteenth card removed from the pocket will be the 10-spot, the top card of the ten-card arrangement.

As each card is removed from the pocket it is held momentarily by the performer before placing it face down on the table. This is done merely to give the spectator an opportunity to call the number 22 and to say "Stop" while the performer still holds a card in his hand. The effect is much greater when the performer still has the card in his hand. When the spectator calls, "Twenty-two, stop," the performer should ask the spectator the name of his selected card before the card is turned face up.

87. JACK GOES TO TOWN

During my tour of Army camps during World War II, I had occasion to see Nick Navarino, a corporal with the Eighth Army Air Force perform this amusing trick for a group of GI's. The rather obvious "method" has absolutely no resemblance to its entertainment value when performed before a moderate-sized audience.

EFFECT

Using a deck of cards, the performer relates a story of a farmer's son, named Jack, who is about to leave the farm. Jack hires several people to help with the chores while he is away, and various incidents occur, the story evolving as the cards are turned up, until the deck is exhausted and the tale is complete.

PRESENTATION AND PATTER

The deck has been prearranged in an order which conforms to the story the performer will tell. Naturally, no hint of such an arrangement is given, though it may be suspected without dire loss of effect. A paradoxical characteristic of this interlude with the pasteboards is that, although the entire deck is arranged beforehand by the performer, no phenomenal memorization is involved. In fact, it is virtually second nature, since the performer need only recall the simple story which he will present audibly later on in order to place the cards in their correct order.

For the sake of convenience, the order of the cards, from top to the face of the deck, is given herewith. (No attempt should be made to memorize this order.) Note that only the card values are given—except in the first three instances—as the suits are immaterial.

KS, QS, JS, 3, K, K, K, 7, 3, Q, Q, Q, 7,
3, J, J, J, 7, A, A, A, A, 2, 2, 2, 2, 6,
3, 6, 5, 7, 6, 4, 8, 4, 4, 4, 10, 8, 8,
8, 6, 9, 9, 9, 9, 10, 10, 10, 5, 5, 5.

The performer removes the deck of cards from its case and has a spectator cut the cards, completing the cut. Additional single cuts of this kind may be made without in any way altering the order of the cards, even though there is a change in the position of the cards.

Subsequently, the performer looks through the deck and removes the king, queen, and jack of spades, placing them face up on the table. The deck is cut casually at that point to bring the 3-spot to the top.

"This is the story of a farmer, his wife, and their son, Jack," says the performer, pointing in turn to the cards on the table. "It seems that the time came, one fine day, for Jack to go to Agricultural College.* Now, Jack was a husky lad for his age and his chores on the farm were considerable. Naturally, with

* When I saw Nick Navarino do this, he had Jack going off to war. In view of the passing years, I have taken the liberty of changing Jack's destination.

158

his imminent departure, it was necessary to get some labor replacement for the work to be done on the farm. 'Leave everything to me,' said Jack to his father and mother. 'I'll take care of everything. I'll go to town and get some hired hands.' "

At this point, the jack is placed on top of the deck, face down, and a spectator is invited to cut the deck once, completing the cut. The performer then takes the deck and starts dealing cards from the top of the deck, face up on the table (one on top of another), stopping only when the jack of spades is reached.

"Yes, Jack went to town," continues the performer as he goes through the dealing process. "He walked, and walked, and walked. He had to get help for the farm. . . . Finally, he arrived in town." (The jack is reached and placed in its former position, next to the king and queen. The cards face up on the table are turned face down and the balance of the deck left in the hand is placed on top.)

" 'How much help did you get?' asked Jack's parents when he got back to the farm. 'I hired three workers,' replied Jack." (The top card of the deck—a 3-spot—is turned over and placed face up on the table.) " 'I got three men.' " (The next three cards—kings—are turned over and placed face up on the table.) " 'Their wages will be $7 a day.' " (The 7-spot is turned over.)

"Well, the men worked just one day and found that everything was satisfactory, except that they were quite lonesome. 'I'll fix that,' said Jack. 'I'll go to town again.' "

Again, the jack is placed on top of the deck (face down), the deck is cut, and the performer proceeds to deal off the cards in the same manner as before, stopping when the jack of spades is reached.

"Off went Jack again, all the way to (local township). He walked, and he walked, and he walked. . . ." (As before, the jack is removed, the cards on the table are turned face down, and the cards in hand are placed on top.)

" 'How much more help did you get?' Jack was asked when he got back to the farm. 'I hired three more people,' said Jack." (Turn over 3-spot.) " 'Three women.' " (Turn the three queens over.) " 'Their wages will be $7 a day, too.' " (The next card—a 7—is turned over.)

"Then it was found that the men and women got along so well that the work suffered, even though morale was high. More help was needed, and Jack found that he had to make another trip to town."

(Once more, the "Jack Goes to Town" process is gone through, as before.)

"This time Jack got three more men." (The 3-spot is shown.)

"They were all young men, about his own age." (Show three jacks.) "They received the same pay—$7 a day." (Show the 7.)

"The young men were drinking men and soon demanded some liquor. There was none on the farm, so Jack had to go to town again." (The "Jack Goes to Town" routine may be repeated once more; this, however, is optional.)

"When Jack got back, they asked him what he had gotten. 'Four bottles of whiskey,' said Jack." (Four aces are turned over.) " 'Fine . . . did you get any chasers?' they asked. 'I sure did,' said Jack. 'Four bottles of ginger ale.' " (Four deuces are turned over.) " 'What did it cost?' Jack was asked. '$6 each for the liquor and the chasers,' said Jack." (The 6-spot is turned over.)

"As they started to drink to Jack's health and good fortune, one of the men said, 'You must be pretty smart to go to Agricultural College. What do you have to know—how many days there are in a year?' Jack decided to humor him. 'Sure,' he said. 'And don't think I don't know. There are 365 days in a year.' " (Turn over 3, 6, and 5.)

" 'That's right,' said the man. 'And how many days are there in a week?' 'Seven,' said Jack." (Turn over the 7.)

" 'And how many working days are there in a week?' Jack was asked. 'Six,' Jack answered." (Turn over 6.)

" 'How many states in the country?' was the next question. 'Forty-eight,' replied Jack." (Turn over 4 and 8.)

"Without anything special to do that night, the group decided to play a game of Poker." (Performer deals a Poker hand on top of each of the three kings, four cards to each hand, the king making up the fifth card. The first hand is composed of three 4's, a 10, and a king. The second hand is three 8's, a 6, and a king. The third hand is four 9's and a king.)

"The first man bets $10." (Turn over 10-spot.) "The second man calls the $10." (Turn over another 10.) "The third man puts in $10 and raises them $5." (Turn over 10-spot and then 5-spot. "The first and second man each put in $5 to stay." (Turn over two more 5-spots.) "Of course, the third man won, with his four 9's, and that ended the Poker game. And that, incidentally, ends the trick!"

All of the cards have been used, and the audience will somehow be left with the impression that either the cards have fallen magically in line with the story or that the performer has amazingly memorized the fifty-two cards of the deck—or both! In any case, the effect is all that may be desired and you should receive many requests to "Do that again!"

88. LYLE'S FOUR OF A KIND

*This trick in which the performer matches the spectator's se-
lected card with three cards of the same rank comes from Art
Lyle, the magician.*

PRESENTATION AND EFFECT

The performer riffle shuffles the deck and says to the spectator, "I am going to make two rows of cards and give you your
choice of either row." With this remark the performer deals
four cards off the top of the deck face down in a row on the
table. Then he deals the next four cards, in the same manner,

below the top row, thereby forming two rows of four cards
each.

The performer requests the spectator to point to a row he
likes. The performer scoops up the other row of face-down
cards, places them back into the deck, and remarks that the
spectator didn't care for that row. The performer shuffles the
deck one or more times after having replaced the undesired
four cards.

The performer then says, "We have four cards left. Would
you please point to one of those four cards." The performer
pushes the card pointed toward the spectator, and replaces the
three remaining cards on the botttom of the deck.

The spectator is told to note his selected card and to remember it, not letting the performer see its face value.

The performer riffle shuffles the deck one or more times,

places the deck face down on the table, and says to the spectator, "Now, would you be kind enough to cut the deck, and from your cut portion I am going to make three piles of cards." While making these remarks, the performer picks up the bottom portion of the cut deck and proceeds to deal off the top of this group three cards in a row face down on the table. This method of dealing one card on top of each pile continues until the cards in the performer's hand have been exhausted.

Upon turning face up the top card of each pile, we find that each card is of identical rank, and these three cards match the spectator's selected card.

THE SECRET

The performer removes two sets of four of a kind from the deck, preferably the four aces and the four kings. The four kings are placed face down on top of the deck, and the four aces are put on top of the four kings.

The performer gives the deck a riffle shuffle, making sure that he does not disturb the position of the eight arranged cards on top of the deck.

He then deals the four aces in one row, and the four kings in another row. When the spectator is requested to point to a pile, it doesn't matter which one he points to because each pile has four of a kind. The performer picks up the other four cards, replaces them in the deck, and shuffles the deck several times. This shuffle is done for two reasons. One, to separate the four of a kind the performer just returned to the deck; the other reason is psychological, because later the spectator remembers that shuffle and believes the performer shuffled the deck very thoroughly at the start of the trick and toward the ending. It is suggested that the performer shuffle the deck more than once at this particular time to help impress the above on the spectator's mind.

Now, when the spectator points to one of the four remaining cards, the performer pushes that card toward the spectator for him to look at and memorize, and assembles the three other face-down cards together and drops the remainder of the deck on top of these three cards. This procedure is more favored than that of picking up the three cards and putting them on the bottom of the deck. It seems to be more casual and eliminates any suspicion of placing cards.

The performer riffle shuffles the cards but makes sure not to disturb the bottom three cards in the deck. Then the spectator is requested to cut the deck, and the performer picks the bottom cut group and deals the cards into three piles. Naturally, the bottom three of a kind will appear on top of each pile, and thereby will match the spectator's selected card.

89. CARDINI'S COLOR DISCERNMENT

A card trick in which the performer correctly guesses the number of red and black cards in a group of cards selected by a spectator. Created by the author and Cardini, the top-flight vaudeville magician.

PRESENTATION AND EFFECT

The performer requests a spectator to shuffle a pack of cards. "While you are shuffling," he says, "I want you to think of a number between twenty and thirty. What number are you thinking of?" The spectator names the number which he had in mind. We will assume that he called the number 20. The performer then says, "You thought of the number twenty. Will you please count twenty cards from the top of the deck face down onto the table. Take this packet of cards in your hands and give me the remainder of the deck." The performer pretends to weigh his packet in his hand. "Although you have shuffled the cards yourself, I can tell you that you have six less black cards in your packet than I have red cards in my packet." (The performer may also say, "I have six more black cards than you have red cards.")

To verify this first statement, the performer counts the red cards in his packet while the spectator counts the black cards in his. Sure enough, the performer's statement is found to be correct. Let us assume that the spectator counts ten black cards in his packet while the performer counts sixteen red cards in his packet. These cards are returned to their proper packets, and the performer and spectator trade packets. The performer then says, "You shuffle your cards, and I'll shuffle mine. This way, we will have no idea of the order or arrangement of the black and red cards in either packet."

The performer then requests the spectator, "Deal some cards one at a time from your packet to the top of mine." Let's say the spectator deals four cards on top of the performer's packet. "Now, cut my cards," the performer requests. Looking first at the spectator, and then at the packet in his hand, the performer says, "My packet contains two less black cards than your packet has red." (Or, he can say, "I have two less red cards than you have black.") The performer counts the black cards in his packet and the spectator counts the red cards in his. Once again the performer is correct. Let us assume that his packet contains ten black cards and the spectator's packet contains twelve red cards.

Once again the performer shuffles his packet and the spectator shuffles his. The performer reassembles the deck by placing his packet atop the spectator's.

"Possibly," says the performer, "you think that this trick is based on a mathematical principle. To prove such is not the fact, we will use only part of the deck for the last part of the trick." He then picks up the deck with his right hand, and with his left hand removes about one-third of the deck from the bottom of the pack of cards. These cards he places to one side. He then places the remainder of the deck on the table, face down.

Turning to the spectator, he says, "Will you please cut off about half the cards from this packet and place them in your

pocket. Don't let me see them." The performer takes the remaining group of cards which are resting on the table and looks through them; then says, for example, "You have a total of fourteen cards in your pocket. And these fourteen cards are comprised of five blacks and nine red cards." The spectator checks and finds that the performer was correct in all his statements.

THE SECRET

Despite the performer's remarks to the contrary, the above trick is based on the mathematical principle that when the spectator and performer each have twenty-six cards, the number of red cards in the performer's packet is equal to the number of black cards in the spectator's packet. By the same token, the number of black cards in the performer's packet is equal to the number of red cards in the spectator's packet.

Therefore, the key number the performer must remember is 26. When the spectator calls his number, in this case 20, the performer subtracts the spectator's number (20) from his key number (26). The number which is obtained by this subtraction, in this case 6, tells the performer that he has six more red cards than the spectator has black cards. It is also true that the performer has six more black cards than the spectator has red. The performer can make either statement and still be correct.

Should the spectator call a number larger than 26, the performer asks him to count down that number of cards and give them to him. In any event, the spectator always is given the smaller packet of the two.

When the performer and spectator exchange packets, it is done to balance the number of cards in each packet, for the spectator will soon deal several cards onto those held by the performer. If the spectator had held twenty cards and then dealt ten cards onto the performer's packet, the performer would then have forty-two cards and the spectator would have only ten. The trick is much more baffling when the two packets are nearly equal.

When the spectator deals cards on top of the performer's packet, the performer counts these cards mentally as they are dealt onto his packet, and adds this number to the original amount. In our example, twenty cards were in the smaller packet. Let us suppose that the spectator deals four cards onto this packet for a total of twenty-four. Subtracting twenty-four from the key number (26) the performer then knows that he holds two red cards less in his packet than the spectator has black in his packet, or two less black cards than the spectator has red cards.

Should the performer hold more than twenty-six cards—for example, thirty cards—he subtracts 26, his key number, from the total number of cards he holds, and gets an answer of 4. He then says, "I have four more red cards in my packet than you have black cards in yours." Or, he may say, "I have four more black cards than you have red."

For the final part of the trick the performer must remember three essentials: 1. The number of cards in his packet. 2. The number of black cards in his packet. 3. When he places his packet on top of the spectator's, he must secretly glimpse the bottom card of his packet and remember it. This is his key card. Let us suppose it is the 3 of clubs.

The performer in the above example would:

1. Remember that he had twenty-four cards in his packet.
2. That ten of these cards are black.
3. That his key card is the 3 of clubs.

Now, when the performer removes about one-third of the deck from the bottom of the deck, he must take precautions not to take too many cards for fear of removing the key card.

When he picks up the packet on the table and casually looks through these cards, he locates his key card, the 3 of clubs, and secretly counts the number of cards starting with the key card and continuing to the left. Let us suppose the total was 10. Subtracting 10 from 24 (the number of cards which were in the original top packet) he finds that the spectator holds fourteen cards. Then, counting the number of black cards to the left of the key card, and including the key card if it is black, he subtracts his total from the total number of black cards that were in the original top packet, ten in our example.

Let us assume that he counted five black cards to the left. Subtracting 5 from 10, he finds that the spectator has five blacks. Subtracting this number from the total number of cards held by the spectator, he determines the number of red cards the spectator possesses, in this case nine.

The performer in the above example would say to the spectator, "You have a total of fourteen cards in your pocket, five of which are black and nine of which are red." The spectator checks this by taking the cards from his pocket and counting them. Again the performer is correct. A fitting climax to a great trick.

90. MIRASKILL

An unusual and streamlined card trick created by the Canadian magician Stewart James—with a few subterfuges added by the author.

PRESENTATION AND EFFECT

The performer hands a spectator a deck of cards and asks him to shuffle it. While the deck is being shuffled, the performer produces a pencil and paper and asks the spectator, "What is your favorite color, red or black?" Regardless of what color the spectator names, the performer writes a message on a piece of paper, taking precautions that the spectator does not see the writing. He then folds the paper up with the writing hidden on the inside, and places it on the table to one side.

The performer now says, "I have written a prediction on that piece of paper, which I believe will prove to be correct. Well, let us get on with the trick. You have shuffled the deck and called out the color red." (Assuming the spectator called red.)

The performer continues instructing the spectator, "Place the deck face down in your left hand, deal two cards at a time from the top of the deck, and turn both of them face up as you

166

deal them. If the two dealt cards are red (the color you called) put them on the table face up in front of you. If the two dealt cards are two blacks, place them face up in front of me. If the two dealt cards are of opposite colors, one red and one black, place them in a third pile which we shall call the discard pile."

The spectator is told to do as directed above until the entire deck of cards is exhausted. In other words, the spectator continues dealing the cards off the top of the deck in pairs and putting them in their correct piles until the entire deck has been dealt into three piles.

When the entire deck has been dealt, the performer asks the spectator to unfold the paper and read the written prophecy.

It reads, "Your pile has four cards more than my pile."

The performer's and the spectator's cards are counted and the prediction is shown to be correct.

The performer starts putting some cards back into the card case, then, as if a thought has just come to him, he removes the cards from the card case and has a second spectator shuffle and do exactly as the first spectator did.

The performer asks the second spectator's favorite color. He calls black (for example) and the performer writes a second prophecy. At the completion of the trick, the prophecy is read and it reads, "Your pile has two cards less than my pile." The cards are counted and the prediction is correct again.

The performer puts the deck into his right-hand coat pocket without the card case. Then, seeing the card case on the table, he removes the cards from his coat pocket and places them into the card case and leaves it on the table while the spectators discuss the trick.

The performer then decides to do the trick once again. The performer requests a spectator to remove the deck from the card case and shuffle the cards, remarking at this time, "I am going to write the prediction without asking the spectator which color he prefers." The performer writes down the prediction and puts it to one side, and informs the spectator that he can put the red or the black cards before himself, whichever he prefers.

The deal is completed in the same manner as the two previous deals. The prophecy is read and it says, "Your pile contains the same number of cards as my pile."

"And that, my friends," says the performer, "proves that I'm one hundred per cent correct in my prediction."

The Secret

The trick practically works itself. It is based on the mathematical principle that regardless of how much the cards are shuffled, if the entire deck of fifty-two cards is used, and the cards are dealt into three piles—as described in Presentation and Effect—the black and red piles must have the same number of cards.

Therefore, to do the trick successfully, before starting the trick the performer secretly removes four black cards. Two of these cards he places inside the card case, and the other two he places inside the right-hand coat pocket of his (the performer's) coat. The card case is then placed into the same pocket.

In other words, the performer has forty-eight cards in the deck when he does the trick the first time. At the completion of the trick the first time, the performer takes the card case out of his coat pocket and puts a few cards back into it. Then, when he changes his mind and decides to do the trick for the second time, he takes all the cards from the card case, including the two extra black cards (we are supposing the performer removed four black cards before the start of the trick). He leaves the card case on the table, and pushes it to one side.

After having done the trick the second time, the performer places the entire deck into his right-hand coat pocket. He now notices that the card case is still on the table. He takes the deck out of his coat pocket, plus the other two black cards (which were placed there before the start of the trick), and places the entire deck into the card case and leaves it on the table.

Later on when the performer decides to do the trick for the third time, the spectator is told to take the deck out of the case himself. Naturally all fifty-two cards are there now.

The prophecy works regardless of which color the spectator selects. Should he call for black, the "short color" (short meaning four black cards were taken from the deck), the performer writes, "Your pile has four cards less than my pile."

Should the spectator call for red, "the long color" (because deck contains more reds than blacks), the performer writes, "Your pile has four cards more than my pile."

Naturally, when two cards are missing, 2 will be the key number. And when the entire deck is employed, the performer writes, "Your pile contains the same number of cards as my pile."

91. LORAYNE'S MIND READING CARD TRICK

This card trick has been used professionally by the magician Harry Lorayne for a number of years; therefore, I call it Lorayne's Mind Reading Card Trick.

The performer shuffles a deck of cards and places the deck face down on the table directly in front of the spectator. The performer says, "I will turn my back, and while my back is turned I will give you instructions. Will you follow them, please?"

The spectator agrees to follow instructions.

The performer tells the spectator to stick his finger in the deck and remove any card, look at it and memorize it. He is to place it on top of the deck and cut the deck, completing the cut (put the bottom cut portion on top of the portion taken from the top of the deck). Now the spectator's card is lost somewhere in the center of the deck.

The performer now turns around to face the spectator, and asks him to shuffle the deck thoroughly. The performer then takes the deck from the spectator and says, "While my back was turned you selected a card, noted its value, put it back in

the pack, cut the deck, and later shuffled the pack. Therefore, there is no way of knowing the name of the card you selected without reading your mind."

The performer looks through the deck, and now and then looks at the spectator asking him to concentrate on his selected card. "Think harder," the performer says. Finally the performer places the deck on the spectator's hand and has the spectator call the name of his selected card. The performer tells the spectator to turn over the top card of the deck. It is the card the spectator selected.

The performer glimpses the top and bottom cards of the deck, prior to shuffling the deck. Then, when starting to do this trick, he shuffles the cards without disturbing the top and bottom cards. This is quite easy to do by using a riffle shuffle. The deck is then placed face down in front of the spectator. The selected card is placed on top of the deck. When the deck is cut, the selected card lies between the two glimpsed cards.

The performer then instructs the spectator to shuffle the cards. During the first shuffle, the performer holds his hand out as if to take the cards, but does not take them from the spectator. This gesture will as a rule "force" the spectator to hand the performer the deck after one shuffle.

When the performer is handed the deck he looks for the two key cards, and the card between is the selected card. It is placed on top of the deck and turned face up after the spectator names his card. Or, if the performer prefers he can put it face down on the table, or call its name himself before the spectator names it.

The reason for putting the card on top of the deck is that sometimes during the shuffle, another card slips in between the two key cards. If such is the case, the performer places one on top of the deck and the other on the bottom. Should the spectator call the top card, the performer tells him to turn the top card over; should the selected card be the one on the bottom of the deck, he tells the spectator to turn the entire deck over.

Should the spectator shuffle the deck more than once, it still doesn't matter. If more than two cards are between the two key cards, the performer asks the spectator if his card was red or black. This question usually eliminates all but two cards. Should the performer still have more cards to eliminate after this question, he asks if the card was high or low.

The above "outs" are mentioned in case the performer gets into a spot, which seldom happens. If it does, however, he can get himself out very gracefully, although the effect isn't so great.

92. THE QUICKIE CARD TRICK

This is one of those fast tricks that can be done any time. It is a great favorite with my friend Milton Berle, the ace comedian and clever amateur magician.

PRESENTATION AND EFFECT

The performer has the spectator shuffle a pack of cards and place them face down on the table. The spectator is told to cut off a small number of cards from the top of the deck. "From about five to fifteen cards," the performer says.

After the spectator cuts his cards off the deck, the performer cuts a group off the top for himself. The performer turns away from the spectator and requests the spectator to count the number of cards he cut, and to let the performer know when he has completed his count. Upon completion of the count, the performer tells the spectator to concentrate on the total.

The performer faces the spectator and says, "I have as many cards as you, three extra, and enough cards left over to make your cards equal seventeen." (The number 17 is used here for an example. The total called may be one of many.) For example, the spectator has cut ten cards. He now counts his ten cards onto the table. The performer counts ten cards of his onto the table at the same time with the spectator. The performer puts three cards to one side, and places the remaining cards in his hand on top of the spectator's ten cards. The spectator is told to count them, and there are seventeen cards.

THE SECRET

The performer notes the approximate number of cards the spectator cuts, and makes sure to cut more than the spectator. For instance, if the spectator cuts approximately ten cards, the performer cuts approximately twenty (ten cards more than the spectator cut is about right).

The spectator is now told to count his cards and to concentrat on his total. The performer turns away, and without saying a word about his own cards, he rapidly and silently counts them. If the spectator sees him counting, it doesn't matter, but it is best not to mention the counting done by the performer.

After the performer knows the total of his cards, he subtracts 3 from that total, and calls his answer as the spectator's final total. It is quite elementary, but fools most everyone.

For example, the performer has twenty cards in his group. He would say, "I have as many cards as you, three extra, and enough left over to make your cards equal seventeen." It would not make any difference what number of cards the spectator had, provided the performer cuts *at least four cards more* than the spectator.

For example, the spectator cuts eleven cards, and the performer cuts eighteen cards. In this case the spectator's total will be fifteen. The spectator counts eleven cards onto the table, the performer counts eleven cards. The performer puts three cards to one side. The performer has four cards left. Placing these cards on top of the spectator's packet, the spectator has fifteen cards.

The performer doesn't have to use number 3 as the number of cards put to one side. He may use 2, 3, or 4, but the author does not recommend the use of number 1.

93. SCARNE'S BIRDS OF A FEATHER

This trick was originated by the author, and has never been performed by anyone except the author prior to the publication of this book.

PRESENTATION AND EFFECT

The performer produces two decks of cards in their cases, each of contrasting color. He hands one to a spectator to examine and shuffle, remarking that it is a standard deck. The performer removes his deck from the case and gives it a riffle shuffle face up. The performer says that he is going to try a card experiment based on telepathy, stating that he understands that if two people think the same they probably will do the same things.

The performer says, "Therefore, it is essential that the spectator and the performer follow exactly the same course in this

card experiment. So that the performer and the spectator will not have any outside, or visual, influence to distract them, everything is going to take place under the table."

The performer requests the spectator to place his deck under the table, and he does the same.

The performer instructs the spectator to shuffle his deck, and he does the same.

The performer says, "To make certain both decks are thoroughly shuffled, let us exchange decks."

The performer instructs the spectator to shuffle the deck he now holds, and he does likewise with the deck he holds. The performer also instructs the spectator to cut the deck; he does the same.

The performer asks the spectator to pick out a card from the deck he is holding and hand it to the performer, who inserts it into the deck he is holding.

The performer now tells the spectator to cut his deck, and he does the same.

The performer now selects a card from the deck he holds, and hands it to the spectator, who is instructed to insert it into the deck he is holding.

The performer tells the spectator to shuffle his deck, and then to bring it into full view again, placing the deck on the table in front of himself. The performer does the same.

The performer now instructs the spectator to deal the cards face down onto the table one at a time until the entire deck is dealt, and to remove the card of the contrasting colored back and to put it face down to one side. The performer does the same.

The performer instructs the spectator to turn his card face up, and he does likewise with his card. A real card miracle has been performed. Both cards are found to be the same, proving that telepathy works.

THE SECRET

A little secret preparation is required. The performer removes a card from each deck, but the cards must be identical. Placing both of these cards on the bottom of one of the decks, the performer makes sure to place the card with the contrasting colored back second from the bottom of the deck. Both packs are returned to their cases. One pack contains fifty-one cards, the other fifty-three. The performer after this secret preparation is now prepared to perform this card miracle. The performer hands the spectator the deck containing the fifty-one cards, taking the deck with the duplicate card for himself.

The performer requests the spectator to take the cards out of the card case, examine them (the spectator will never notice a card is missing), and shuffle them. The performer removes his deck from the card case, taking the cards from the case face up so as to prevent the spectator from getting a glimpse of the different-colored back card. For this same reason the performer riffle shuffles the cards face up on the table, taking precautions not to disarrange the arranged cards (the bottom cards of the deck). It is not necessary for the performer to shuffle his cards at this time, if he prefers not to.

Now, when the performer and the spectator place their cards under the table, the performer secretly drops the bottom card of his deck onto his lap. When the spectator and performer exchange packs, the performer adds the card he placed on his lap to this deck. At this point each has a fifty-two card deck, and each pack has the identical card of a contrasting colored back. Now the spectator and performer freely shuffle the pack each holds.

When the spectator selects a card from his deck and hands it to the performer, the performer places this card on his lap. Then, after the shuffling of cards has taken place, and the performer states that he is going to select a card from the deck he is holding for the spectator to insert in the pack he holds, the performer actually takes the card which is on his lap and hands it back to the spectator. This is the same card the spectator just handed him. This trick is now complete as far as the deceptive moves are concerned, and the cards are now brought into full view onto the table.

Note: Remember that all the moves take place under the table.

94. FIVE NINE KING

An effect by magician Martin Gardner, in which a spectator, through a series of deals, locates three cards of the same value as a previously selected card.

PRESENTATION AND EFFECT

The performer removes a pack of cards from the card case, riffle shuffles them once, and then places them face down on the table. He then asks a spectator to cut the cards and complete the cut. Picking up the deck, the performer says, "I'd like to show you a card trick, but unfortunately this trick doesn't work with jokers, so I'll take the joker out of the deck first." Looking rapidly through the deck, he removes the joker and places it face up on the table, but off to one side. Squaring up the cards, he places the deck face down on the table and asks one of the spectators to "cut the deck into three piles of nearly equal size." After this has been done, he spreads one pile face down on the table and asks a spectator to "pull out one of these cards, look at it, and place it face down on the table in front of you."

Squaring up the pile and returning it to its place on the table, the performer points to one of the three packets of cards and asks the spectator to "pick up that pile and deal off one card for each spot on the selected card. Thus, if the selected card is a three, deal off three cards; if it is a seven, deal seven cards; if a jack, eleven cards; if a queen, twelve cards; or, if a king, thirteen cards. After that, deal one card from the pile in your hand on top of each of the other two piles. Now place the pile back in its original position on top of the cards which have just been dealt onto the table." The performer points to a second pile and instructs the spectator to perform the same actions with these cards. The spectator is then instructed to follow exactly the same procedure with the remaining pile.

The performer now looks at the spectator and asks, "Well, what do you think of this trick so far? Pretty good, isn't it?"

In most cases, by now the spectator thinks the performer is playing a trick on him, and he usually admits that the trick isn't so good. Regardless of the spectator's answer, the performer asks, "Well, what card did you select before? Turn it face up on the table. Hmm, that's a very pretty card. Now, please turn up the top card of each pile." When the spectator does so, he finds that all four cards, the one he selected and the top card of each pile are of the same value: all fives, or nines, or kings.

THE SECRET

The performer secretly places the following cards on the bottom of the deck: the joker, any three cards, all the 5's, all the 9's, and all the kings. The kings are on the bottom of the deck. He then places the cards in the card case and keeps the case in his pocket until it's time to perform the trick. He then removes the card case from his pocket, and takes the cards out of the card case. He riffle shuffles the pack, taking precautions not to disturb the sixteen-card arrangement on the bottom of the deck. If the performer desires, he can dispense with this shuffle and merely have the cards cut.

When the performer states that he must remove the joker from the pack, he looks through the cards and locates the joker. He separates the deck into two packets at the exact position at which the joker is found. The left hand holds the top portion of the deck; the right hand holds the bottom portion of the deck, with the joker uppermost, as the performer moves to the center of the table and drops the joker face up on the table. When the two packets are put together again, the original bottom packet is placed on top of the original top packet, which was held in the left hand. The fifteen-card arrangement, minus the joker, is now on top of the deck.

When the deck is cut into three piles, the performer keeps his eye on the pile that contains the fifteen-card arrangement. This is the pile that the performer spreads face down on the table. The spectator is then instructed to select a card from this spread.

In most cases the spectator will select either a 5, a 9, or a king. In the event that the spectator attempts to select one of the top three indifferent cards, the performer tells him to take a card from some place in the pile, not from the top of the pile. Similarly, if the pile contains more than fifteen cards, and the spectator attempts to select one of the bottom cards, the performer tells him to select a card from some place in the pile, not from the bottom of the pile. This pile is then squared up and placed on the table next to the other two packets of cards.

In asking the spectator to pick up one of the piles to be dealt, the performer points to that pile which is furthest away from the one containing the fifteen-card arrangement. After the spectator finishes with that pile, the performer points to the center pile, the other one which does not contain the fifteen-card arrangement. Finally the performer points to the remaining packet of cards, the one containing the prearranged group.

There is nothing else for the performer to do or to remember. The trick is mathematically perfect and will work every time if the above instructions are followed carefully.

Variation

When the spectator selects his card from the spread pile, by noting its position from the top the performer can tell which card has been selected. In this method of performing, the spectator is instructed *not* to look at his card, but merely to place it face down on the table in front of himself. Knowing the value of the card, the performer then instructs the spectator to deal either five, nine, or thirteen cards from each pile, and concludes the trick as above with the exception that the spectator does not know his selected card.

95. THE EIGHT ACE ROUTINE

This is one of those routines that will take about five minutes of the performer's time, and not once does a spectator have to select a card. From magicians Otis Manning, Phil Sevush, Charles W. Nyquist, and Jack McMillen.

PRESENTATION AND EFFECT

The performer removes eight aces from a pinochle deck or from two standard decks of cards having the same color backs

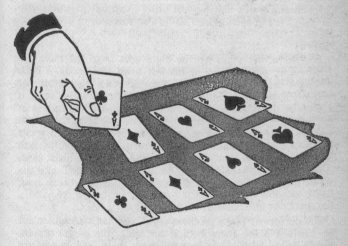

and designs. The eight aces are placed face up on the table. The performer picks up four aces of different suits and places them face down on the table. Then he picks up the other four aces from the table (these are also of different suits) and places these four aces on top of the other four aces. The performer has a spectator cut these cards and complete the cut. This is done as often as desired by the performer.

177

Effect 1

The performer picks up these cards, places them behind his back without looking at the faces, and states that he is going to bring the cards out in pairs of the same suits. For example, the first two cards brought forward will be the two aces of clubs, next two cards will be the two aces of spades, etc. This the performer does, placing the cards on the table as he brings them forward.

Effect 2

The performer picks up the aces from the table, in this order: red, black, red, black, etc. The cards are again cut, and the performer states that he will bring out two cards of similar color but of different suits. For example, he brings out the ace of diamonds and the ace of hearts, ace of spades and ace of clubs. This procedure is followed through four times.

Effect 3

The performer picks up the eight aces from the table the third time, and after having the cards cut, places them behind his back and states that he will bring them out in pairs, with black and red in each pair. This he also succeeds in doing.

Effect 4

The performer picks up the eight aces from the table the fourth time, places them in his left hand and spells R-E-D, moving a card from the top of the packet to the bottom for each letter spelled, and turning up the next card and placing it face up on the table. It is a red card. (When spelling red, as in this case, the card turned up on the table would be the fourth card from the top of the packet.) The performer then spells B-L-A-C-K in the same manner and turns the next card (sixth card from top of packet) face up on the table. It is a black card. This procedure of spelling Red or Black is continued until the last card is left in the performer's hand, which is a black card.

Effect 5

The performer picks up these cards and has a spectator cut the cards. Placing them behind his back, the performer instantly brings both hands into full view again, and in one are all the black aces, and in the other all the red aces.

THE SECRET

The performer picks up the eight aces in the following suit order: clubs, diamonds, hearts, and spades; clubs, diamonds, hearts, and spades. The last four are in the same suit order as the first four, colors alternating. This is done so that the spectator can see that they are being picked up in a mixed fashion. The cards are then turned face down for the spectator to cut, completing the cut each time. This cutting and completing the cut can be continued by the spectator as long as the performer desires. It does not disturb the position of the suits.

Effect 1

The performer places the cards behind his back, counts four cards from the top of the deck without disturbing their positions, and turns face up the remaining four bottom cards. This little piece of business puts the four aces on the bottom in the same position as the four aces on the top, except that the bottom four aces are face up. The performer takes a card from the bottom and one from the top. They are aces of the same suit, but the performer must reverse one of these aces before bringing them forward, so that they both will be facing in the same direction. Repeat the above three more times, and all the duplicate aces come out in pairs.

Effect 2

The performer picks up the cards in the following order. The first four aces are picked up in the same order as for the first effect: clubs, diamonds, hearts, and spades. But the next four are picked up as follows: spades, hearts, diamonds, and clubs, exactly the reverse of the other aces. Again the cards are cut by the spectator, and as stated before, the cutting does not disturb the position of the suits.

The performer now brings out pairs of the same color but of different suits. These are found behind the back in the same manner as described for the first effect, when the pairs were duplicate aces. Throughout this routine, the performer must always inform the spectator what he intends to do when the cards are behind his back.

Effect 3

This time the performer picks up the four red aces and places the four black aces on top of them. The cards are cut, and the performer uses the same method behind his back to bring out a red and black ace at the same time, as described above.

Effect 4

The performer picks up the cards in the following order and places them face up in his left hand: two blacks, two reds, one black, two reds, one black. Turning the cards face down, the performer spells out the colors, as described under Presentation and Effect. In this effect the performer does not put the cards on the table to be cut.

The performer picks up the cards in the alternate color position that they now occupy—red, black, red, black, etc.—bringing this to the attention of the spectator, who is asked to cut the cards. The cards are then placed again behind the performer's back, and as the red and black cards alternate, it is only necessary for the performer to put the top card on top of his index finger (between index finger and thumb of right hand), the second card below his index finger (between index finger and middle finger of right hand), the third card above his index finger, the fourth below his index finger, etc., until he has two groups of four cards each. The performer brings out the two packets. One has the red aces, the other the black aces.

96. SCARNE'S LIE SPELLER

A creation by the author from an idea suggested by Martin Gardner, the magician.

PRESENTATION AND EFFECT

The performer riffle shuffles the deck, spreads the deck face down in his hands, and requests the spectator to select a card. The performer then places the deck on the table, asks the spectator to note and remember his selected card and to place it face down on top of the deck. The performer has the spectator cut the deck and complete the cut.

The performer places the deck behind his back and says that he is going to reverse (turn face up) a card in the deck. If the card he reverses is red, the spectator must answer truthfully any questions asked by the performer. If the card is black, the spectator is told that he has the privilege of telling the truth or telling a lie, whichever he prefers.

The performer says that he has reversed a card in the deck, and brings the deck forward. He spreads the cards in his hand, face down, looking for the reversed card. He locates it and brings it to the top of the deck by cutting the deck at the position where the reversed card is located.

The performer says to the spectator, "Since the reversed card is black, you may either lie or tell the truth when answering three questions I am going to ask you." In the meantime the performer has turned the reversed card face down on top of the deck. The performer now looks at the spectator and inquires, "Is your selected card red or black?" If the spectator says it is black, the performer spells B-L-A-C-K and deals a card face down on the table from the top of the deck for each letter spelled. In other words, if black is called, the performer deals five cards off the top of the deck. If red is called, he deals three cards off the top of the deck.

The next question the performer asks the spectator is, "Is the value of your card above or below seven, or is it a seven-spot?" The performer spells the answer, either A-B-O-V-E or B-E-L-O-W or S-E-V-E-N, and deals for each letter one card off the top of the deck face down onto the table.

The third and last question asked is as follows: If the spectator called black, the performer asks him if the selected card was a club or a spade. If the spectator had called red, naturally

the performer asks the spectator if the card is a heart or a diamond.

The performer spells the suit named and holds the last card to be dealt face down in his hand. Asking the spectator to name his selected card, the performer turns over the card he holds, and it proves to be the spectator's selected card.

The Secret

The performer reverses the fourteenth card from the bottom of the deck making sure it is a black card. This he does before the start of the trick.

When the performer riffle shuffles the deck, he must make certain not to disturb the fourteen bottom cards of the deck. If the performer would rather not shuffle the cards in this manner, he may skip the shuffle.

The performer now spreads the deck in his hand and asks a

spectator to select a card. The performer only spreads the top part of the deck. Therefore the spectator cannot see the reversed card near the bottom of the deck. The performer now squares the deck and places it face down on the table. The spectator replaces his selected card face down on top of the deck, and cuts the cards.

The performer picks up the deck and places it behind his back. He only pretends to turn a card face up at this time, but the spectator is led to believe when the deck is brought forward that the performer just happened to reverse a black card in the deck.

Now, when the performer cuts the deck where the black card is reversed, it becomes the top card of the deck. The spectator's selected card is fifteenth from the top, so 15 is the key number required to do this trick.

The performer turns the black reversed card face down on top of the deck and asks if the selected card is red or black. Then he asks if it is above or below 7, or a 7-spot. The above two questions are spelled correctly by the performer.

But, when spelling the answer to the third question concerning the suit of the selected card, the performer must remember the following. If the spectator has called black, we have taken five cards off the top, and five more for either above, below, or 7. Each of these words has five letters. Therefore we have dealt ten cards off the top of the deck. The performer knows that the fifth card from the top is the selected card. So, on the last question, if the spectator answers clubs, the performer spells C-L-U-B-S, and holds the card that spelled S as the selected card.

If the spectator calls spades, the performer spells S-P-A-D-E, leaving off the end S.

If the spectator called red, the performer would have removed a total of eight cards for the answers to the first two questions. We still have seven cards to remove to reach our key number of 15. Should the spectator call hearts, the performer spells H-E-A-R-T-S, a total of six letters, and takes the next card off the top of the deck. This proves to be the selected card. If the spectator calls diamonds, the performer spells D-I-A-M-O-N-D, leaving off the end S. In the above manner, the performer always will locate the selected card.

97. SCARNE'S TAPPIT

In this trick the performer stops on the spectator's mentally selected card when the spectator's mental count reaches twenty. Originated by the author.

The performer riffle shuffles a deck of cards and says to the spectator, "For this experiment of mine, I require seven cards of any rank or suit. Therefore, to make my choice haphazard, I am going to remove seven cards from the deck while the deck is hidden from view under the table." To illustrate this, the performer places the deck under the table and removes two

or more cards from the deck and places them into a pile face down on the table. This procedure is continued until the performer has removed seven cards from the deck. The performer then places the remainder of the deck to one side, with the remark, "I have no further use for the remainder of the deck."

The performer hands the spectator the seven face-down cards and asks him to select mentally one of those seven cards. Then the spectator is instructed to shuffle the group and hand it back to the performer.

The performer states that he is going to pick out the card that the spectator is thinking of. He places the cards under the table in such a manner that only he can see the faces of the cards. The performer says to the spectator, "Please concentrate on the name of your mentally selected card—it will be a much easier task for me to find it."

The performer plays around with the cards for a while, and then says to the spectator, "I don't believe you are a good subject as far as suits of cards are concerned. I don't seem to be able to get any impression whatever regarding the suit of your card." He then goes on to say, "I will try this experiment in a different manner."

With this remark the seven cards are brought into full view, face down in the performer's hand.

The performer deals the top three cards singly off the deck

face down in a row starting from left to right. The next three cards from the top are dealt, in the same manner, directly below the first three cards dealt. The last card is dealt directly below the second card in the bottom row.

This being done, the performer produces a pencil or any pointed object, and says to the spectator that as he taps his pencil on the backs of the face-down cards in a haphazard fashion, the spectator is to count the taps mentally. But, he must begin with a number that is equal to the numerical value of the card he is thinking of, and continue his count until it reaches a total of 20. For example, if the spectator's selected card is an ace, he starts his count with number 1. If the card is a deuce, he starts with number 2; a 3 starts with 3, etc. Jack carries a numerical value of 11; queen, 12; and king, 13. Therefore, if the spectator's card is valued at 9, he counts the performer's first tap as 9, his second tap as 10, third tap as 11, etc. When the spectator's count reaches 20, he is instructed to say, "Stop."

The performer turns over the card on which his pencil is resting as the spectator calls, "Stop," and it proves to be the card that the spectator is thinking of.

THE SECRET

Before the start of the trick, the performer secretly removes an ace, 3, 5, 7, 9, jack, and king of any suit and places them on top of the deck in any order. At the start of the trick, when he riffle shuffles the deck, he makes certain not to disarrange the top seven cards. When the performer places the deck under the table to remove seven cards at random, he removes the top seven cards. It is suggested that the performer remove these cards one, two, or three at a time. It is not wise to remove the seven all at one time.

The spectator is then asked to think of one of these cards. After taking the cards back, and placing them under the table in such a manner that only he can see them, the performer says that he is trying to find the selected card. This is only a pretension. What the performer really does is arrange the cards in the following sequence: king, jack, 9, 7, 5, 3, and ace.

When the performer deals out the cards, as described under Presentation and Effect, the first dealt card will be a king, and the last the ace.

The secret of tapping is as follows. The performer may tap any cards for his first seven taps, but for his *eighth tap he must tap the king*. Thereafter he must tap the cards in the following manner: 9, any card; 10, the jack; 11, any card; 12, the 9; 13, any card; 14, the 7; 15, any card; 16, the 5; 17, any card; 18, the 3; 19, any card; 20, the ace.

If the above directions are followed, whenever the spectator says, "Stop," the card being tapped at that time will be the selected card.

98. THE PIANO CARD TRICK

This trick, in which a card travels from one pile to another, is a non-sleight-of-hand specialty performed by Nate Leipzig, Dai Vernon, John Mulholland, and Francis Carlyle.

PRESENTATION AND EFFECT

The performer is seated at a table directly opposite the spectator. He says to the spectator, "Kindly place both your hands on the table in a position similar to the one you would use if you were playing a piano." The spectator places his hands on

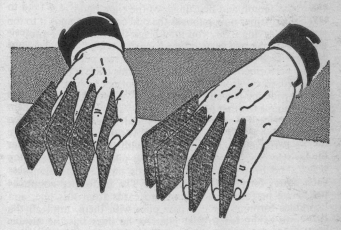

the table as instructed. The performer then places two cards between the fourth and third fingers of the left hand, and says, "Here is a pair." Next he places two cards between the third and second fingers of the left hand, and says, "Here's a pair." Then he places two cards between the second and first fingers of the left hand, and says, "Here is a pair." He places two cards between the first finger and thumb of the left hand and says, "Here is a pair."

The same procedure and patter are continued with the right hand except that the performer does not place two cards between the first finger and thumb of the right hand. The performer takes one card and places it between the thumb and first finger of the right hand, and says, "Here is an odd card."

The performer then reiterates, pointing to each two cards, saying, "Here is a pair, here is a pair," etc. Then, pointing to the one card, he says, "And one odd card."

The performer now says, "I want you to watch carefully everything I do." The performer removes two cards from the spectator's left hand, saying, "Here is a pair." He separates these two cards and places both cards face down in front of the spectator's outstretched hand, each card about two inches from the other. Then he removes two more cards, saying, "Here's a pair." He separates each and places one card on top of each of the face-down cards on the table. This procedure and patter are followed until the spectator no longer holds any cards in his left hand. Then the same procedure is followed with the three pairs held in the spectator's right hand.

Now all the spectator holds is the odd card (one card) between the thumb and first finger of the right hand.

The performer now removes the odd card and hands it to the spectator, saying, "Sir, you may place this odd card on top of any one of the two piles of cards on the table." The spectator places it face down on top of one of the two piles.

The performer says, "The object of this trick is to make that odd card travel from this pile" (performer points to pile on which spectator placed the odd card) "over to this pile" (performer points to other pile).

The performer snaps his fingers and says to the spectator, "Did you see it go?" He continues, "Well, it did."

The performer picks up the pile with the odd card and removes two cards from the top of the pile, saying, "Here is a pair." And he places these two cards on the table alongside each other, forming two new piles. The performer continues the above performance, taking two cards from this pile, and continues forming the two new piles with them, until all the cards are exhausted in that pile. As he does this, he always says, "Here is a pair," as he separates them into the two piles. The performer will have removed four "pairs," and the odd card has gone. The performer does the same with the other pile—takes off two cards and adds them to the two piles he is forming. But here he finds that at the end he has one odd card, proving that the trick was successful.

THE SECRET

The performer does everything as described in Presentation and Effect. The trick is self-working and requires no arrangement beforehand. What actually happens is this. The spectator is actually holding four pairs in his left hand and three pairs in his right hand, plus an odd card in his right hand.

When these seven pairs are separated into two groups, there are actually seven cards in each pile. The odd card is added to any one of the two piles, making that pile an even-number pile. The other pile remains an odd-number pile. The reason for calling two cards a pair, reiterating this continually, is purely psychological and is done to impress the spectator with "pairs," so he does not think that when these pairs are separated they will each hold an odd number of cards. The performer must always call two cards a "pair" when performing this trick.

99. CROSS SUITS

Featured by magicians Martin Gardner, Johnny Albenice, and Bert Feinson.

PRESENTATION AND EFFECT

The performer removes a pack of cards from its case, turns the two top cards of the deck face up, and calls attention to the value and suits of the two cards; for example, the 9 of diamonds and 8 of hearts. After carefully showing these two cards, he places them face down on top of the deck. The performer then cuts the deck once, riffles the ends of the cards, and says, "I command those two cards to reverse themselves in the pack." He spreads the cards and reveals the two cards, turned face up in the center of the deck.

Cutting these two cards to the top of the deck, he inserts them face down into different sections. In placing them in the deck, he leaves no doubt that they are really going into different parts of the deck. This is accomplished by inserting the first card halfway into the deck about twenty cards from the top, and the other about thirty-five cards from the top. While doing this he says, "I shall place these cards in different parts of the deck, one high and one low." After showing these two cards protruding part way out of the deck, and in different parts of it, he squares up the cards, pushing the two into the pack. Riffling the ends of the cards, he says, "Now to bring these cards to the top of the deck." Turning over the top two cards, he again reveals the 9 of diamonds and the 8 of hearts.

THE SECRET

The 9 of diamonds and 8 of hearts are, of course, on top of the deck. On the bottom of the deck the performer has secretly placed the 9 of hearts and the 8 of diamonds, face up. The deck, thus arranged, is placed in the card case.

After removing the cards from the card case, the performer turns up the top of two cards, and calls attention to their identity, naming the cards. Placing these cards face down on the top of the pack, and cutting the deck, brings them directly under the two face-up cards now in the center of the deck. When the performer spreads the cards, he reveals the 9 of hearts and the 8 of diamonds, but when naming them he merely

says, "The red nine and the red eight." This conveys the impression that they are the original two cards.

Cutting the two face-up cards to the top of the deck brings the 9 of diamonds and the 8 of hearts third and fourth from the top of the deck. When the 9 of hearts and the 8 of diamonds are buried in the deck, the original two cards are once again atop the pack. In revealing these two cards, the performer once again names them, fixing their identity in the spectators' minds, and causing them to believe that the same two cards were used throughout the trick.

In this effect, any two cards of the same color may be used, but the high-number cards of the red suits have been found to be most suitable. Naturally, one of the originals must be a diamond and the other a heart. The two face-up cards must be of the same values as the originals, but of the opposite suit.

The misrepresentation of the cards may seem rather bold as you read this, but in actual performance no one suspects that these cards are not the original two. This effect is sure to give you the reputation of being capable of manipulating a pack of cards with great skill.

100. THE CARD ON THE WALL

This trick is frequently performed by magician Johnny Paul of Cicero, Illinois; Howard Thurston; and the New Jersey magician Richard Du Bois.

PRESENTATION AND EFFECT

The performer removes a pack of cards from a card case and places the cards face down in his left hand. He then deals the top card face up onto the table; the next card is dealt face up on top of the first dealt card; and the next card is dealt face up on top of this card. After dealing about five cards in this manner, the performer says to the spectator, "Stop me any time you desire; merely call the word stop, and I will discontinue dealing the cards."

Let us suppose the performer is commanded to stop, and that the last card dealt was the 4 of spades. The performer says, "You stopped me on a 4-spot. Am I correct? Therefore, I want you to count down four cards from the top of the pack and memorize the fourth card." The performer hands the spectator the pack of cards. The spectator notes the card which is fourth from the top of the deck. The performer then states, "Please reassemble the deck and shuffle the cards very well."

The performer then takes the cards and looks through the deck, apparently trying to locate the spectator's chosen card. Seeming to have little success with his search, the performer picks up the card case and says, "So that the cards can't escape, I will place the entire deck back into the card case." He does so. "As you can see, the cards are securely bound by the card case," he says as he shows the case on all sides. Walking over to a wall or door, the performer holds the deck high in front of the wall, and patters, "I shall now cause your card to jump out of the card case." So saying, he slaps the case against the wall and lets it drop. The card case falls to the floor, but the selected card is found tacked to the wall.

THE SECRET

First, place a tack in your right-hand jacket pocket where you can get at it easily. Second, the card case must be one of the regular type with a flap, not one of those fancy two-piece affairs. Third, the top sixteen cards of the deck must be secretly arranged before the deck is placed into the card case.

Let us suppose that the performer desires to have the spectator choose the ace of spades. To accomplish this feat, he arranges the top sixteen cards in the following manner (the X's represent any indifferent cards):

X X X X X 10 X 8 X 6 X 4 X 2 X and the ace of spades.

Suits do not matter for any of these cards, with the exception of the ace of spades. These cards are placed in the deck so that the first five cards are the indifferent cards and the sixteenth cards is the ace of spades. Now the performer is ready to do the trick.

In performing the trick, he removes the cards from the card

case and deals the five indifferent cards onto the table, then he pauses for a moment to instruct the spectator to tell him to stop any time he wishes. Now the performer deals the cards much more slowly, merely to get the spectator to stop him before he has dealt fourteen cards from the top of the deck. The performer must make sure that the spectator stops him after the first five cards are dealt, and before the fourteenth card is turned face up. Should the last face-up card be one of the indifferent cards when the spectator calls to stop, the performer turns up the top card of the deck to indicate the number of cards which the spectator is to count down. Should the last dealt card be one of the *five key cards*—that is, the 10, 8, 6, 4, or 2—the performer uses that card to indicate the spectator's count down.

If the above instructions are followed correctly, the spectator must take the ace of spades for his selected card.

After the spectator has shuffled his selected card (which is already known to the performer) into the deck, the performer looks through the cards and secretly places the selected card on top of the deck. This can be accomplished readily by cutting the deck and bringing the chosen card to the top.

The performer then places the deck of cards in the card case in such a manner that the flap will close on the top card. He closes the flap, but in so doing, places the flap between the top card and the rest of the deck. The performer squeezes the sides of the box while closing the flap. This causes the top few cards of the deck to arch upward slightly, permitting him to insert the flap under the top (chosen) card with no difficulty.

The performer can now show the card case on all sides merely by placing his thumb over the semicircular cut that is in front of the flap. As the performer shows the card case with his left hand, his right hand removes the thumb tack from his pocket. He turns and walks toward the wall, and as he walks he slides the selected card part way out of the case and pushes the tack through the card so that the point is away from the deck. The performer then pushes the selected card back into the case. The point of the tack now protrudes from the semicircular cut.

When the performer reaches the wall or door, he holds the pack in front of it, with the tack pointing toward the wall, and hits the cards forcibly against the wall. He lets the card case fall. The chosen card, now tacked to the wall, will remain in place while the rest of the deck falls.

Note: It is not advisable to perform this effect against a plaster wall. In the first place, the tack may not stick; second, the tack may chip out some of the plaster, leave a hole in the wall, and make you an unwelcome visitor in the house. A wooden door or a wall made of pine paneling is best suited for this effect.

101. VARIATION ON CARD ON THE WALL

This is a variation of the preceding trick which eliminates the use of the tack. It is greatly favored by Melbourne Christopher, the magician.

This variation is presented exactly as described above, and all the instructions outlined are followed by the performer until he has the deck back in the card case, and has inserted the flap under the selected card.

The performer places his thumb over the semicircular cut that is in front of the card case. Now the performer tosses the card case into the air, keeping his thumb on the selected card. The card case will fall to the ground, and the performer will be left holding the selected card. A little practice in tossing the card case will prove how easily this can be done.

102. SCARNE'S RED AND BLACK SPELLER

Most spelling tricks have one disadvantage, and that is the performer must memorize the setup, or the cards must be arranged beforehand. This trick was created by the author in such manner as to eliminate these hazards. As a matter of fact, the spectator does almost all the dirty work himself. A favorite of Dell O'Dell's, America's top lady magician.

PRESENTATION AND EFFECT

The performer requests a spectator to remove six black cards from the deck and place them face down on the table. Then he is to remove six red cards and place the red cards face down on top of the six blacks previously removed.

The performer then picks up this group of cards, turns them face up toward himself, counts the cards, and places them face down in his left hand.

He then spells R-E-D for red, and removes a card from the top of the packet and places it on the bottom of the packet for each letter spelled. After spelling the word, he turns the top card of the packet face up, and places it on the table. In other words, the word red is spelled with three letters. Therefore, the performer removes three cards from the top of the twelve-card pile, one at a time, and places them on the bottom of the pile, one at a time. The fourth card from the top is now turned face up and placed on the table. It turns out to be a red card.

The performer now spells black, B-L-A-C-K, takes a card off the top of the pile, and places it on the bottom of the pile for each letter spelled in that word. He then turns up the next top card of the pile and places it face up on the table. It is a black card.

Next, the performer spells red, and works it out exactly as before; then he spells black, then red, etc. This procedure is continued until the performer has one black card left in his hand. In other words, the performer alternates between npelling red, black, red, black, etc.

THE SECRET

The performer picks up the pile of twelve cards, six red on top of six blacks. He turns the cards face up in his left hand, but keeps them out of the spectator's vision. He then counts five cards off the bottom of the pile (to himself), and places them face down on the table. These are five blacks. The performer does not count the cards out loud, but tries to give the impression that he counted six cards.

He now holds seven cards in his left hand, six reds and one black. The black card is the top face-up card of that group.

He now counts three cards and reverses their position in his right hand. Counting three to himself, he changes his mind about the count and says, "Yes, we have six reds and six

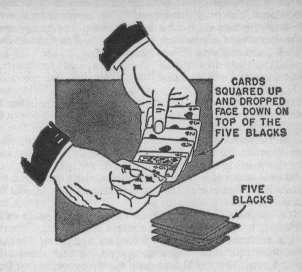

CARDS
SQUARED UP
AND DROPPED
FACE DOWN ON
TOP OF THE
FIVE BLACKS

FIVE
BLACKS

blacks." The three cards in his right hand are added to the bottom of the remaining four cards and they in turn are dropped on top of the five cards restng face down on the table.

They are now in a position to be spelled out. That simple three-card count has done this: It has placed one black card between the reds, four reds on top and two below this black card. And, when dropped on top of the five blacks face down on the table, they are arranged in the following order: four reds, one black, two reds, and five blacks.

103. SCARNE, PLEASE HELP ME

This cute spelling trick was created by the New York lawyer and magician, Joseph Linman.

PRESENTATION AND EFFECT

The performer riffle shuffles the deck of cards, spreads the cards face down in his hands and has a spectator select a card, look at it and remember it. The spectator is then told to put the selected card on top of the deck, which has been squared up by the performer. This is done while the performer is holding the deck. The cards are then cut by the spectator and the cut completed.

The performer now patters, "I'm sorry, I forgot to remove the joker in the deck. This trick cannot be done with the joker, that's what Scarne told me once." The performer faces the cards toward himself, looks through them, and removes the joker. Squaring the cards up, he places the deck face down in his left hand and says, "Scarne told me that if I spell the sentence 'The chosen card is here,' and remove a card for each letter spelled, I will five times out of ten find the spectator's selected card."

The performer deals one card face down on the table for each letter spelled: T-H-E C-H-O-S-E-N C-A-R-D I-S H-E-R-E. The performer spells aloud as he does this. For example, the performer spells T and deals the top card of the deck face down on the table; he spells H and deals the second card face down on top of the first dealt card; he spells E and deals the third card face down on top of the second dealt card. This procedure is continued until the entire sentence is spelled out. The last spelled card is turned face up.

It is apparent from the spectator's expression, if not from his exclamation, that this is not the selected card.

The performer feigns disappointment and turns this card face down. He states, "Scarne advised me that should this occur I may call upon him for help merely by spelling 'Scarne, please help me.' " So saying, the dealt-off cards are returned to the top of the deck, and now the performer spells S-C-A-R-N-E P-L-E-A-S-E H-E-L-P M-E, dealing off one card for each letter spelled in the same fashion as before. Turning the last dealt card face up, it is found to be the spectator's selected card.

THE SECRET

The performer places the joker next to the bottom (second card from bottom). When riffle shuffling the deck, he must take precautions not to disturb the position of the two bottom cards. The selected card is placed on top of the deck and the deck is cut. The performer then mentions that he can't do the trick with the joker in the pack. He looks through the deck, finds the joker, and removes it. While removing the joker, the performer separates the deck into two parts, at the exact spot where the joker was removed, and places the bottom group of cards on top of the former top group. This maneuver brings the selected card second from the top of the deck.

The spelling of THE CHOSEN CARD IS HERE automatically puts the selected card at the correct position after the dealt cards are returned to the top of the deck.

It must be remembered that when the last card is turned face up after spelling "The chosen card is here," then that card is turned face down and becomes the top card of the deck when the dealt pile is returned to the top of the deck.

104. CARLYLE'S MIGRATING DECKS

This unusual card trick in which two decks change places— except for the two selected cards—was created by Francis Carlyle, the top-notch card manipulator. A few new twists have been added by the author.

PRESENTATION AND EFFECT

The performer produces two card cases, each of which contains a deck of cards with differently colored decks. Any two decks of contrasting color can be used, provided the two decks are of the same size. For clarification, we will refer to the backs of the decks as red and blue.

The performer removes a red deck from the card case, spreads the cards out in his hand face down, and has a spectator to his left select a card and hold it for a while. The performer then turns the deck face up in his left hand, deals one or more cards face up on the table, and drops the remainder of the deck on top of these dealt face-up cards. He pushes the deck to his right, still leaving it face up on the table.

The performer now removes the blue deck from the card case and has a second spectator, one to his right, select a card in the same manner as described above. While this second spectator is still holding his card, the performer turns the blue deck face up and deals one or more cards onto the table, singly, and drops the remainder of the deck, still face up, on the dealt cards which are face up on the table. He now picks up this deck, squares it up, and lays it on the table to his left, still face up.

The performer now patters about the fact that each spectator must remember his selected card (the card each still holds in his hand), and to make it easier for the performer to do this trick, it is suggested that each spectator concentrate very hard on the name of his selected card.

The performer now picks up the deck on his left and places it face down in his left hand. This is the red-back deck (although only the top card is seen by the spectator, since the deck is squared up). The performer takes the red-back selected card from the spectator on his left, and pushes it face down neatly into the deck, without looking at the face of the card.

The performer now turns the deck face up in his left hand, removes the bottom card from the deck (top card of the deck if the deck were face down), turns this card face down, and

195

sticks this face-down card into the face-up deck, leaving about two-thirds of the card protruding from the deck. Naturally, this card is a red-back card, and the performer remarks that sticking the card into the deck was done merely to keep track of the red deck. The performer now drops this face-up deck, with the face-down card sticking out from its side onto the table, and remarks, "This is the red deck," pointing to the lone red-back card sticking out from its side.

The performer now picks up the blue-back deck and goes through the same business with it as he did with the red deck, as described above.

The performer now says he is going to try a very difficult bit of sleight of hand. He is going to make both of these decks change places so rapidly that it will be impossible for the eye to follow.

He picks up the deck to his left, with the identifying red-back card sticking out of it, and says, "Go." With this remark, he turns the deck face down, and it has changed into the blue deck, except for the identifying red-back card which is now face up. The performer does the same with the other deck, and it also has changed.

The performer now takes the two face-down cards that are protruding from the side of each deck and places each on its own deck (deck of same color as card).

The performer says that although both decks have changed places under the spectators' eyes, something just as remarkable

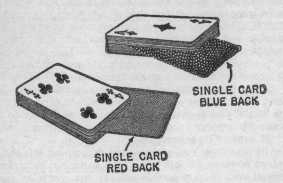

SINGLE CARD
BLUE BACK

SINGLE CARD
RED BACK

has also occurred at the same time. The two selected cards are the only two cards that did not migrate. They remain in the exact position as originally placed. Spreading each deck out, the performer discovers one red-back card in the blue-back deck, and one blue-back card in the red deck, and each proves to be one of the selected cards. Truly a remarkable finish for this wonderful trick.

THE SECRET

Before starting the trick the performer secretly places a blue-back card on the bottom of the red-back deck, and a red-back card on the bottom of the blue-back deck. With this preparation they are put into their respective card cases.

At the start of the trick the performer removes the red deck from the card case, has a spectator select a card as described in Presentation and Effect, but takes such precautions that the bottom blue-back card is not noticed by the spectators. The performer now turns this deck face up in his left hand and deals one or more cards from the face-up deck onto the table. What occurs is that the single blue-back card is the top card of the face-up deck and is dealt onto the table as the first card, and the remainder of the deck is dropped on top of it. When the deck is turned face down, a blue card is on top of the red deck and the spectator is led to believe that the entire pack is blue. The reason for dealing more than one card face up onto the table is purely psychological, and the number of cards dealt is discretionary with the performer.

The same situation is duplicated with the other deck. The preformer put the red deck to his right and the blue deck to his left merely to confuse the spectators. This procedure is very subtle, since the deck with the red-back card will be closest to the spectator who holds the red-back selected card, and the same holds true with the other deck and selected card.

The performer now picks up the deck to his left, turns it face down on his left hand. It is actually the blue-back deck with the red-back card on top of it. So when the red-back card is inserted into this deck, it is being pushed into the blue deck. The opposite holds true for the blue deck.

The performer must be careful—when turning the bottom card of the face-up deck and inserting it into the face-up deck to identify its color—not to expose the backs of any of the other cards which are of the opposite color.

Note: If the performer prefers to shuffle the deck (instead of dealing the opposite colored card onto the table and dropping the pack on top of the dealt cards) so as to put the opposite colored card on the bottom of the face-up deck, he may do so; but it is suggested that he practice it a bit before attempting it in public.

105. BUCKLE UP

The performer finds a selected face-up card in a group of face-down cards without ever seeing the cards. This effect is a favorite with magicans Le Paul, Zingone, Marlo, Jimmy Herpick, and Al Cohn, the New York City magic dealer.

PRESENTATION AND EFFECT

While seated at a table the performer hands a spectator a pack of cards to shuffle and cut. "Now," says the performer, turning his back to the spectator, "remove ten cards from any place in the deck. Select one of these cards, look at it and remember it. Then, place it *face up* in the face-down ten-card packet. Now shuffle the cards again. Hold the cards under the table so that I can't see them when I turn around."

Facing the audience once again, the performer reaches under the table and asks that the spectator place the packet of cards in his hands. Keeping his eyes pointed straight ahead, preferably looking one of the spectators directly in the eye to show that he is not peeking at the cards, the performer states that he can feel the difference between a face-up and a face-down card. To illustrate, he brings the cards to the top of the table one at a time and places them face down on the table. Finally he says, "I have one card left in my hand; it is your card. Will you please name the card which you selected." As soon as the card is named the performer brings the selected card to the top of the table, face up. The performer concludes with the remark, "It's easy to tell the difference between a face-up and face-down card when you know how."

THE SECRET

This trick is based upon a little-known principle. To illustrate this principle to the reader, take a pack of cards that has been used for some time. Remove one card from the pack and hold it face down from above, with your thumb on one edge and your second finger on the other edge. Permit your index finger to hang down so that it almost touches the back of the card. Now apply pressure to the edges by pressing your thumb and second finger toward one another. You will notice that the center of the card arches upward and touches your index finger. Now turn the card face up and repeat the application of pressure. You will notice that the card arches away from your index finger and does not touch it. Thus, with a pack of cards that has seen some use, you can tell if a card is face up or face down.

Now, back to the performer. After the spectator hands him the packet of cards under the table, the performer holds the cards in his left hand and deals them one at a time from the top of the packet into his right hand. With the right hand he applies pressure to the edges of the cards with his thumb and second finger, as described in the preceding paragraph. If the card touches his index finger he knows that it is face down,

and he places it on top of the table. If it does not touch his finger he knows that it is face up, and he places it on the bottom of the pile in his left hand. He continues to test the remaining cards so as to be sure that there is no mistake about which card is face up. When he has only the face-up card remaining in his left hand he stops. He then announces that he has only one card left, and declares that it is the selected card. After the spectator names his card, the performer reveals the card which he still has, and shows that he has no other cards under the table.

It is important that the performer remember that this effect will work only with a deck that has been used for some time. This trick *should not* be attempted with a brand-new deck. If the performer has any doubts about a pack of cards he should secretly apply the pressure before beginning the trick.

It is necessary that the performer test all the cards under the table for two reasons.

1. To stump some smart alec spectator who has turned more than one card face up.

2. If a deck has been used for a very long time, occasionally a face-down card will tend to buckle downward in the same manner as a face-up card.

To minimize the possibility of embarrassment to the performer, the author suggests that if the performer finds he has two cards left, and he tests these cards again and still can't decide which is the face-up card, he should turn both cards over before bringing them to the top of the table. The performer then states, "I have turned your card face down." He brings the two cards forward. If both cards are face down he knows that the spectator turned two cards face up. If one card is face down and one face up, he knows that the deck is too old, and that some of the cards are weak. This procedure is not recommended as a different effect, but only as a possible method of concluding the trick in the event the performer has difficulty in determining which is the selected card. Any method of revealing the selected card is better than admitting defeat.

Note: It is recommended that the performer use a standard (Poker width) pack of cards when performing this trick; the results obtained with the narrower Bridge-width decks are not satisfactory.

Important: The buckling of the cards described in this effect applies to a deck in which the overhand shuffle is almost consistently used. If the deck employed has been riffle shuffled most of the time, the buckling of the cards will be just the opposite. When the card arches upward, the card is face up, when the card arches downward it is face down.

106. DOUBLE EMPATHY

A card trick in which the performer finds the spectator's selected card and the spectator finds the performer's selected card. A joint effect much used by magicians Bill Nord and Sol Stone.

PRESENTATION AND EFFECT

The performer states, "Very few people are aware of it, but the subconscious mind does more for a person than he ever suspects. When you walk up the street to your home, it's the power of your subconscious mind that directs you. When you get up in the morning and go immediately to the washroom, you are being directed by your subconscious mind. When you kiss your wife, you don't think about it, you do it subconsciously, or possibly unconsciously.

"As a matter of fact, I get better results when I do card tricks subconsciously than when I do them consciously. Permit me to demonstrate. Somebody please shuffle the pack of cards."

After the cards have been shuffled, the performer takes the deck and squares the cards up by tapping the edges of the pack on the table top. Holding the pack face down in his left hand, he riffles the front edges of the cards from the bottom up, and asks the spectator to call a stop any time he wishes. When he is told to stop, the performer removes all the cards below the point to which he has riffled, and hands them to the spectator. Let us suppose that the spectator commanded the performer to stop after he had riffled about twelve cards from the bottom of the deck.

The performer then takes the remainder of the deck and cuts approximately the same number of cards from the top of the deck, although a few more will do no damage. The performer then instructs, "Count your cards, dealing them face down onto the table one at a time. I will count my cards also." Should the performer's pile contain more cards than the spectator's, he discards the extras; if he has less, it does not matter.

The performer now says, "So that the subconscious mind will have all the latitude necessary to function properly, please try to do exactly as I do."

The performer places his packet of cards face down on his left hand.

The performer removes the top card of the packet and inserts it into the center of the packet, instructing the spectator to do the same.

The performer removes the bottom card of his packet and places it into the center of the packet, as the spectator imitates his actions.

The performer instructs the spectator to peek at the top card and to remember this card; the performer does the same with his packet.

The performer now instructs the spectator to "Write the name of your card on this piece of paper. Be sure that I don't see what you are writing. While you are doing that, I will write the name of my card on this other paper. After you've done that, fold the paper with the writing inside, and place the paper on the table in front of you. I'll do the same and put my paper in front of me."

After this has been done, the performer says, "Shuffle your cards and I'll shuffle mine. Now let's exchange packets. You look through my cards and see if you can find the card which I selected. I'll look through your cards and see if I can find the card you selected."

The spectator is, of course, unsuccessful in locating the performer's card, nor does the performer have any better luck with the spectator's card. The performer says, "Maybe we will have better subconscious luck in finding the cards if we exchange our folded papers, but let's not open them yet. I have one other subconscious test that we can try. If this fails we may as well be conscious about the whole matter and forget the trick entirely.

"I want you to remain in your subconscious state and do exactly as I do. First, spread the cards which you have face down on the table in front of you. I'll spread my cards in front of me. Now hold your hand above the cards. Pass your hand back and forth over the cards slowly, but relax while you are doing this. The relaxing gives the subconscious mind more freedom, and therefore we get better results. When you feel an impulse to stop and touch a card, do so. Push this card out, away from the rest of the cards. I'll do the same thing with my cards."

After this has been done, the performer picks up the card which the spectator has pushed forward, and without looking at its face, places it in his pocket. The spectator is instructed to do the same with the card which the performer pushed out.

The performer now unfolds the paper on which the spectator had written the name of his card. "Will you please remove the card which you have placed in your pocket?" asks the performer. The card which the spectator removes from his pocket is his selected card, as can be verified by the writing on the paper. The performer removes the card from his pocket and places it face down on the table. He then asks the spectator, "Will you please open the paper on which I wrote the name of my card, and read what I have written." The spectator reads the name of the performer's card; the performer turns his card face up. It is the card just named by the spectator.

THE SECRET

Before starting the trick, the performer secretly removes a card from the pack, memorizes its value and suit, and places it in his coat or trouser pocket. When the pack has been shuffled by the spectator and taken back by the performer, he secretly glimpses and memorizes the card which is second from the bottom of the deck. This is done while tapping the edge of the deck on the table to square the cards. This is accomplished by holding the cards in the right hand with the thumb across the face of the bottom card. By moving the thumb upward slightly, the bottom card will slide up sufficiently for the performer to see the second card.

When riffling the cards for the spectator to call "Stop," the performer makes sure that the group contains at least twelve cards, and no more than twenty. Should the spectator fail to stop him before he reaches about the twentieth card, the performer merely starts riffling again.

The counting of the cards under the pretense of obtaining an equal number of cards is very important. This action brings the glimpsed card to a position second from the top of the packet of cards held by the spectator. After removing the top card and placing it in the center of the packet, the glimpsed card becomes the top card of the packet. This is the card at which the spectator peeks.

When the performer peeks at the top card of his packet he ignores it completely. Instead of writing the name of this card on the paper, he writes the name of the card which he had secretly placed in his pocket.

After the packets of cards are exchanged, when the performer and spectator are unsuccessful in finding each other's cards, the performer looks for the spectator's card (the one he glimpsed second from the bottom of the deck) and notes its position from the top of the deck. He does this so that when the cards are spread face downward on the table he knows the exact location of the spectator's card, and is able to slide the correct card out of the spread. Thus, the spectator places his selected card in his pocket.

The performer, on the other hand, has very good reason for not wanting anyone to see the face of the card which the spectator pushes out to him. He places this card in the pocket where he had secretly hidden the card whose name he wrote on the paper. When the time comes for him to produce his card, he merely switches cards in his pocket, bringing the previously hidden card into view, and leaving the card pushed to him by the spectator in his pocket.

107. SCARNE'S SIX-WAY BAFFLER

This effect in brief: Two spectators are handed packets of cards and instructed to place them into their pockets. The performer names the exact number of cards in each spectator's packet. Then, for a startling climax, names the exact number of red and black cards comprising each packet. These six baffling revelations can be performed, if necessary, with a borrowed deck thoroughly shuffled several times during the performance of this trick, which was created by the author.

PRESENTATION AND EFFECT

The performer has a spectator thoroughly shuffle a deck of cards one or more times. The deck is then placed face down in the center of the table. "Well," says the performer, "top-flight card manipulators can cut any number of cards called, merely by using their sight and sensitive touch. A person can't appreciate how difficult this feat is, unless he tries to do it himself."

The performer says to the spectator, "Listen carefully to the conditions I propose. First, you are permitted to cut the deck in two; you may place the two cut packets flush against each other so that you can gauge them. Then, if you desire, you may transfer one or more cards from one packet to the other in an effort to place twenty-six cards in each packet." This is done to prove this feat is more difficult than it seems even with the above aids given to the spectator.

After this has been done, the spectator is instructed to pick up one of the packets and count the cards. The performer picks up the second packet and counts it to verify the spectator's count.

The performer asks the spectator, after he has completed counting his cards, "What is the total?" Should the spectator's packet contain twenty-six cards, the performer says, "Not bad for an amateur." Should his packet contain either more or less than the desired twenty-six, the performer says, "I told you it was very difficult to do."

The performer now asks the spectator to shuffle the packet he holds and he in turn picks up the other packet and shuffles it. The performer and spectator then exchange packs and shuffle them. The spectator is told to place his packet face down on

the table, and the performer places his packet face down on top of this packet, squaring the deck immediately and leaving it on the table.

The performer now says to the spectator, "Let's see how good I am at this guessing game. But, to make things a bit more difficult, I am going to turn my back, and while my back is turned, just cut off a group of cards from the top of the deck. Let's say, any number from one to twenty, and then put this cut group of cards in your pocket."

The performer says, "Under these conditions, I'll try to guess how many cards you took away."

When these instructions have been complied with and the performer turns around again, he cuts the remaining cards approximately in half (or another spectator may do this) and the bottom portion is given to another spectator to pocket.

The performer picks up the remaining packet, looks through the cards a moment, and then addresses the second spectator, saying, for example, "You have sixteen cards in your pocket. Don't take them out as yet." Then, addressing the first spectator, the performer says, "You have eighteen cards in your pocket." The performer continues, "Now, will you two gentlemen take the cards out of your pocket and count them face down on the table to see if I am correct in my estimation."

Addressing the second spectator first, the performer inquires, "How many cards have you counted? . . . Sixteen cards? . . . And what was my guess? . . . Sixteen, also? . . . Isn't that amazing? It was just a wild guess, too. Since that was such a lucky guess I might as well stretch my luck a little further. I'll guess that you have six black cards and ten red cards in your packet. . . . Wait, don't count them just yet."

To the first spectator, the performer asks, "How many cards have you counted, sir?" . . . Eighteen cards? . . . Just what I guessed it would be, right? . . . And I might as well guess the breakdown of colors for you. . . . I would guess . . . let's see . . . I'd say that you have five black cards and thirteen red cards."

To both participants the performer now says, "All right, gentlemen, count your cards into respective red and black packets and see if I'm right." When this is done, the performer's "guesses" are again shown to be uncannily accurate.

THE SECRET

While the spectator is counting the first packet to ascertain the number of cards it contains, the performer picks up the second packet and pretends to count the cards merely to verify the spectator's count. But this is what he actually does: he faces the cards to himself and counts the black cards in the second packet. The counting is done from hand to hand. Let's suppose he counts eleven black cards; subtracting this number from 26, which is the total number of black or red cards in a deck, his result is 15, and that is the number of black cards in the spectator's packet.

The spectator is asked how many cards he counted, and we

will further suppose that he says twenty-seven. In this manner, the performer has learned two essentials for his part in the proceedings:

1. The number of black cards in the spectator's packet.
2. The total number of cards in the spectator's packet.

Now, after the two packets have been shuffled, they are exchanged and shuffled again. The performer when placing the packet he holds (the one the spectator counted) on top of the spectator's packet on the table, glimpses the bottom card of that packet and remembers it. Let us suppose again that the glimpsed card is the queen of hearts. This is the third essential fact in the performance of this trick. Now let us recapitulate. The performer must remember three essential factors to do this trick successfully:

1. The number of black cards in the top packet of the deck, fifteen in this instance.
2. Total number of cards in same packet, twenty-seven in this instance.
3. Glimpsed card, queen of hearts in this instance, which is now twenty-seventh card from the top of the deck.

After each spectator has placed his cards into his pocket, the performer takes the remaining cards. Because of the instructions and handling, this packet is certain to contain the key card (queen of hearts). With the cards facing him, the performer begins a mental count of the cards up to, but not including, the key card, starting with the number following the total of cards in the original half-deck packet. (In our example, the start of the count, from the face of the deck, would be from the number 28.) The total reached is merely subtracted from 52, the total number of cards in the deck, which gives the number of cards the *second* spectator holds. Thus, if "36" is reached, the second person holds sixteen cards, and the performer informs him of this, saying, "I would guess that you have sixteen cards—but don't count them just yet."

The performer now starts a mental count, beginning with the queen of hearts, counting the key card as 1 and continuing to the last card at the back of the packet. This total is subtracted from the *key number* (total of cards in the spectator's estimate—twenty-seven) to determine the number of cards the *first* spectator holds. Thus, if nine cards are counted, subtracting from 27, the first man holds eighteen cards. "I would guess," says the performer, "that you have eighteen cards. Now, will both of you count the cards you hold, face down, to see if I have estimated correctly."

While both participants count their cards, the performer again looks over the cards in his hands, preparatory to the next and more amazing stage of the trick. He begins a mental count of the *black* cards from the face of the packet up to, but not including, the key card, starting with the number following the total of black cards in the original half-deck packet. The total reached is subtracted from 26 (total number of black cards in the deck) to get the number of *black cards* held by the *second* spectator. Keeping this number in mind, the performer counts the black cards in the back part of the packet, beginning at the key card. This number is subtracted from the known number of black cards in the original packet to determine how many black cards the *first* spectator holds.

When the performer knows the total number of cards held by each spectator and the number of black cards each has, he merely subtracts the number of black cards the spectator holds from the total number of cards he holds to ascertain the number of red cards he holds. This subtracting is done for each spectator.

The procedure here given has been designed so that the performer does not have too much to remember at any point. Once he names the number of cards in each spectator's packet, it may be forgotten, and he may now concentrate on the calculation of black cards in each packet. Later, the number of cards in each packet is automatically revealed again by the verification of the spectators, and the final calculation for red and black cards is a simple matter. The trick, pruned of superfluous working, should nevertheless be run through in practice a few times so that the successive steps involved become almost second nature. In return for such practice, the performer will be rewarded with a trick that will always confound and impress his audience.

108. VARIATION ON SIX-WAY BAFFLER

A simplified version of the above trick is often performed by magician George Kaplan.

The effect is to omit naming the colors, but just name the number of cards in each spectator's pocket. In this version, the performer can dispense with the spectator's attempting to cut twenty-six cards at the start of the trick. Instead the performer merely looks through the pack once, pretending to look for a joker. While doing this he counts the cards and notes and remembers the twenty-sixth card from the top of the deck. That is his key card. Everything else is done in the same manner as described above in order to ascertain the number of cards in each spectator's pocket.

109. DICE WILL TELL

A noted card is mysteriously located by the throw of a pair of dice. From magicians Howard Thurston and Oscar Weigle.

PRESENTATION AND EFFECT

The performer hands a deck of previously shuffled cards to a spectator, asks him to remove six cards face down from the deck and place them into a little packet face down on the table. The performer takes the remainder of the deck and puts it to one side, saying, "We don't need these cards any longer." This being done, the performer produces a pair of dice which he throws on the table, remarking, "No, I'm not going to start a dice game, instead I'm going to have these dice help me to perform a very remarkable card trick, or should I say dice trick."

The performer turns his back and says to the spectator, "I want you to roll those dice one or more times, and whenever you have rolled a number that is satisfactory to you, I want you to note the number uppermost on one of the dice (either one). This number I want you to remember. Then I want you to count down to the card at that number in the small packet of cards resting on the table. Note and remember its face value, and leave this card at the same position in the packet as it was originally."

The performer continues, "Now take the die used to determine the location of the noted card and place it in your pocket. Say 'Ready' when this has been done."

The spectator calls, "Ready." The performer turns, faces the spectator, and says, "This one remaining die cannot possibly give me any clue as to what number was uppermost on the die you have in your pocket—is that right?" The spectator admits this. "And, therefore, I can't possibly know which one of these cards you have remembered—is that right?" Again an affirmative reply.

The performer places the cards behind his back. "Allow me merely to place the cards behind my back, where I shall attempt to detect your card and change it to another position there." The packet is brought forward and dropped on the table.

"Now," directs the performer, "please bring out the die in your pocket and place it next to the other die with its original number uppermost." The spectator does this. "For the first time I know the total of the numbers thrown—is that right?" This is another undeniable fact.

Taking the total of the numbers showing on the two dice, the performer proceeds to transfer cards from the top to the bottom of the packet (one at a time), counting audibly to the

208

designated number. The card at the last number is placed aside. When the remembered card is named, the isolated card proves to be it.

The secret consists merely of transferring some cards from

the bottom to the top of the packet when the cards are behind the performer's back. The number of cards is determined by the number noted on the die remaining on the table! Thus, if a "4" is the number on the die in view, four bottom cards are transferred to the top. When there's a "6," no alteration is necessary at all, as there are only six cards.

Analysis will show that all that is done is a count-down to the spectator's number, *plus* the number on the die that's seen. Obviously, it must work out.

110. AFFINITY IN NUMBERS

A card trick whereby the spectator goes through a bit of mental calculation and arrives at a two-digit total. These two digits are of the same numerical value as two previously selected cards. Much used by Harry Houdini, Nate Leipzig, and the New York magician Harry M. Levine.

PRESENTATION AND EFFECT
The performer hands the spectator a deck of cards and says, "Would you please shuffle this deck of cards and remove two cards from the deck face down. Then hand me one of the cards and retain one yourself."

The performer asks the spectator to note and remember his

card. The performer looks at his own card at the same time the spectator is noting his.

The performer asks the spectator to place his card face down in the center of the table, and to remember its numerical value. For example, an ace is counted as 1, a 2-spot as 2, a 3-spot as 3, etc. Jack counts as 11, queen as 12, and king as 13. The suit values are disregarded entirely.

The performer now places his card two or three inches to the right of the spectator's card.

"Should I hold a picture card (jack, queen, or king), this card carries a value of zero when held by me," states the performer.

The performer now says to the spectator, "I want you to listen carefully and follow my instructions. I will prove to you that your card and mine have a strange affinity for one another."

To help clarify the following instructions, let us assume that the numerical value of the performer's card is 4 and the spectator's 7. The performer now asks the spectator to mentally do the following: Think of the numerical value of his card. Double its value. Add 2 to the doubled value. Multiply the total by 5. Subtract 6 (the number subtracted depends on the card held by the performer).

The performer now says to the spectator, "Would you please call out your answer?"

Using the above example, the spectator would call 74 for his answer. The performer now turns the two selected cards face up and says to the spectator, "You see the cards are a seven for you, and a four for me; the combined form is seventy-four, proving that numbers do have an affinity for one another."

Following, in chart form, are the performer's comments and the spectator's mental calculations for the above example.

Performer's Directions	Spectator's Mental Results
Think of your number	7
Double it	14
Add 2	16
Multiply total by 5	80
Subtract 6 (6 is key number in this instance)	74
What is your answer? Spectator calls out	74

THE SECRET

The shuffle and the selection of the cards do not affect the trick in any manner. All the performer must do is to note the card that the spectator hands him and subtract this number from 10, and the result is his key number. In the example used under Presentation and Effect, where the performer looks at the card chosen for him by the spectator and finds it to be a 4-spot, he mentally subtracts this number from 10. The difference is 6, the key number. Therefore, when he tells the spectator to subtract a number, it is 6 he must subtract in this instance. The rest of the formula remains the same at all times, but the key number will vary depending upon the number on the card chosen for the performer.

Picture cards chosen by the spectator for himself have values of jack 11, queen 12, king 13, but if chosen for the performer they have the value of zero.

In the event that a 10-spot or picture card is chosen for the performer, the *key number* to be subtracted by the spectator is 10.

The trick is more effective when court cards and 10-spots are not used.

111. GARDNER'S SYMPATHETIC CARDS

This card trick is made to look like a real card miracle in the hands of its creator—magician Martin Gardner.

PRESENTATION AND EFFECT

The performer produces two decks of cards, a red-back and a blue-back deck. The performer hands the spectator the blue-back deck to shuffle, and he shuffles the red-back deck.

Now, at the start of the trick, the performer may say, "In

this experiment I would prefer to have the blue-back deck for a magical reason which I will explain later on."

However, if the performer decides to keep the red-back pack he is holding, he turns the deck so that the faces of the cards are toward him, and instructs the spectator to do the same with the deck he holds.

The performer now says, "I want you to do the same with your deck as I do with mine. Try to follow me exactly. I am going to select a card, remove it from the deck, note and remember its value, place it on the top of my deck, and cut the cards."

The performer hands the spectator his deck, and he takes the deck the spectator is holding. He remarks, "It is easier to find a selected card from a 'stranger deck' than from its 'own deck.'" The performer faces the cards toward himself and has the spectator do the same with the deck he is now holding. He remarks that when the spectator has located his selected card, he is to remove it from the deck and place it face down on the table. The performer removes his own selected card and places it face down on the table. The performer now squares up his deck and places it face down on the table, instructing the spectator to do likewise.

The performer states that there is a sympathy between certain cards. For example, if he (performer) wishes to know the spectator's chosen card which is face down on the table, all he has to do is look at the top card of his (performer's) deck, and it will tell him. So saying, the performer turns over the top card of his deck, then turns over the spectator's selected card. These two cards are identical.

The performer says to the spectator, "You can do the same thing. To ascertain my selected card, all you have to do is note the top card of your deck, and it will be the same as my selected card." Spectator turns up the cards and they also prove to be identical.

THE SECRET

While the spectator is shuffling his deck, the performer tries to get a glimpse of the bottom card of the spectator's deck. Failing to do this, the performer glimpses the bottom card of his own deck, and then exchanges decks, saying, "I would prefer to have your blue deck for a magical reason which I will explain later on." The performer and the spectator almost invariably forget this remark, but should the spectator ask what the magical reason is, the performer laughs and remarks that red-back cards hurt his eyes.

For the purpose of illustration, let us assume that the bottom card of the spectator's deck is the ace of spades.

212

The performer when selecting a card from his own deck looks through the cards and locates the ace of spades. He now removes a card, the card above the ace of spades. "This is my selection," he says, and places it on top of the deck. While the cards are still spread out, facing him, comes the cut. There is a slight separation where the selected card was removed, and the top card below the separation is the ace of spades. The performer cuts the cards and brings the ace of spades on top of the deck. He disregards the card that was supposed to be his selected card. The spectator in the meantime has selected a card and cut the deck (his own deck).

The two decks are now exchanged. The performer looks through the spectator's deck, locates the ace of spades which was the original bottom card of the spectator's deck, and separates the deck at this position.

The left hand stays stationary with the top half of the deck. The right hand takes the bottom group with the ace of spades on top, and moves about a foot to the center of the table, sliding the top card of this group, the ace of spades, onto the table face down.

Next, this group is placed on top of the cards held in the left hand. This maneuver brings the spectator's selected card on top of the performer's deck, and the cutting of the cards is never noticed by the spectator.

All that is left now is the turning over of the cards to complete the trick.

112. THE LAST TWO CARDS

As performed by Harry Houdini and Stewart Judah.

PRESENTATION AND EFFECT

The performer shuffles a deck of cards, has a spectator cut the deck and complete the cut. The performer picks up the deck and deals out six heaps of five cards each. These heaps can be dealt out in groups of five cards each, or the performer can deal out six hands as in Draw Poker, dealing five cards singly into each heap, starting from the left and continuing clockwise until each of the six heaps contains five cards.

This being done, the performer spreads out the remainder of the cards face down in his left hand and has two spectators each select a card, each to note his card and remember it. Then each spectator places his card face down on top of any one of the six packets, but not both cards on the same packet. The performer assembles these six packets into one large packet by placing one on top of the other.

The performer then has a spectator cut the cards and complete the cut. The performer picks up the large packet, faces the cards toward himself, separates the large packet into two packets, and places each packet face down on the table.

The performer now seems to remember something. He places one packet back on top of the other saying, "I must make two packets of cards, but that's not the way to make them."

The performer places the packet face down in his left hand and deals the cards into two face-down packets, left to right, one card dealt at a time. For example, the first or top card of the packet is dealt face down on the table. The second card is dealt alongside the first dealt card to its right. The third dealt card is placed on top of the first dealt card. The fourth dealt card is placed on top of the second dealt card, etc., until all the cards have been dealt into two packets.

The performer then asks a spectator to point to one of the packets (whichever one is indicated—the performer interprets the gesture according to his purpose). If the right-hand packet is indicated, the performer discards it. If the left-hand packet is pointed to, the performer takes it to mean that it is the packet to be retained. In any event, the right-hand packet is eliminated. The original left-hand packet is again dealt into two packets from left to right one at a time, same as before.

The performer eliminates the right-hand packet again, saying to the spectator, "Right was your previous choice, therefore we must again discard the right-hand packet." The same patter and procedure of dealing two packets of cards and eliminating the right-hand packet—then two more deals—are carried on. Upon the completion of two more deals (four in all), the performer is left with two cards face down. The spectators are asked to name their selected cards. The performer turns the two cards face up and they prove to be the selected cards.

THE SECRET

The performer does everything as described under Presentation and Effect—until the two selected cards are placed on top of separate packets. The trick will not work if the selected cards are placed on the same packet.

In collecting the packets, the performer first picks up the one which does not have a selected card on it, puts it on another packet which does not have a selected card on it. This action is done with each hand—that is, each hand collects three packets, and the "chosen card" packets are on the bottom of each set. Finally, one set is placed on top of another. Nonchalance is the keynote, so that the impression given is that the packets are collected at random.

214

The performer then picks up the entire packet, and in the act of squaring it, glimpses and remembers the bottom of the packet. Then he places the packet for the spectator to cut. The performer, looking through the cards, prior to separating the one packet into two, spots the card which was glimpsed on the bottom of the packet and separates the cards at that point, putting the two packets on the table face down, leaving the glimpsed card on the bottom of one group.

The performer then says that the packet should be dealt into two packets instead of cut as he has just done. He reassembles the two packets into one, but makes sure to leave the packet with the glimpsed card on the bottom and places the other packet on top of it. In this way the glimpsed card is again on the bottom of the packet.

With the glimpsed card back on the bottom of the packet, all that remains for the performer is to deal the cards into two packets and eliminate the right-hand packet, as described under Presentation and Effect, until two cards remain in the performer's hand.

113. THREE-IN-ONE CARD TRICK

This mental card trick was created by Warren Wiersbe. A few subterfuges have been added by the author.

PRESENTATION AND EFFECT

The performer produces two decks of cards in their cases, one a red-back deck and the other a blue-back deck. He removes the red-back deck from the card case, shuffles it, and has a spectator cut and complete the cut. The performer then takes this deck and spreads it ribbon style about a foot in length face up on the center of the table in such a manner that the markings of approximately half the deck are visible.

The performer now asks a spectator to think of one of the cards that are visible. While the spectator is thinking of a card, the performer removes the blue-back deck from the card case, looks through it, removes a card, and places it face down on the table in front of himself (the performer takes precautions that the face of this card is not seen by any of the spectators).

The performer says to the spectator, "I received a mental impression from you, and I believe that the card I placed face down on the table is the same in its numerical value and suit as the card that you are thinking of. Would you be so kind as to remove your card from the face-up deck?"

For the purpose of illustration, let us suppose that the spectator removed the ace of spades. The performer says, "I was right," and takes this ace of spades and places it face down on top of the card he removed from the blue-back deck.

The performer looks at a second spectator and has him mentally select a card that can be seen in the face-up deck resting on the table. The performer reads this spectator's mind, so he says, and removes a second card from the blue-back deck he is holding in his hand, placing this card face down on the other two face-down cards. The second spectator is told to remove his selected card from the spread deck.

Let us assume the second spectator removes the 10 of diamonds from the face-up deck. The performer takes this card and places it face down on top of the three-card packet he has on the table. (This packet is now comprised of two red-back cards and two blue-back cards.)

Remarking, "I was right again," the performer patters for a while along these lines: "I have had two spectators think of two cards, and I have placed a card on the table before either one removed his mentally selected card from the face-up deck resting on the table. I would like to have a third card selected, but this one I would like to have selected by chance."

While the performer is addressing the spectators, as described above, he is looking through the blue deck he is holding in his hand. He cuts the deck while he is holding it (the faces of the cards are visible to him during the cutting procedure), then he places the deck face down on the table.

The performer now picks up the face-up deck from the center of the table, squares it up, and places it face down on the table in front of a third spectator.

The performer now says that he is going to cut his blue deck into two parts, and he wants the third spectator to do the same with the red deck.

Instantly, after the performer and spectator have cut their respective decks, the performer picks up the original bottom half of his deck and reaches across the table and puts it criss-cross on top of the spectator's original top half of the deck. He then takes the spectator's original bottom half of the deck and places it criss-cross on top of his original top half of the deck.

The performer does not mention which half is which, but says, "The decks have been cut, one by you and one by me. I am now going to remove the two cards at the cut positions."

The performer removes the red-back cards that are lying criss-cross on top of the blue cards and places these red cards in front of the blue cards. He then takes the top card of the blue-back group and places it face down on top of the four cards that contain the mentally selected cards of the two spectators.

The performer removes the top card of the lower packet in front of the spectator in exactly the same manner as described above. This card is also placed face down on top of the now five-card packet, making a total of six face-down cards, three reds and three blue-back cards.

The performer now cuts this six-card packet and completes the cut. He then picks up these six cards and turns the faces toward himself. He looks at the first spectator and asks, "What was the name of the card you thought of?" The first spectator replies, "The ace of spades." The performer instantly removes and turns two cards face up on the table. Each is the ace of spades. The performer says to the first spectator, "I read your mind correctly."

The performer asks the second spectator to name the card he thought of. The spectator names the 10 of diamonds. Instantly the performer says, "I got you, too," and turns up two 10's of diamonds.

The performer then turns the two cards that were selected

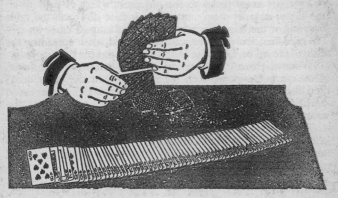

by chance and they prove to be alike also. For example, the two kings of clubs.

The performer concludes his remarks by saying, "Not only did I find two mentally selected cards, but I exerted enough mental influence on your mind" (addressing the spectator who cut the cards at the end) "to compel you to cut at the exact spot in your deck as I did in mine."

THE SECRET

When the performer spreads the red-back deck on the table in ribbon style, he glimpses and remembers the top card of this deck. Let us assume this is the king of clubs. He spreads the cards in such a manner that this card is hidden behind other cards. The performer asks the first spectator to think of a card that is visible in the spread-out deck.

The performer removes the king of clubs from his blue deck and places it face down on the table. The spectator is then requested to remove the card he mentally selected from the face-up deck. He removes the ace of spades. This card is placed face down on top of the king of clubs.

Now, when the second spectator thinks of a card, the performer removes the ace of spades from his deck and places it on top of the ace of spades from the face-up deck. Second spectator is asked to remove his mentally selected card. He removes the 10 of diamonds. This card is placed face down on top of the three-card packet.

The performer now patters about having a card selected by chance. While he is talking he is looking for the 10 of diamonds in his deck. He locates it, and cuts the deck, bringing the 10 of diamonds to the top of the deck. Then he places the deck face down in front of himself.

The performer picks up the red deck, which is face up on the table, squares it up, and places it face down on the table in front of the third spectator. It has the king of clubs on top, the card that the performer secretly noted when spreading the cards face up on the table at the start of the trick.

When the two decks are cut and the lower halves of each deck are put criss-cross on the top halves of the other decks and the two cards removed, as described under Presentation and Effect, the two cards selected by chance are the 10 of diamonds and the king of clubs.

The reason for the performer's cutting the six cards toward the end of the trick is to prevent a spectator from remembering the position of any of these six cards.

114. THE DRUNK PLAYS BRIDGE

This trick, by Howard P. Albright and "General" U. F. Grant, the Columbus, Ohio, magic dealer, is a natural with which to conclude an evening of Bridge, or it can be presented as a regular trick. A few twists have been added by the author.

PRESENTATION AND EFFECT

The performer removes a pack of cards from the card case and says that he would like to demonstrate how "some of the boys played Bridge the other night. They were all slightly tipsy, but one more so than the others. In fact, he was practically drunk, and everybody thought that he didn't know what was going on. When it came his turn to deal he shuffled the cards

218

something like this." Playing the part of the drunk, the performer shuffles the cards in a very haphazard manner. "Then," says the performer, "he started to deal. He didn't seem to care where the cards were going, but eventually each of the four players had thirteen cards apiece."

The performer deals the cards at random, some to West, some to East, some to North, and some to South. Sometimes he deals two or three successive cards to one player and none to another. All this time the performer is playing the part of the drunk, swaying slightly, and speaking thickly, saying such things as, "Two for you, one for you, none for you, one for me, two for you, etc." Then he picks up the hand on his left and counts the cards. If there are thirteen he's happy. If there are more than thirteen he takes away the extra cards. If there are less than thirteen he adds enough cards to bring the number up to the official thirteen. He does this with the other hands, too, to make sure that everyone has the right number of cards.

Continuing with the story of the drunk, the performer goes on to say, "Then he picked up his cards and said, 'I bid seven spades.' Well, the fellows looked at one another and winked. 'Yep,' they thought, 'he's drunk all right.' So they tried to ignore him, but he kept yelling, 'I bid seven spades.' So, they let him play his hand. And would you believe it, he took all thirteen tricks. *A grand slam.*" And the performer reveals the "drunk's" hand and shows all thirteen spades, saying, "There's no need to play the hand, because I can't lose a trick."

THE SECRET

In performing this trick, the performer makes use of a deck known in the magic world as a "one-way deck," or "single enders." These cards have a back pattern that distinguishes one end of the deck from the other. Most Bridge decks have just such a pattern on their backs, and a few Poker-width decks have a small distinguishing mark on one end that is missing from the other end. When all the cards are set, with the back patterns pointing the same way and one card turned so that its pattern is upside down, anyone looking for this turned-around card can easily notice the difference in back pattern.

In preparing for this trick, the performer selects a pack of cards having a one-way back design, and arranges all the cards with the backs pointing in the same direction. He then places the thirteen spades in the deck so that their back patterns point in the opposite direction, and places the cards in the card case.

As previously mentioned, most Bridge decks have such a back design. Should the performer wish to present this trick at the conclusion of an evening of Bridge, after the last hand is played, he can arrange the cards as he picks them up to place them in the card case. If he is the host, he can have a duplicate deck prepared in advance; then, during the post-game discussion, it is an easy matter to switch this deck for the one previously used. Of course, if he desires, he can perform the trick as the opening effect of a series of card tricks.

When ready to perform the trick, he removes the cards from the card case and begins the story about the drunk. He can shuffle the cards as much as he desires, provided he does not turn them around end for end. Playing the part of the drunk, he deals the cards haphazardly, apparently not caring where any of the cards go. In reality this is a cover-up for his dealing himself all the spades. Every time he comes to a card having its back pattern turned the wrong way, he knows it is a spade, and he deals it to himself. The story and the drunk act cover his operations perfectly, and usually even get a laugh. Instead of arousing suspicion, the method of dealing seems perfectly natural under the circumstances, and no one suspects what the performer is actually doing.

When the performer deals the cards in the manner described, it is almost impossible to deal each player the correct number of cards. Therefore, it is necessary to count the number of cards in each of the other hands just in case someone wants the performer to play the hand out. In this case, the performer might well be embarrassed by having the hand called a misdeal because of a player's having too few or too many cards.

115. SCARNE'S PHONE MIRACLE

Created by the author—the most direct of all telephone card tricks.

EFFECT AND PRESENTATION

The performer calls a friend on the teephone and says, "Will you please get a pack of cards and bring them to the telephone with you." After the friend returns, the performer instructs, "Shuffle the cards and then cut off a packet of cards and push the remainder of the deck to one side. I am thinking of a card, but I have to be sure that the card I am thinking of is in the packet which you have in your hand. So, will you please hold the cards which you have face down, and deal them face up one at a time onto the table and call off the names of the cards."

After the friend has called the names of all the cards in his packet, the performer says, "Yes, the card which I have in mind is in that packet. Now pick up the packet of cards again and hold them face down in your hand; deal the top card onto the top of the deck that is on the table; place the next card on the bottom of the packet you have in your hand; and continue to deal the cards alternately onto the deck and onto the bottom of the packet until you have just one card left in your hand. Do not look at this card, but place it face down on the table and push the rest of the deck out of the way. Tell me when you have done this."

When the cards are all dealt back onto the deck, and the last card is face down on the table, the performer says, "Remember, I have been thinking of a card. You have one card on the table in front of you. Please turn this card face up. I was thinking of the ten of clubs. This is the card which you have in front of you." The performer is correct. Most people seeing this card trick done begin to wonder if maybe there is something to this telepathy business after all.

THE SECRET

The performer is alone when he makes this phone call. The only preparation required is that the performer have with him a pen or pencil and a piece of paper with the numbers 1 to 52 written in a column on it. He must also remember five key numbers: 2, 4, 8, 16, 32.

When the person on the other end of the telephone line calls out the cards which he has cut from the deck, the performer jots down the names of the cards next to the numbers on his paper, in the following manner:

        (1)   3 C (3 of clubs)
        (2)   K D (king of diamonds)
        (3)   A S (ace of spades)
        (4)   8 H (8 of hearts), etc.

He can thus list the cards as fast as they are named.

While the cards are being dealt alternately to the top of the deck and to the bottom of the packet, the performer notes how many cards are in the packet by noting the number of his last entry on the paper. Let us assume that there are twenty cards in the packet. The performer then subtracts the nearest lower key number, in this case 16. The difference is 4. He doubles this number and gets an answer of 8. Looking at his chart, he determines the identity of the eighth card in the packet, in this case we will assume it to be the 10 of clubs. He remembers this card. When he is told that all but one of the cards have been dealt to the top of the deck, this is the card that he names as being the remaining one. If these instructions are followed completely, the trick will always work, for it is mathematically perfect.

The formula is to determine the number of cards in the packet; subtract the nearest lower key number; double the difference. The card at that position is the card which will remain in the hand of the person who has the cards.

The reason for the performer's instructing the person with the cards to deal them face downward onto the deck is very simple. This is done to destroy any evidence as to the number of cards that were in the packet. This way, no mathematically inclined spectator can get any idea of how the trick was done by trying to check back on it later.

116. SCARNE'S KNOCKOUT CARD TRICK

This card trick is one during which the performer never sees the faces of any of the cards in use, but still finds the spectator's selected card and commands it to reverse itself in a mixed group of cards, which are also commanded to arrange themselves all face down. And all this is done in the spectator's hand! This trick was created by the author.

PRESENTATION AND EFFECT

The performer says to the spectator, "I am going to try an experiment in cardology that was never attempted before. Will you please assist me? Thank you, sir." The performer continues, "You will have to listen to me closely, because I am going to turn my back and tell you what to do. And remember, if you don't do exactly as I instruct you, it's no use trying this experiment."

The performer hands a spectator a deck of cards and the performer turns his back. He requests the spectator to shuffle the deck to his heart's content, then cut the deck and complete the cut. The spectator is then instructed to deal out two piles of cards, an equal number in each pile, not exceeding twenty-one cards in each pile, and not less than nine cards in each. While the spectator is counting the cards into the two piles, the performer tells him to count the cards so softly that he cannot hear the sound of the cards as they are being counted and dealt.

This being done, the spectator is asked to pick a card from either one of the two piles, note its value, remember it, and place it face down on the table close to the two piles of cards. The spectator is then told to assemble the two piles into one, and place these cards face down in his left hand.

The performer now tells the spectator to deal the top card of the pile face down onto the table, then deal the next card face up on top of the first dealt card; the next card is dealt face down, the next face up, and this procedure of dealing one card face down and one face up is continued until the entire

222

pile of cards has been dealt into one pile in the manner described above.

The performer then tells the spectator to put this entire pile of cards on top of the face-down selected card, then to cut

SELECTED CARD

these cards, completing the cut, then to cut the cards once again, and again complete the cut. Next, he is to turn the cards over on the table and cut the deck again.

The performer now tells the spectator to place the entire pile of cards into the performer's hand, which is behind the performer's back. Then, behind his back, the performer counts the cards out loud: one, two, three, etc. until the entire number of cards has been counted. The performer now calls out the number of cards in the group—for example, twenty cards—and says to the spectator, "Take the cards from behind my back and place the entire group between the palms of your hands."

The performer faces the spectator at this moment, and tells him to hold the pile of cards tightly between the palms of both hands. The performer reivews what has happened up until this point: the spectator selected his own number of cards, selected a card while the performer had his back turned, reversed a number of cards, cut the deck, etc.

The performer says, "All that I did was to count the cards behind my back. Never once did I see the backs or faces of any of the cards. Now I am going to do the impossible. While the cards are held tightly in your own hands, I am going to command all the cards in your hands to assemble themselves one way, that is, all face down—and the only card that will be face up will be your card. What was the name of your selected card?"

For example, the spectator calls the 5 of clubs. The performer says, "I command you, the five of clubs, to reverse yourself in this gentleman's hand, and I command the remainder of the cards to turn themselves all face down."

The spectator is requested to open his hands and spread the cards. All the cards are face down with the exception of the selected card.

THE SECRET

The trick is practically self-working. The reason for having the spectator deal out two piles of the same number is so that the entire total of cards used will be an even number, since this trick cannot work with an odd number of cards.

When the spectator drops the mixed pile on top of the selected card, they are the only two cards together that are face down. All the other cards are separated by opposite facing cards. So it doesn't matter if the pile is turned over during the cutting or when handed to the spectator.

The only thing the performer does in this trick is done when the cards are placed behind the performer's back to be counted. He does as follows, counting the cards at the same time. He holds the deck in his left hand and deals the top card into his right hand, holding it between his thumb and index finger. He then deals the second card between his index finger and second finger (middle finger). He deals the third card into his right hand between his thumb and index finger, just as he did the first card. The fourth card is dealt between the index finger and second finger (middle finger) of his right hand, just as the second card was dealt. This dealing, described above—alternating between thumb and index finger, index finger and second finger—is continued until all the cards have been dealt from the right hand. The performer now takes the cards which are held between the thumb and index finger into his empty left hand and reverses this group (turns them over). He then places these cards on top of the cards between the index finger and second finger of his right hand, forming one group. The cards are all facing one way with the exception of the selected card.

The spectator now takes the group of cards and places them in his hands. The performer then goes into his patter, as described under Presentation and Effect.

The performer usually can see the back or face of a card while held in the spectator's hand. If the card is face up, the performer turns the spectator's hands over. If the top card is face down, he merely asks the spectator to deal them as they are.

117. THE STOPPER MIND READING TRICK

A clever mind reading card trick, much favored by Charles W. Nyquist, magician, and Edward Dart, writer on magic subjects.

PRESENTATION AND EFFECT

The performer requests a spectator to shuffle a deck of cards and place them face down on the table. The performer backs away from the table and requests the spectator to cut the deck at any point. The spectator is requested to note and memorize the card at the bottom of the cut-off group, after which the spectator is told to replace the cut portion back on top of the deck and square up the deck.

The performer says to the spectator, "You have just noted a card. I want you to concentrate on it—and I will attempt to read your mind. You realize, of course, that mind reading is done by association. That is, I must force you to think of two similar things. You are already thinking of a card, and since cards are usually associated with numbers, I will ask you to think of a number. You may choose it yourself. Which do you prefer to use, four, five, or six?"

The performer requests the spectator to state his choice (for example, the spectator states that he wants number 5). The performer tells the spectator, "To impress the number on your mind, I want you to deal five cards in a row face down on the table." (Naturally if the spectator calls for number 4, four cards are dealt on the table; for number 6, six cards are dealt.) The performer continues, "To impress further the number on your mind, I want you to continue to deal cards singly on top of the cards on the table until the entire deck has been dealt." The spectator deals one card at a time starting from left to right as he would deal in a card game. Upon completing the deal, the spectator is asked to pick up the packets and look through each without disturbing the position of the cards, and to retain in his hand the packet that conains this card.

The spectator is asked to place the cards in this packet in his left hand and to deal them face down on the table, putting one on top of the other as they are dealt. The performer says to the spectator, "You must concentrate on your card while you are dealing these cards."

The performer permits the spectator to deal all these cards onto the table. The performer then states that he has not received an impression, and he would now like the spectator please to concentrate a little harder and deal the same cards again onto the table, only this time to deal them very slowly.

As the spectator deals again, this time he is abruptly stopped by the performer, who takes the card that the spectator is holding in his hand at the time. Asking the spectator to name the card he is thinking of, the performer turns the card he holds face up, and it proves to be the card the spectator named.

THE SECRET

The performer watches the spectator as he cuts the deck, noting the bottom card of the cut portion. While this is going on, the performer merely *guesses* the amount of cards cut off. This is not as difficult as it sounds. With a little practice, it is

possible to guess within four or five cards or closer, and even to the exact number at times. This is all that is required.

For example, the performer guesses the number of cards cut to be twenty. The spectator names 5 as his number. The performer mentally divides 5 into 20, which is 4. When the cards are dealt by the spectator into five piles, as described in Presentation and Effect, the remembered card would be the fourth card from the bottom of the group the spectator says contains his card. After the spectator deals this group for the second time, the selected card will be fourth from the top. All the performer does is to say, "Stop," as the spectator is ready to deal the fourth card, and that card proves to be the spectator's selected card.

If the performer has been "away off" in his approximation of cards cut off and the card he holds at the finish is not the named card, all is not lost. He blithely informs his audience that the card he holds is a "magic" card. It is touched to the back of the card that would be the next card dealt (the fifth card in the above example). That card is then turned over and revealed to be the correct one.

Note: It is suggested that the performer also note in which dealt pile the selected card is. That is, the first pile dealt to the left is number 1, second number 2, etc. This is important for the success of the trick. For example, if the performer calculates the spectator's number of cut cards at eighteen, and five piles have been dealt by the spectator—dividing 5 into 18, we get 3⅗. Assuming that eighteen was the exact number of cards cut by the spectator, the card the spectator looked at would be dealt fourth from the bottom instead of third. The above tip is added as a note so as not to complicate a wonderful trick.

118. CARDOLOGY—OR, A CARD TRICK WITHOUT CARDS

The following trick—suggested by Blackstone, the great magician—does not require the use of a deck of cards.

PRESENTATION AND EFFECT

The performer starts his patter: "You have seen or heard of many ways in which a performer can ascertain what cards have been selected by his audience. I have developed a science which gives me one hundred per cent accuracy without seeing a card, touching a card, in fact, without using any cards at all. I call this science cardology. All of you are invited to participate in this demonstration, and I hope time will permit me to answer all. Simply follow my instructions, and as you complete this test in cardology, raise your hand. Ready? I want you to think of any card in the deck, double its value (if it is an ace count it as one, two as two, etc., up to ten. If you think of a jack the value is eleven, Queen is twelve, and King is thirteen. Now, after doubling its value, add one and multiply this total by five. Has that been done? Fine.

"Now listen to my final instructions. If the card you are thinking of is a spade, add nine to the last total; if it is a club, add six; if a heart, add eight; and for the diamond add seven. As soon as you have your answer raise your hand."

The performer continues, "You, sir, say that your total is seventy-four; then the card you thought of was the six of spades. That is correct, you say? Thank you.

"This gentleman has one hundred and thirty-one, and he thought of the queen of clubs. The lady who called out eighty-two was thinking of a seven of diamonds. Thank you.

"For your answer to fifty-three—you, sir, thought of the four of hearts. Thank you, ladies and gentlemen, for helping me."

The final total announced by the spectator will give the performer the clues to both suit and value of the selected cards. If the total ends in 1, remember that it will be a club; if it ends in 2, it will be a diamond; an end 3 will be hearts, and an end 4 will be spades.

The first number, or the first two numbers minus one, determines the value of the card. For example, the number that the first spectator called was 74, and this proves to be the 6 of Spades (doubling its value made it 12, adding 1 made it 13, and multiplying by 5 gave him 65. Adding 9 for spades gave a final total of 74.) The last number being a 4 indicates that the selected card is a spade.

A further example: the value of the second card called was 131. The final 1 indicates a club; the first two numbers are 13 (minus 1 makes 12, and 12 means the Queen); therefore, the card is the queen of clubs.

To be certain, when you start your demonstration, impress your audience with the idea of concentrating on the selected card and also to listen to your instructions. It is also important to make it plain that the ace counts as 1, 2 as 2, etc., up to 10, after which the jack counts as 11, queen as 12, and the king as 13. You can vary the presentation in a mixed group by asking the ladies, for example, to think of hearts and diamonds, and the men, spades and clubs. Using this system—if a lady calls out a number you will know that the selected card will be either hearts or diamonds. This effect can be done with as many people as time will permit.

119. CARD ON THE CEILING

This trick has probably been more talked about by spectators than any other card trick. It was used at one time or another by such great magicians as Harry Houdini, Howard Thurston, Blackstone, Max Malini, Nikola, Carl Rosini, and numerous top-notchers.

PRESENTATION AND EFFECT

The performer removes a pack of cards from the card case and requests a spectator to call a number from 10 to 19. This being done, the performer counts down to the number named by the spectator, dealing that number of cards on top of each other, equal to the number the spectator called. Picking these cards off the table, the performer adds the first and second digits of the number called, and counts down to that number. For example: The spectator calls number 13, the performer deals thirteen cards onto the table one at a time, placing each card on top of the previously dealt card. Picking up the thirteen cards, he adds the first and second digits of 13, saying, "One plus three totals four." He then counts four cards from the top

RUBBER BAND

of this group of thirteen cards and places the fourth card to one side. All the remaining cards are reassembled.

The performer now requests a spectator to note that card (which was left on the table), place it in the deck (which is on the table), and shuffle the deck thoroughly. The performer takes the deck back, looks through it as if trying to find the selected card, but does not say a word to this effect.

He then removes three rubber bands from his pocket, and has the spectator place two of the rubber bands around the width of the pack and one around the length. The performer watches the spectator to see that this is properly done, or, if he cares to, the performer may place the rubber bands around the deck himself.

The performer places the deck in his left coat (jacket) pocket and remarks that he will name the exact position in the deck of the selected card. However, the performer remarks that, since he looked through the cards before, naming the position of the selected card is quite simple.

With that remark, the performer removes the pack from his pocket and throws the pack against the ceiling, and the result is—the selected card remains stuck to the ceiling.

The performer requests the spectator to pick up the deck, which has fallen to the floor, remove the rubber bands, and look through the cards to see if there is a duplicate of the selected card in the deck. The spectator finds the deck is comprised of fifty-one cards and the selected card, the fifty-second, is stuck to the ceiling.

The performer requires two decks of cards exactly alike in size, color, and design; six rubber bands; and a piece of beeswax, or, if wax is not available, a piece of gum just previously chewed or paste may be used.

The performer decides what card he wants to have stick on the ceiling. For example, the jack of spades. He removes the jack of spades from one of the decks, places the queen of diamonds on the bottom of the deck, and places the three rubber bands around the deck in the same manner as described in Presentation and Effect. The piece of wax is put on the back of the jack of spades, in the center of the card.

This jack of spades is now placed face down on top of the deck and put into the performer's left-hand coat pocket.

The other deck is prepared as follows: The performer places the jack of spades so that it is the tenth card from the top of the deck, and the spectator is requested to name a number from 11 to 19. Regardless of the number named, the performer does as described in Presentation and Effect, and the spectator's chosen card will be the jack of spades. (If the performer has his own favorite method of compelling the spectator to select the jack of spades, it is suggested he use it.)

After the spectator has noted the jack of spades, returned it to the deck, and shuffled the deck, the performer looks through the deck, apparently looking for the selected card, in this case the jack of spades, but instead he finds the queen of diamonds and places it on the bottom of the deck. (*Note:* The queen of diamonds is the bottom card of the deck in the performer's pocket.) The rubber bands are now placed around the deck and the deck placed into the same pocket that holds the duplicate deck with the prepared jack of spades.

After the performer informs the spectator that he will name the exact position in the deck that the selected card occupies, and remarks that this is easy to do, the performer removes the duplicate pack from his pocket, plus the prepared jack of spades which is free from the rubber bands.

The performer holds the deck with the jack of spades on top of it so that the top card (the jack) is close to his body and the spectators cannot see that this card is free from the deck.

The performer now quickly grips the deck (plus the jack of spades) with his right hand, as shown in the illustration, and throws it quite violently against the ceiling, with a sort of circular motion. The result is that the jack of spades is stuck to the ceiling.

It is suggested the performer practice this trick before trying it in public, and also make sure that the type of wax or gum or paste used will stick.

120. VARIATION ON CARD ON THE CEILING

Do not pass this variation by. It has been a great success with magicians Frank Garcia, Clayton Rawson, and Paul Fleming.

PRESENTATION AND EFFECT

The performer brings the spectator into the room where he intends to do this trick; however, he doesn't mention anything about the trick at this time. Pointing to a chair, he asks the spectator to be seated and to make himself comfortable. After some small talk back and forth with the spectator, the performer decides to do this particular trick.

He "compels" the spectator to select the jack of spades, for example, in the manner described in "Card on the Ceiling" (see page 230), by having the spectator call out a number from 10 to 19. Dealing down to the number called, the performer adds the two digits of that number, and counts down to that card from the small packet of cards he just counted off the deck. When he arrives at the correct number, he takes that card and places it face down on the table. He reassembles all the remaining cards. He has the spectator note and remember the card that is on the table, and asks him to place it in the deck and shuffle the pack thoroughly.

After this has been done, the performer looks through the cards, then places the deck in his pocket. He remarks that he is going to find the selected card in his pocket, but since he looked through the cards, it will be easy to do. Therefore, he will do a more difficult trick.

He takes the deck out of his pocket, and throws the cards at the ceiling. The cards fall every other which way all over the floor, except the one card which sticks to the ceiling. It is found to be the spectator's selected card, the jack of spades. Upon picking up the deck, it will be noted that it does not contain a jack of spades.

THE SECRET

The performer has the card he is going to use in this trick— for example, the jack of spades—already pasted on the ceiling. It is put there by the method described in "Card on the Ceiling" (see page 231). Of course, it is best that the performer choose a high-ceiling room for this trick. The spectator will rarely notice that there is a card pasted on the ceiling, since the performer never mentions card tricks until he has the spectator in the right room and seated in the right chair. The chair the performer requests the spectator to sit in is placed so that the card on the ceiling will be behind the spectator, and even if he does glance up, it will be out of view.

In order to perform this variation, the performer must have a duplicate jack of spades pasted on the ceiling. This card does not have to be of the same color back, since the back will be stuck to the ceiling. The performer then places the identical card (as that on the ceiling), the jack of spades in this example, to be the tenth card counting down from the top of the deck. When the spectator calls a number from 10 to 19, using the same procedure as described on page 230 in "Card on the Ceiling" the spectator will be forced to select the jack of spades.

The performer now has the spectator look at and remember his selected card (jack of spades), return it to the deck and shuffle. Now the performer takes the deck, looks through the cards, places the jack of spades on top of the deck (unseen by the spectator), and states that he is going to find the selected card while the deck is in his coat pocket. He illustrates by placing the deck in his coat pocket for a moment. He then changes his mind and says, "I will do a better trick." Out comes the deck into full view again. But the performer has dropped the jack of spades in his pocket merely by letting it fall off the top of the deck.

The performer now has a deck in his hand minus a jack of spades. He throws the deck toward the ceiling, as described, and when the cards are picked up from the floor, the deck is minus the jack of spades, and that card is found to be on the ceiling.

121. LEIPZIG'S POCKET CARD TRICK

During my associations with Nate Leipzig, the great card manipulator and magician, I remember his doing a card trick which was one of his pets. Briefly, Leipzig would name the number of cards that a spectator had placed in his pocket in addition to finding the selected card. Here is that trick.

PRESENTATION AND EFFECT

The performer requests a spectator to give the deck a thorough shuffle. Then he instructs the spectator to remove ten cards from any part of the deck and put them into his pocket.

Next the spectator places the remainder of the pack face down on the table. The performer tells the spectator that he (the performer) is going to turn his back, but first he wants the spectator to know what he is to do when the performer's back is turned.

"Here is what you do when my back is turned. Take any number of cards out of your pocket that you desire, note the bottom card of that group, and place that group on top of these cards." The performer points to the deck resting on the table.

The performer turns his back and tells the spectator to do as instructed. After all this has been done, the performer faces the spectator, picks up the cards, and deals ten cards in a row face down on the table.

The performer does a bit of concentrating, after which he turns up one of these ten cards. It proves to be the selected card. "Furthermore," the performer states, "you have —— cards in your pocket." The number the performer names proves to be exactly the number of cards the spectator has in his pocket.

THE SECRET

The performer carries some salt in his pocket. After the spectator has put the ten cards into his pocket, the performer moistens his fingertip slightly by touching his lips. Then he places his hand into his pocket containing the salt, touches the salt with his wet fingertip and a few grains of salt adhere to his fingertip.

Prior to turning his back, the performer instructs the spectator to take any number of cards out of his pocket and note the bottom card of *this group,* then to put this group on top of the deck. The performer illustrates by hitting the top of the deck with the finger which has the grains of salt adhering to it. This gesture causes a few grains of salt to fall on the top card of the deck.

Then the performer turns his back, and the spectator after noting the bottom card places the cards taken out of his pocket on top of the deck. The spectator squares the deck, then the performer faces the spectator again, and picks up the pack. He puts a slight pressure of the thumb on the top and side of the pack, causing a packet of cards to break away from the remainder of the cards. (*Note:* The salt causes the cards placed on top of it to slide a little and creates a slight separation at the point where the salt is.)

The performer keeps his eye on this separation, counting the top cards that have been separated while he is dealing the ten cards onto the table. For example, if six cards are in this separate group, the performer subtracts 6 from 10, and knows that the spectator has four cards left in his pocket. And, the sixth card dealt is the card that the spectator noted. A bit of practice is necessary to get the right spot to press your thumb. If the reader desires to try this trick, it is best to drop a few grains of salt on the top of the deck as described above, and then place five cards on top of the salt spot. Then try sliding the cards. With a little practice it will come easy.

If the performer finds this a bit difficult, he should try this. After the spectator has replaced his cards on top of the deck, the performer cuts the deck. In doing so he notes the bottom card of the deck. The performer places the deck on the table and gives the side of the deck a sharp blow with his hand, so that the cards will slide apart at the point where the salt is. This separation is your cut, the bottom card of the separated group (the card which was placed on top of the salt) is the spectator's selected card.

To ascertain the number of cards the spectator has in his pocket, the performer counts the selected card as number 1, and continues counting until he reaches his glimpsed card. Subtracting the number counted from 10, the performer arrives at the number of cards in the spectator's pocket.

122. THURSTON'S CARD MYSTERY

One of the first tricks I ever saw performed by Howard Thurston, the great magician of years ago, was this effect, which I call "Thurston's Card Mystery."

PRESENTATION AND EFFECT

The performer hands the spectator the deck to be shuffled (although shuffling is not necessary). The performer turns his back and instructs the spectator as follows:

Put two rows of cards on the table, each to contain the same number of cards, one row above the other. The number of cards in each row is left to the discretion of the spectator.

The performer tells the spectator to remove one card from the bottom row and put it back on the top of the remainder of the deck.

The performer asks the spectator, "How many cards would you like to remove from the top row?" The spectator, for example, specifies five. The performer then tells him to remove five cards from the top row and place them on top of the remainder of the deck.

Now the performer instructs the spectator to remove from the bottom row as many cards as are left in the top row and to put them on top of the deck.

The performer now tells the spectator to remove all the remaining cards in the top row and put them on top of the deck.

The performer then tells the spectator the number of cards left in the bottom row. In the above instance the number of cards remaining would be four.

THE SECRET

The performer instructs the spectator to do exactly as described above. All the performer has to do to know the exact number of cards is to subtract 1 from the number of cards that the spectator desires to remove from the top row. (The spectator calls that number out loud.) The performer must bear in mind that the entire trick is performed behind his back.

123. SCARNE'S MIRACLE CARD-FINDER TRICK

This perplexing mystery—the spectator finds the card the per-former has in mind—was originated by the author.

PRESENTATION AND EFFECT

The performer patters along these lines: "Magicians have had to change the method of working their tricks to suit the trend of times. Illusionists today, on a night club floor surrounded by people, can perform tricks that were never even dreamt of by magicians of years gone by. I have been asked what card manipulators do today that wasn't even heard of a few years ago. Well, my friends, card magic has advanced so rapidly in the past few years that tonight for the first time I am going to have a spectator who knows nothing about the art of legerdemain find a card that *I* am thinking of. I am now going to think of a card. I have thought of one," continues the performer. "You have no idea what I am thinking of or where in the pack my card may be. But, regardless of these hazards, you will find my card. Shuffle the deck to your heart's content, and so that the method of choice may not be too long, please call a number from eight to forty."

This being done, the performer then instructs the spectator to deal the cards face up on the table, placing each dealt card on the previously dealt card and stopping at the number called. "The reason for the spectator's dealing the cards face up is," the performer says, "so that I can ascertain if my mentally selected card is in the dealt group."

After the given number of cards has been dealt, the performer states that the card he mentally selected is in that group. The performer then writes down the name of his card on a piece of paper and places it face down on the table. The writing, of course, cannot be seen.

The spectator is now instructed to pick up the group he just dealt face up onto the table and hold them face down in his hand. (The remainder of the pack is put to one side and is not used.) The spectator is instructed to give the performer the top card of the pack, put the next card on the bottom of the packet, give the performer the next card, put the card after that on the bottom of the packet, hand the performer the next card, put the next on the bottom of the packet, etc. This action is continued until the spectator has only one card left in his hand. The spectator is told to hold that card face down. The performer then remarks, "If that is the card I am thinking of, you are a better magician than I."

The performer names the card he is thinking of, the spectator turns the card he holds face up—and it proves to be correct, as does the writen message on the piece of paper.

THE SECRET

When the performer states that he is thinking of a card at the start of the trick, it is only a bit of misdirection. So the performer has the spectator deal the cards face up on the table to see if his mentally selected card is in that group. The performer always answers that his card is there. But what the performer actually does is note the card that is at the correct position in the group so as to be the last card dealt.

And here is how it is done. A simple mathematical formula is used. The key numbers are 2, 4, 8, 16, and 32. They are easy to remember; starting with 2 each following number is doubled. At the time the spectator calls out his number (number of cards to be dealt), the performer mentally subtracts from it the key number next below the called number, and multiplies the answer by 2. The final result is the position of the card to be mentally noted in the dealt group of cards when they are face up.

For example, the spectator calls number 29. The performer mentally subtracts 16, the next key number below 29; 29 minus 16 leaves 13; 13 multiplied by 2 is 26. The spectator is told to count his cards face up. So all the performer does is note the twenty-sixth dealt card. Since the cards are turned face up during the deal, and the entire group is then turned face down, the twenty-sixth card dealt will remain in the same position when the group is turned face down. This same holds true at all times. The card being noted, the performer now writes the name of the card in the twenty-sixth position in the group on a slip of paper, naming this as his selected card.

Now all that is left is for the spectator to do as instructed: Give the performer the top card of the group, put the next card

236

on the bottom of the group, etc., until the spectator has only one card left in his hand. It will be the card called by the performer as his selected card.

124. THE SPIRIT CARD TRICK

This version of the "Hands-off Miracle" (page 61) has a very spooky effect upon the audience. It is greatly favored by Audley Walsh, the racket exposer, and Jerry Lukins, the magician.

PRESENTATION AND EFFECT

The performer tells a story along these lines: "You may not know this," the performer states, "but all magicians, when sworn into a magical society, sign an oath that after death they must try to come back from the spirit world and communicate with one of their brother magicians.

"You probably have read of magician friends of Houdini's, who each year upon the anniversary of his death sit in a room by themselves at a specified hour, hoping that Houdini will be able to contact them from the spirit world, as he promised to do when he was alive.

"I don't know how successful these magicians have been, but I have been quite successful with my own séance. A brother card trick artist of mine, whom we shall call Harry, always helps me to do a card trick if I call upon him, especially when I am sincere and my audience does not laugh at me while I am calling upon him.

"Promise me that you will not ridicule this experiment, and I will attempt it now."

After the spectators promise not to ridicule the experiment, the performer starts the trick.

The performer speaks to a spectator. "Please shuffle this deck of cards," he says. "Now, will you please stand up and place your left hand in front of your body, palm up and arm outstretched."

The performer then places the deck of cards on the spectator's hand, and requests the spectator not to close his hand, but to keep his palm flat so that the deck can rest on it.

The performer addresses the spectator. "Would you mind cutting the deck with your right hand, and then note the bottom card of the cut portion. Now replace the cards back on top of the lower group." (The performer points to the group resting on the spectator's hand.)

Squaring up the cards, the performer says, "I will now call upon my friend Harry in the spirit world to find the selected card."

The performer calls, "Harry, Harry, help me find the right card." And, with this bit of patter, the performer takes hold of the spectator's left elbow and slowly pushes the elbow back and forth. (He pushes the elbow back and forth for the distance of

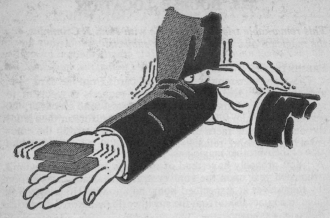

about an inch.) Since the spectator is not clutching the cards, but merely has them resting on his flat outstretched palm, the cards will sway a little. But then a very weird thing occurs; the cards start to separate at one particular spot. The performer then stops pushing the spectator's elbow, and says, "Harry, my spirit friend, thanks a million."

The performer asks the spectator to name his selected card. The performer then cuts the cards at the separation, and it is found that the selected card is at just that spot. This is truly a very weird effect.

THE SECRET

The performer requires some salt to perform this trick. He has the salt in his pocket, and prior to asking the spectator to cut and note the bottom card of the cut portion, the performer puts his hand into his pocket and touches the salt with his forefinger. Some grains of salt will adhere to the fingertip or under the fingernail.

Then, when the spectator has cut the deck and noted the bottom card, the performer instructs the spectator to replace the cut packet on top of the bottom packet. He illustrates this by tapping the top card of the bottom packet which is resting on the spectator's outstretched hand. This gesture causes a few grains of salt to fall on the top card of this packet.

Then, when the other packet (top half of deck) is placed on

top, and the performer pushes the spectator's elbow, the cards must separate at this exact position. A little practice will prove this.

125. DOUBLE LOCATION

This remarkable trick is a favorite with John J. Crimmins, Jr., the magician and writer on magic subjects.

PRESENTATION AND EFFECT

The performer removes a deck of cards from the card case, and spreading them out in his hand, requests a spectator to select a card from the deck. Turning to a second spectator, the performer has him select a card, also. The performer then holds the deck with the faces toward himself, and passing the cards from hand to hand, remarks that it would be a good trick if he could name the two selected cards.

The performer then separates the deck into two parts and hands a packet face up to each of the two spectators, requesting each to insert his selected card into the group he holds, and then to shuffle that group thoroughly so that there will be no clue for the performer to follow when trying to find the selected card.

After each spectator has shuffled the packet he holds, he is instructed to return the packet to the performer. The performer places one packet on top of the other, and requests one of the spectators to cut the cards and complete the cut.

The performer takes the deck in his hands and remarks, "It would be a good trick if I could name the two selected cards after all this."

He then faces the deck toward himself and looks through the cards. The performer goes through the business of taking a card out of the deck, then putting it back, putting a card on the bottom, then saying that he cannot find the selected cards.

After a bit of byplay along these lines, the performer, holding the deck face down in his right hand, stands up and *backs* away from the table. His hand turns slightly (he turns his wrist to the left), and the deck of cards falls to the floor with the exception of two cards that are still in the performer's hand.

The performer apologizes for his clumsiness and remarks, "Wouldn't it be a remarkable accident if these two face-down cards in my hand were the two cards selected by the two spectators."

The performer asks each spectator to name his selected card, and when the faces of the two cards in the performer's hand are shown, they *are* the two selected cards.

"Proving that when you know your stuff," says the performer, "even accidents can't hinder a good trick."

The deck is arranged into odd and even cards. The odd cards —ace-3-5-7-9-jack-king of all four suits—are placed together, and the rest of the deck—2-4-6-8-10-queen of all four suits—is placed on top of the odd cards. In this arrangement the performer places the deck into the card case.

When ready to perform, he removes the deck, spreads it face down, requests a spectator to select a card—but makes certain that the spectator selects one of the top twenty-six cards (which must be an even card). Should the spectator pick one from the bottom twenty-six cards, the performer must remember that it is an odd card.

The performer then requests the second spectator to select a card from the deck, and tries to make him select one from the twenty-six cards opposite where the first card was selected.

The situation is this: one spectator has selected an even card, and one an odd card. The performer faces the deck to himself and separates the deck at the exact position where the odd cards meet the even cards.

He then hands the spectator, holding the odd card, the group comprised of even cards, and does the opposite with the other spectator. Should both spectators select a card from the same group, the performer merely requests each spectator to place his card in the group handed him. The performer retains the other half of the deck.

Naturally, if they both select even cards, the performer hands them the odd group, or vice versa.

When both groups are placed together and cut, this does not disturb the arrangement of odd and even cards. The performer merely locates the opposite card or cards in one or both groups, and they prove to be the selected cards. For example, an odd card in the even group, or an even card in the odd group, would be the selected card.

These two cards are placed—one on the top of the deck and one on the bottom of the deck—by the performer during the act of looking through the deck.

The performer then wets the fingers of his right hand slightly, by putting them up to his lips, before backing away from the table, and holds the deck in his right hand, with the thumb on top of the deck and the fingers on the bottom. The performer turns his hand over slightly, and all the cards fall out of his hand except the top and bottom cards, and they are of course the two selected cards. (The performer must hold the deck loosely so that all the cards between the top and bottom of the deck will fall out.)

126. RIBBON SPREAD

This is Chet Miller's and "Rusduck the Magician's" trick.

PRESENTATION AND EFFECT

The performer requests a spectator to shuffle the deck, then to select a card and place it in his (spectator's) pocket without looking at the face of the card.

The performer then takes the deck from the spectator and spreads it face up on the table, in a long ribbon fashion. The performer makes certain that the markings of all the cards are visible.

The performer now says that he and the spectator will draw cards alternately at random from the cards on the table, and that the performer will compel the spectator to leave until last a card which will indicate to the performer the name of the chosen card in the spectator's pocket.

The performer instructs the spectator to remove any card from the spread-out deck. The performer now removes one card. The spectator removes another card, then the performer does likewise. This is continued until only one card is left on the table. The performer studies that card for a moment, then names the card the spectator has in his pocket. The spectator removes the selected card from his pocket, and the performer is correct.

THE SECRET

The performer pairs hearts and spades, and pairs clubs and diamonds. In other words, if the spectator draws a heart card, the performer draws a spade card, or vice versa. The same procedure is followed for clubs and diamonds. If the spectator draws a club card, the performer draws a diamond, and vice versa. This process takes care of the suits.

Now, for the numerical value of the cards: When the spectator takes a card, the performer must take a card that will bring the combined total of the spectator's and performer's cards to 13. This simple calculation is made mentally by the performer. All cards carry their own numerical value: ace is 1, 2 is 2, 3 is 3, etc. Jack carries a value of 11; queen, 12; king, 13.

Following are a few samples: Spectator takes the 4 of hearts, the performer must take the 9 of spades (4 plus 9 equals 13, hearts and spades must be paired).

Spectator takes the 3 of diamonds, performer must take the 10 of clubs (10 plus 3 equals 13, diamonds and clubs are paired.)

Spectator takes a king of spades, performer takes the king of hearts (since king carries a value of 13, the performer must take a king also, but he must take the king that pairs, such as, in this example, spades and hearts).

When the spectator draws a card and the performer cannot pair it, that missing card (which the performer needs to match the spectator's) is the selected card. The performer could name the card in the spectator's pocket at this time, but it is much more effective to continue taking cards alternately until only one card is left. However, from this point on, the performer can take his cards indiscriminately. This tends to break up any sequence which could give the spectator a clue to the method employed.

The performer should practice spreading the pack on the table, and practice locating the corresponding cards so that he can do this with ease. When performing the trick he must not give the spectator the impression that he is making a mental calculation.

127. THE ODD WILL

The idea for this trick was suggested to the author by Bruce Elliot, editor of The Phoenix, the magazine of magic.

PRESENTATION AND EFFECT

The performer relates a story about an early settler in Virginia. This old settler, who was a farmer, died, and upon reading his will, it was found that his farmhouse, buildings, equipment, and all of his livestock with the exception of his herd of cows, were mortgaged for their full value.

The only thing left, this herd of cows, he willed to his three sons and his next-door neighbor, Farmer Brown.

With the three sons and Farmer Brown present, the will was read, and it was found to contain the statement that in order to prevent bitterness and quarreling among the three sons, the herd was to be divided among them by making use of a pack of cards.

The will read: "Bill, my oldest son, you shuffle the cards." (Performer illustrates by shuffling the cards, playing the part of Bill, the oldest son.) "Bill," the will continued, "put the cards on the table and let Joe, your brother, cut the cards." (At this point the performer has a spectator cut the cards and square the deck.) "Now let your youngest brother, John, cut the deck and square the cut." (Performer has a second spectator cut the cards and square the deck.)

"Bill," the will went on, "take three aces out of the pack and place them in a row face up on the table. Each will represent the top half of a fraction." (The performer looks through the deck and does exactly as the will directed.)

Continuing, the will read, "Place the deck face down on the

table, Bill. Take off the top two cards. The value of those two cards will represent the number of cows you and your brothers will divide. The remainder of the cows in my herd I will to Farmer Brown."

The performer turns up an ace first, then a 7. The digits of the two cards form the number 17. Therefore 17 is the number of cows the three brothers are to divide.

"Bill," continued the will, "take the top card of the deck, turn it face up, and place it below the first ace in the row you formed so that it slightly overlaps the ace. That card forms the bottom part of your fraction."

The performer takes the top card of the deck and does as the will directed. The card is a 2-spot. Therefore, Bill gets one-half of the cows. The performer takes a card off the top of the deck to form the bottom part of Joe's fraction. This card is a 3-spot. Therefore, Joe, the second brother, is to get one-third of the cows. The performer takes the third card off the top of the deck to form the bottom part of the fraction for John, the youngest son. This card is a 9-spot. Therefore, John is to get one-ninth of the cows. He wasn't as lucky as his other two brothers.

Now the brothers begin to argue. It seems they cannot divide seventeen cows evenly, and to cut a cow into sections would do none of them any good. So, in order to settle the problem, they asked Farmer Brown's advice.

After a long wait and careful consideration, Farmer Brown decided to give the brothers one of his cows to help solve the problem. Bill, the oldest brother, remarked at this, "There must be a joker somewhere. Farmer Brown is so stingy he wouldn't give a penny away."

Farmer Brown, accompanied by the three brothers, went out to the barnyard, and rounded up the seventeen cows willed to the brothers, and Farmer Brown added a cow of his own to make the total eighteen.

The performer illustrates this by dealing seventeen cards from the top of the deck face down onto the table one at a time, counting out loud as he deals, and placing each dealt card on top of the card previously dealt. After dealing seventeen cards, he takes another card from the top of the deck and places it on top of the seventeen cards, making a total of eighteen.

"Now," said Farmer Brown, "Bill, you get one-half. One-half of eighteen is nine." (The performer picks up the eighteen cards and deals nine cards face down below Bill's ace-2 fraction.) "Joe, you get one-third, or six cows." (The performer deals six cards below the ace-3 fraction.) "And John, you get one-ninth, or two cows." (The performer deals two cards below the ace-9 fraction.)

The performer still has one card in his hand, and that represents the cow the wise old Farmer Brown took back to his own barnyard. The performer turns the card face up, and it is the joker. He says, "Bill was right. Farmer Brown was joking when he said that he would give a cow away."

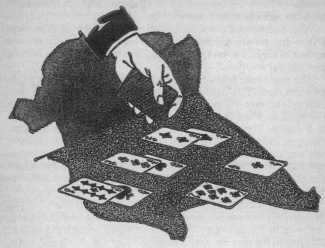

THE SECRET

The trick is almost self-working. The performer merely sets up nine cards: the four aces on top of the deck, followed below by a 7, a 2, a 3, and a 9-spot, and below the 9-spot he places the joker.

The cards are on top of the deck. The performer riffle shuffles cards, making sure that the top nine cards are not disturbed, then has the cards cut, squared up, and cut again.

All the performer has to do now is look for the four aces which are together, take the top three aces and drop them on the table face up. After the three aces have been taken out of the pack, the performer will have two groups of cards in his hand. He merely puts the group containing the ace on top of the other group and follows the instructions described in Presentation and Effect—and he's all set to perform "The Odd Will" trick.

128. THE UNINVITED JOKER

This swell spelling trick, where the joker always gets into the spectator's spelling, is a favorite with George Karger, the ace photographer and clever amateur magician.

PRESENTATION AND EFFECT

"Ladies and Gentlemen, this evening we are going to hold a spelling bee." With this remark the performer takes a deck of cards out of the card case. He then riffle shuffles the deck *once*. Turning the deck over, he states that he is going to remove the spade suit from the deck. The performer looks through the deck and says, "I have taken out all the spade cards including the joker." (As each card is removed from the deck it is turned face down on the table, one on top of the other.)

The performer puts the remainder of the deck to one side, and picks up the packet of spade cards plus the joker, and places them face down in his left hand. He states, "I am going to spell from ace to king in the following manner." He spells A-C-E, removing a card from the top of the packet and placing it on the bottom of the packet for each letter spelled. After spelling the word ace, the next card on top of the packet (fourth card from the top originally) is turned face up, removed from the packet, and placed face up on the table. This card is the ace.

The above procedure is followed by the performer until the thirteen spade cards have been correctly spelled and removed from the packet. Occasionally, however, the performer hands the packet to the spectator to spell out the next card, and the spectator upon completion of the spelling always turns up the joker instead of the proper card. The performer then spells the card in the same manner as the spectator, but he always succeeds in turning up the card he spelled.

THE SECRET

The spade cards plus the joker are arranged face down on the table in the following order, as preparation for this trick: queen, 3, 5, king, ace, 10, 9, joker, 2, 8, 7, jack, 6, 4—the 4-spot being the bottom card of the group and the queen the top card. These fourteen cards are then placed on top of the remainder of the deck and the deck is placed in the card case.

At the start of the trick the performer removes the deck from the card case and riffle shuffles the deck *just once*. The arrangement of the spade cards is not disturbed by this shuffle. They are only distributed throughout the deck in their arranged order. The performer now picks up the deck and faces the cards toward himself, stating that he is going to remove all the spade cards. The first spade card he sees is the 4 of spades. He removes it from the deck and places it face down on the table. Next card he removes is the 6 of spades. This he places face down on top of the 4 of spades already on the table. He continues removing the spade cards and the joker in the order that he finds them in the deck, until he has removed twelve spade cards and the joker. The last spade card in the deck is the queen of spades.

245

This one he does not remove. Instead he puts it on top of the deck, face down. Then he places the face-down deck in front of himself so that no one will take the deck, since the queen of spades must be used a little later on in the trick.

The performer now picks up the packet of twelve spade cards plus the joker in the exact setup as described above (although the queen is not included in this setup), starts to spell A-C-E for ace, and follows through as described in Presentation and Effect.

Here is the full spelling routine:

The performer spells ace.

The performer spells two.

The performer spells three.

The spectator spells four, and gets the joker.

The performer places the joker on the bottom of the packet, then spells four.

The spectator spells five, and gets the joker.

The performer places the joker on the bottom of the packet, then spells five.

The spectator spells six, and gets the joker.

Performer puts the joker on the bottom of the packet, then spells six.

The performer spells seven.

The performer spells eight.

Spectator spells nine, and gets the joker.

Performer puts joker on the bottom of packet and hands the cards back to the spectator. Spectator spells nine once again, and gets the joker.

Performer puts joker on *top* of packet and spells nine.

Performer spells ten.

Performer spells jack.

The performer then says, "You know that I can spell the queen and king." And, with this remark, he places the two cards he still holds on top of the deck. Then he says, as if he has overheard a spectator, "Oh, you're not so sure that I can?" The performer goes on, "We still have the queen, king, and joker to spell out." And so saying, he removes the three top cards instead of the two he placed on top. Regardless of whether the spectator notices this move or not, the performer takes three cards, and says, "You can't spell three cards with only two cards." If the performer takes pains in handling the last few spelled cards the spectator will not notice that the performer had only two cards left at this point.

The performer spells queen.

The performer spells king.

The performer turns up the joker and says, "Ladies and gentlemen, the joker never gets in my way."

129. THE IMPOSSIBLE LOCATION

This trick is from Martin Gardner, the author and magician.

PRESENTATION AND EFFECT

The performer removes a deck of cards from the card case and asks a spectator to cut approximately seventeen cards off the top of the deck (about one-third of the deck) and to put these cards to one side. The performer then requests the spectator to cut the remaining group in half.

The spectator is instructed to shuffle the group that was the top part of the deck (first group cut off) and to place the cards face down on the table. The spectator then is told to shuffle the group that was the bottom portion of the pack. When he has finished shuffling, the spectator is told to note and memorize the bottom card of this group, and then to place the group on top of the other shuffled group which was formerly the top part of the deck.

The spectator is then requested to shuffle the group which was formerly the middle portion of the deck, and to place these cards on top of the other group (which is now comprised of the top and bottom portions of the deck).

The performer instructs the spectator to cut the deck and complete the cut. The performer himself cuts the deck and completes the cut, also. This procedure is repeated as often as desired by the performer.

The performer states that he will try the impossible, and locate the noted card. Taking the deck, he walks away from the table, faces the cards toward himself, and removes a card, placing it face down on the table.

Requesting the spectator to name his card, the performer has the spectator turn this card face up, and it is found to be the card that the spectator chose.

THE SECRET

The deck is prepared by having all the red cards separated from the blacks, placing the red cards on top of the black cards.

With this setup, the spectator follows directions as stated in Presentation and Effect.

For his first shuffle, he mixes all red cards; and on his second shuffle he mixes all black cards. Therefore, when he notes the bottom card of this group and places the group of cards on top of the first shuffled group, the selected card will be the first black card on top of a long string of red cards.

The shuffle of the former center part of the deck will mix red and black cards. The cutting of the cards will not disturb the order of that long block of red cards and the long block of black cards. Therefore, the performer merely locates the seventeen or more red cards in a goup and removes the black card on top of this group. It will be the card noted by the spectator.

It is suggested that the performer, after placing the spectator's selected card face down on the table, shuffle the entire pack so that upon inspection any trace of the prearrangement will be eliminated.

130. THE COMPLEMENTARY CARDS

This is one of Nate Leipzig's effects.

PRESENTATION AND EFFECT

The performer requests a spectator to shuffle a deck of cards, divide it into two groups, shuffle one of the groups and hand it to the performer. The performer takes the group handed to him, and immediately places it in his right-hand trouser pocket without looking at the faces of any of the cards. The spectator then shuffles the other group, and the performer places this group into his left-hand trouser pocket.

Upon completion of instructions outlined above, the performer says, "I cannot know the position of any cards in the deck. The deck has been shuffled and cut into two halves, both of which are in my trouser pockets." Turning to a spectator, the performer asks him to name any card in the deck. For example, the spectator calls out the ten of diamonds.

The performer says, "I will first take out a card whose suit value is the same as that of the card you called." Reaching into his pocket, he comes out with a card. Turning it face up, it proves to be a diamond.

Then he continues, "I am going to pick out two more cards whose total will be ten, the numerical value of the card called." (Occasionally, the performer will include the same card he used in denoting the suit as one of the cards making up the total of the numerical value of the called card.) The performer states that if the spectator calls out a jack, the numerical value is 11; queen, 12; and king, 13.

Regardless of what card is called, the performer is always successful in picking a number of cards from his trouser pockets to represent the correct suit and the numerical value.

THE SECRET

The performer secretly removes the ace of clubs, and the 2 of diamonds and places these cards in his left trouser pocket. Then he removes the 4 of hearts and the 6 of spades and places them in his right trouser pocket. He must make sure, when the cards are placed in the pocket, to leave the two planted cards on the bottom of the group so that they can easily be taken out.

The performer must use his own calculations to arrive at the given number (always remember jack is 11; queen, 12; and king, 13). With the four planted cards any number called can be made, also the suit can be determined.

For instance, the spectator calls the 7 of diamonds. The performer first removes the 2 of diamonds from his pocket, turns it face up, and says, "This is the diamond suit." Then he reaches into both pockets and removes the ace spot from his left pocket and the 4-spot from his right trouser pocket, and states, "The total of these three cards equals the value of the card you named. One plus two plus four equals seven."

Should the spectator call the king of clubs, the performer removes the ace of clubs first and states that this is the suit of the called card. Then he proceeds to remove the other three planted cards, stating that the total equals 13, which stands for king.

When a card is called, and the performer finds that the card he uses to denote the suit value is not needed to make up the numerical value also, he proceeds as follows. For example, the spectator calls the ace of diamonds. The performer takes out the 2 of diamonds, and before showing it, he says, "This card will determine the suit value." He turns it over and says, "Diamonds, correct." He places this card to one side and continues, "The next card that I take out of my pocket will determine the numerical value." And the performer takes out the ace.

Naturally, if the spectator calls out one of the four planted cards, you merely reach into the pocket, take it out, and you have performed a miracle.

The performer can produce cards from his pocket to equal any card called by using a little simple arithmetic and common sense.

131. BEHIND MY BACK

A fast trick that requires no previous preparation, from Bert Feinson, the New York magician.

PRESENTATION AND EFFECT

The performer produces a deck of cards and says, "Some people believe that I actually can see what card is taken. To dispel that idea, I will shuffle this deck and will perform this card trick behind my back—everything will be done behind my back."

The performer hands the deck to the spectator, turns his back, and instructs the spectator to shuffle the deck. Then he is told to remove from fifteen to twenty-six cards from any part of the deck, and to hold these cards in his hand. (For clarity we shall call the packet of cards the spectator holds packet number one.) The spectator is told to place the remainder of the deck (packet number two) on the performer's outstretched hand, which the performer holds behind his back.

The spectator is then instructed to shuffle carefully the cards he holds (packet number one) and then to select any card from that packet, memorize it, and then place it face down on the table. After this has been done, the spectator is instructed to take as many cards from the group he holds (packet number one) as will equal the numerical value of the selected card, and to place these cards on top of the selected card which is face down on the table. For example, if the spectator selected an ace, the spectator places one card on the selected card; if he selected a 2-spot, he places two cards on top of the selected card, etc. The jack, queen, and king count 11, 12, and 13, respectively.

The performer says to the spectator, "Now shuffle the remainder of the cards you are holding" (part of packet number one), "then place this group into the center of the group I am holding behind my back" (packet number two). The performer may aid the spectator by cutting the group he holds behind his back so that it will be easier for the spectator to place his group into the center of the group the performer is holding.

The performer now tells the spectator to shuffle the remaining group of cards left on the table (comprised of the selected card plus the added cards), to place them on top of the deck, and to cut the deck.

After all this has been done, the performer brings the deck into full view, walks to the far end of the room, and starts looking through the deck of cards, quite openly. Walking toward the spectator, he takes one card from the deck and holds it aloft, face hidden from the spectator. He then asks the spectator, "What is the name of your card?" The spectator reveals the name of his selected card, and the performer shows the face of the card he holds. It proves to be the selected card.

"Now, all of this perhaps," says the performer, "proves that I can see behind my back."

THE SECRET

After the spectator has taken fifteen to twenty-six cards from the deck and returned the remaining part of the deck (packet number two, to the performer's hand, the performer quickly turns and addresses the spectator, telling him to shuffle the cards thoroughly (packet number one). The performer secretly notes the top and bottom card of the group he holds (packet number two). The spectator is busy shuffling his cards and pays no attention to this ruse. That is the secret.

Eventually, when the original card and those added are placed on top of the deck, and the cards cut, this small packet will be between the top and bottom cards the performer glimpsed and made note of. Now, at the end of the trick, the performer looks through the entire deck. He locates the former top and bottom cards and starts counting. If, for example, the spectator picked an 8-spot, there will be nine cards between the top and bottom cards noted. To ascertain the selected card, always count between the two location cards minus one. Again, in this case, where the performer has nine cards, he is told the 8-spot was selected. All he does is look through this group and locate the 8-spot among the group of nine cards. Should there be two 8's, or more, he then asks if the card is red or black. By a process of elimination he finally brings the selected card out of the deck. The important points to remember are: note mentally the top and bottom cards of the deck the spectator places on the performer's hand; and then, after the cut, count the cards between these two cards less one. In other words, the performer must allow for the original selected card plus those added.

132. SI STEBBIN'S MASTER MEMORY TEST

This effect, whereby the performer names the exact positon in the deck of any card called by a spectator, has long been a favorite with many magicians, and particularly with Si Stebbins, the magician who was one of the first to use such an effect on a vaudeville stage. Since Si Stebbins first made use of the principle that is used in this trick, numerous additional effects have been developed based on the same principle. Following is the Presentation and Effect as developed by the author.

PRESENTATION AND EFFECT

The performer begins his patter along these lines, "Ladies and gentlemen, tonight I am going to present one of the greatest memory feats possible to the human mind. I am going to name the fifty-two cards in the deck without once renaming the same card. No, I am not going to call all the spades first, then the clubs, etc. But I am going to name the cards in a sort of mixed order. And, ladies and gentlemen, if you think I have a code for doing this, you are sadly mistaken. May I go further and state that after I call the entire deck, I will name the exact position in the deck of any card named by a spectator."

The performer shuffles the deck, and hands each of four or five spectators a group of cards. The number of spectators and cards in each group is optional with the performer, although the larger the number of spectators holding cards, the speedier the trick.

The performer then calls out the 3 of spades for his first card, and requests the spectator holding that card to hand it to him. He calls the 6 of diamonds next. He continues calling names of cards, taking each named card from the person holding it, until he has the entire deck.

The performer states that in order to prove that he has actually done the previous part of the trick by memory, he will allow any person to name a card and he will call out the exact position from the top of the deck that the named card is located.

For example, a spectator names the 10 of spades. Instantly the performer says, "Then ten of spades is exactly the twelfth card down from the top of the pack." The performer counts twelve cards off the top of the pack, turns over the twelfth card, and it is found to be the card named, the 10 of spades in this instance. This procedure is continued as long as the performer desires, proving without a doubt that he is endowed with a remarkable memory.

THE SECRET

Although the performer told the spectators that he does not use a system, he really does use one, and when properly used by the performer, it eliminates all suspicion in the spectator's mind that a system is being used. The system is quite simple to follow, and no great memory is required. Here it is in a nutshell.

All cards have a numerical value: Ace counts 1; 2 counts 2, etc., up to 10. The jack counts 11; the queen, 12; and the king, 13.

The suits must eventually be placed as follows: clubs, diamonds, hearts, and spades (this order is similar to the rank of suits in Bridge).

The performer must always add 3 to the numerical value of the previously named card, and name the next suit that follows that of the previous card to give suit value to the card he is calling.

With the above information at hand the performer can name the entire fifty-two cards without ever repeating the name of a single card. The performer merely adds the number 3 to the previous card called, and combines the numerical value with the following suit.

When adding 3 to the previous card, if the total goes above 13, the performer stops at 13 and then continues counting, starting with 1, 2, etc. For example, the queen of spades was the last card named. Since the queen counts 12, adding 3 would bring the total over 13. So the performer counts the king as the first card, the ace as the second, the 2 as the third. The card he names is the 2 of clubs.

At the start of this trick, the performer names the 3 of clubs as his first card. The performer can name another card first and the result will be the same, but the author has found that the 3 of clubs is the best card to start with. The person who holds it hands it to the performer, who places it face up in his left hand. Adding 3 to the value of this card, he knows that the next card must be a 6, and that the diamond suit follows clubs; therefore, he names the 6 of diamonds. The next named card is the 9 of hearts, the fourth named card the queen of spades, fifth the 2 of clubs, etc.

The system is quite simple to learn, but to mislead anyone who might guess the method, the performer may skip one or two cards now and then. For example, the 3 of clubs is called. The 3 of clubs is placed in the performer's hand. He knows the next card to be called, according to the code, will be the 6 of diamonds, but instead he adds 9 to the 3 and calls a queen of spades, which is the third card that should be called after the 3 of clubs. The performer calls the 6 of diamonds now, or the 9 of hearts, following with the next card.

If cards are called in this manner every now and then, the most observant of spectators will be mystified. It is not difficult to do this, for the simple reason that the performer can always look at the last cards called and easily ascertain which code cards are missing, and then call them correctly.

In order to make this trick effective, the performer must pretend he is concentrating much harder as the number of cards diminishes in the spectator's hands.

After the performer has called the fifty-two cards correctly, without repeating any, he places the deck face down in his hands.

Following is a chart showing the arrangement of the fifty-two cards from the top of a face-down deck. The chart reads from left to right, the 3 of clubs being the top card of the deck and the king of spades the bottom card.

Clubs	Diamonds	Hearts	Spades
3	6	9	queen
2	5	8	jack
ace	4	7	10
king	3	6	9
queen	2	5	8
jack	ace	4	7
10	king	3	6
9	queen	2	5
8	jack	ace	4
7	10	king	3
6	9	queen	2
5	8	jack	ace
4	7	10	king

With this arrangement it will be noted that every card of the same numerical value is thirteen cards apart and in the same order as the value of suits in a Bridge game where clubs are low.

For example, the 3 of clubs is on top of the deck, the 3 of diamonds is thirteen cards away, or the fourteenth card down from the top of the deck, the 3 of hearts is the twenty-seventh card down, and the 3 of spades the fortieth card down. The performer will note that each card of the same suit is separated by three cards of different suits. This setup lends itself to a mathematical formula which permits the performer to calculate the exact position of any card in the deck called by the spectator.

To accomplish this the performer must do as follows:

Glimpse the card of the same suit nearest the bottom of the deck, or, better still, memorize the four bottom cards of the deck. This will come easy if you merely remember the system.

Subtract the numerical value of the card called from the value of the nearest card from the bottom of the deck having the same suit. For example, the 10 of spades is called by a spectator. The performer subtracts 10 from 13 (because the king of spades is on the bottom of the deck and carries a value of 13); 10 from 13 leaves 3; this is multiplied by 4, and our result is 12. The 10 of spades, therefore, is the twelfth card from the top of the deck.

Should a suit of the card called fail to be on the bottom, subtract the number of cards below this card from the final total, and that is the location of the card from the top of the deck. For example, a spectator calls the 3 of hearts. The second card from the bottom is the 10 of hearts. The performer subtracts 3 from 10, giving him 7. He multiplies by 4, result is 28. He then subtracts 1 (for the one card which is below the 10 of hearts) and the performer knows that the card called the 3 of hearts is the twenty-seventh card from the top of the deck.

Should the card nearest to the bottom of the same suit as the card called be of a lower numerical value, add 13 to this number, then subtract.

The performer must remember, when counting the cards to verify the fact that the named card is at the number called by the performer, not to disturb the position of these cards. They must be placed back on top of the deck in the same positon as before.

133. SI STEBBINS' MASTER TRICKS

The author suggests that before the performer attempts to perform these, he should become thoroughly acquainted with the workings of "Si Stebbins' Master Memory Test." The effects in these tricks are performed with an approach different from the "Memory Test."

PRESENTATION AND EFFECT

The performer removes a deck of cards from the card case, places it on the table, and has a spectator cut the deck. This is done one or more times.

The performer then requests a spectator to name a card; and instantly the performer names the exact location from the top of the deck, where the named card can be found. Counting down to the number named by the performer, the card called by the spectator is found. This is done as often as the performer desires.

The performer asks that a card be selected, and names this card. This also is done as often as the performer desires.

The performer has a spectator select a group of cards, all in one portion, and the performer correctly names the cards taken by the spectator.

The performer has a spectator take out a group of cards, all in one portion, from the deck, and the performer names the correct number in the group taken.

For his final trick, the performer has the deck cut one or more times, then states that he is going to deal out a Bridge hand to four people, including himself. He deals thirteen cards to each, dealing clockwise one card at a time to each player until the entire deck has been dealt out. Upon turning up each player's hand, it is found that each holds thirteen cards of the same suit; but the performer holds the thirteen spades—which is the best hand. This is the finish of this remarkable demonstration.

THE SECRET

The cards are arranged the same as in the chart for "Si Stebbins' Master Memory Test" (see page 254). The cutting of the cards does not disturb the position of the setup. Therefore, to ascertain the location of any card, follow the same procedure as described in the aforementioned trick.

To find the name of a selected card, the performer cuts (separates) the cards at the exact position where the selected card was removed, and puts the bottom half of the pack on top of the top half. The performer knows that the selected card has a numerical value of 3 higher than, and the suit next in order to (see page 253), the bottom card of the deck, so he peeks at the bottom card and determines the value of the selected card.

The same holds true when the spectator selects a group of cards. They are named in the same manner, by peeking at the bottom card. The performer requests the spectator to hand him each card as he names it. When the spectator hands the performer his last card, the performer ceases naming cards.

To find out the number of cards removed in one portion from the deck, the performer must cut the cards at the position where the cards were removed, and place the bottom group on top of the former top group of the deck. Then the performer notes the bottom card. He also notes the card of the same suit nearest the top of the deck. Now he subtracts the numerical value of the card of the same suit nearest the top from the value of the card on the bottom of the deck; multiplies the result by 4; and subtracts the number of cards above the card of the same suit as the bottom card plus one from the result arrived at from the multiplication. The difference is the number of cards removed.

If the numerical value of the necessary top card (nearest card of same suit to top of deck) is greater than the bottom card of the deck, add 13 to the numerical value of the bottom card.

The performer must remember never to disturb the setup of the cards when doing an effect with this particular method.

And, last, when ready to deal out the Bridge hands, the performer has the deck cut until a spade appears on the bottom of the deck. He makes certain of this by squaring up the deck and glimpsing the bottom card.

134. THE MISHAP POKER DEAL

A favorite with George Schindler and Bob Condon, the New York magicians.

PRESENTATION AND EFFECT

The performer begins his patter as follows: "For years, people have been under the impression that card cheaters only cheat when dealing cards from the bottom of the deck. I'd like to show you how untrue that actually is. Let's get a nice Poker hand." (The performer looks through the deck and picks out the four aces and a king.) "Here is a good hand," he says as he places these five cards on the bottom of the deck so that the ace of spades becomes the bottom card of the deck.

"Now, let us suppose," continues the performer, "that we are playing a five-handed game of Draw Poker. Here's how the bottom dealer would do it." The performer deals the first four cards off the top of the deck and very openly takes one from the bottom for his own hand. The performer remarks that, "Of course, this should be done a bit more quickly so that it cannot be detected, but then again, if I could do it undetectably, I wouldn't be here showing it to you." The performer continues dealing out the five Poker hands, dealing himself the bottom card of the deck each time.

The performer now turns up each hand dealt and shows the value of it, then immediately after showing the hand, he turns

each face down on the table. He then turns up his own hand—and, naturally, he holds the four aces. He turns his hand face down, and continues.

"Suppose we eliminate the bottom deal." (And the performer gathers the five previously dealt hands and places one on top of the other, then places all of them on top of the deck.) "This time," says the performer, "I will deal from the top. You can watch me very carefully, and you won't see a thing wrong, but I still will get the four aces."

The performer deals out five hands again. After the five hands have been dealt out, the performer turns up the four hands and leaves them face up (pretending not to see that three of the aces have been dealt to these hands). He says, "Of course, we find that the winning hand, the four aces, are in my hand." The spectators will call attention to the fact that the performer made a mistake.

"Well," says the performer, "gamblers will make mistakes, so the only way out of this is to beat the four aces." The performer turns up a Royal Flush as his hand. (This is the first time the performer shows his hand on this deal.)

THE SECRET

The performer secretly removes the 10, jack, queen, and king of spades, and places them on top of the deck. This can be done beforehand, or when taking the four aces out of the deck. The performer must make certain to have the ace of spades as the bottom card of the deck when dealing the aces from the bottom.

When the performer deals out the five Poker hands, he must make certain to deal each card of the hand directly on top of the previously dealt card, to prevent a card in any of the Poker hands from slipping under the first dealt card of each hand. When the performer puts each dealt hand on top of the other, he must make certain to leave the bottom card of each hand exactly in the same position as it was dealt. In other words, none of the cards in the hands can have its position disturbed.

Then, all the performer need do is deal the cards out, and every fifth card is his (the bottom card of each hand), and so he gets the Royal Flush.

135. THE TWENTY-ONE CARD SPELLING TRICK

From the Chicago magician Martin Sunshine.

PRESENTATION AND EFFECT

The performer hands the deck of cards to a spectator, instructing him to shuffle the deck as much as he desires, then to deal three piles of seven cards each face down onto the table. The remainder of the deck is then put to one side.

The performer now invites the spectator to pick up any one of the piles and memorize one of the cards in that pile. The performer assembles the piles, putting one on top of the other, after the spectator has chosen a card. Now the performer deals three cards in a row face down on the table, and continues dealing the remaining cards on top of these three face-down cards in proper dealing order until each pile contains seven cards.

The spectator is told to guess which pile now contains his card. After he points to the pile, the performer exhibits it to him by spreading the cards before the spectator's eyes. If the spectator says, "It's there," the performer compliments him. If the card isn't in that pile, the spectator is given another try. This byplay is continued until the spectator has seen his card.

The performer again deals three piles of seven cards each, rotating the deal in the same manner as previously described, and the guessing again takes place. Or, if the performer prefers, he shows the three piles face up and asks the spectator which pile contains the memorized card. The performer takes that pile, places it face down in his left hand, and then starts to spell: T-H-I-S I-S T-H-E C-A-R-D Y-O-U T-O-O-K.

For each letter spelled, he takes one card from the top of the seven-card packet and places it on the bottom of the packet. At the end of each word, he pronounces the word, and then tosses the next top card of the packet onto the table. For example, after T-H-I-S has been spelled the performer says, "This," and tosses the next card onto the table. In this case he would be tossing the fifth card from the top of the original pile, etc.

259

After spelling the last word, "Took," and tossing the next card away, the performer has just one card left in his hand. He says to the spectator, "This is the card you took." Turning the card face up in his hand, it proves to be the selected card.

THE SECRET

The performer always puts the pile that contains the chosen card between the other two piles. After this is done twice, as described, the trick works by itself, following the procedure given in Presentation and Effect.

136. THE FUTURE DECK

This is a very good trick, but probably will be little used, for the simple reason that it requires considerable preparation. But once prepared, it will become one of your favorites. This is magician Jack Vosburgh's trick.

PRESENTATION AND EFFECT

The performer takes a deck of cards from the card case, places it behind his back, and states that he is going to select a card from the deck behind his back. "On second thought," he says, "I will write a prediction on the face of this card that I have selected at random behind my back." He places this card on the bottom of the deck and tilts the entire deck so that the face of the card is toward him. He then takes a pencil and writes a prediction on the left-hand corner of the card, taking pains that the spectator does not see the face of the card or the written prediction. Then he puts the card face down in a borrowed hat.

The performer now spreads out the deck of cards face down on the table, and requests a spectator to touch any card he desires. The performer informs the spectator that he may change his mind and touch another card, if he desires. This bit of byplay is continued by the performer until the spectator is perfectly satisfied with the card he has touched.

The performer now tosses the card (the spectator touched) into the hat, face down. The performer states that he has written a prediction on a card, and he names the card (with the written prediction on it) he had previously placed in the hat. If he is successful, he says, the spectator will have selected the card whose name is written on the face of his card. The performer instructs the spectator to turn the hat upside down over the table, and out drop the two cards. It is found that the performer has correctly written the name of the spectator's selected card on the face of the other card.

The Secret

The secret is quite simple, and still Jack Vosburgh and the author have fooled plenty of clever magicians with this trick. A prepared deck is used. The performer takes out the 10 of clubs (for example) from the deck, and on the face of all the other cards in the deck, in the upper left-hand corner near the identification, he writes "Ten of Clubs." This is written on all fifty-one cards. He then puts the 10 of clubs on the top of the deck and the joker on the bottom of the deck, and places the entire deck into the card case.

The performer when ready to perform this trick takes the cards out of the case, with the joker showing, puts the pack behind his back, and pretends to pick a card out at random but actually takes the 10 of clubs from the top of the deck. He then openly puts the 10 of clubs on the bottom of the deck below the joker, although he does not allow the value of the card to be seen. The performer takes the pencil and *pretends* to write in the upper left-hand corner of the face of the bottom card. He writes nothing, merely wiggles the pencil in the semblance of writing. The face of the deck is tilted away from the spectator when the supposed writing is taking place.

The performer then takes the 10 of clubs, turns it face down, and puts it in the hat.

The performer holds the deck with the joker on the bottom

ALL CARDS
ARE PREPARED AS SHOWN
IN ILLUSTRATION

and fans the cards, faces toward the spectator, showing that the cards are well mixed and all different. The writing on the cards is concealed at the lower and almost unfanned ends by the left fingers, and the joker covers the writing on the bottom card. The performer now turns the deck face down and removes the joker, saying that he doesn't need it. The performer gives the deck an overhand shuffle, then spreads the deck face down on the table with a wide movement, and has the spectator point to a card.

After the spectator's selected card has been tossed into the hat, the performer scoops up the deck, putting the joker back on the bottom of the pack, and holds the cards in his hand while the hat is turned upside down and the two cards fall out. He then quietly puts the cards (he is holding) into his pocket. When the trick is finished he erases the writing off the one card which was in the hat, takes the cards out of his pocket again, adds the two cards (from the hat) to the deck, puts them all back into the card case, and now into his pocket.

It is advisable to have another card case containing another deck of the same color and design, so that the performer can switch to the unprepared deck in his pocket and continue to do more tricks.

This trick actually works backward. The performer puts the supposedly selected card into the hat, and the spectator without knowing it puts into the hat the card with the prediction written on it.

137. LEIPZIG'S SYMPATHETIC CARDS

The principle on which this trick is based—which makes use of two decks of cards and two handkerchiefs—came from that great card expert Nate Leipzig.

PRESENTATION AND EFFECT

The performer produces two packs of cards, which may be borrowed. He asks a spectator to shuffle one of the decks thoroughly. The spectator is then asked to spread his own handkerchief on the table, after having shuffled and cut the deck. The spectator is requested to place the pack in the center of the handkerchief, being careful not to allow anyone to see the faces of any of the cards. The performer then states that he is going to wrap the deck in the handkerchief so that no one can possibly see any of the cards, picks up the deck with the handkerchief, and proceeds to wrap it up as he is making the statement.

The performer then inquires, "Is there a joker in the second pack of cards?" Then, looking through the second pack, he removes the joker, or, if the pack fails to have a joker, he states, "No, there is no joker in this pack." The performer then shuffles the second deck and places it under a handkerchief. The deck is placed face down and completely covered with the handkerchief. The performer then inserts his hand into the folds of the handkerchief which contains deck number one, and his other hand under the handkerchief which contains the second deck. Taking a card from each deck, he brings the two cards out into full view. Upon examination, they are found to be identical.

THE SECRET

The performer, while tightly wrapping deck number one in the spectator's handkerchief, naturally turns the deck at the same time. By wrapping very tightly, the linen becomes taut and he can easily see the bottom card of the deck through the hand-kerchief. Knowing this card, the performer, while pretending to look for the joker in deck number two, secretly locates the identical card in this pack, and places it on the bottom of the deck. The performer shuffles deck number two, being careful not to disturb the bottom card, then places deck number two under the handkerchief. The performer now has only to remove the bottom card of each deck and the trick is completed.

138. THOUGHT ABLAZE

This fiery trick comes from Charles Roe, the magician.

PRESENTATION AND EFFECT

The performer requests a spectator to call out a number from 11 to 19. For example, the spectator may call out number 15. The performer then deals out fifteen cards onto the table one at a time, placing each dealt card on top of the card previously dealt. Stopping, after he has dealt the fifteen cards, he picks up this group and says to the spectator, "You called number fifteen. I am going to add the two digits: One plus five equals six." The performer then deals face down, from the group of fifteen cards he holds, five cards onto the table, counting out loud as he deals. Arriving at number 6 (the total of the two digits of the called number), he places this sixth card face down on the table to one side. He puts all the remaining cards, fifty-one in all, to one side, and says to the spectator as he hands him a piece of newspaper about five by eight inches, "I want you to write the name of the selected card (face-down card on the table) on any white space you find on this piece of newspaper, then crumple the paper into a ball."

The spectator looks at the selected card and writes its name on the newspaper, being careful not to let the performer see the card or what he writes. He crumples the newspaper and hands it to the performer.

The performer then burns the ball of paper in an ash tray. Rolling back his shirt sleeves, he dusts the ashes across his arm. After the ashes are cleared away, the picture of a card appears very distinctly on the performer's arm. It is the 3 of clubs minus the number 3. In other words, three clubs are perfectly formed one below the other on the performer's arm.

Upon turning over the face-down card on the table, we find that it is the 3 of clubs.

THE SECRET

To prepare for this trick, the performer must take an old soft deck of cards, from which he removes the 3 of clubs. Taking a razor blade, he cuts out the three club spots, making a stencil out of the card. With two heavy rubber bands and this stencil card in his wallet he is prepared to do this remarkable trick, "Thought Ablaze."

Before starting this trick, the performer places the stencil card on his arm, and holds it in place with the two heavy rubber bands. Then he takes a piece of soap and dampens it. Now he takes the soap and applies it to each cut-out pip on the stenciled card, using one of the corners of the soap to do this. This procedure transfers the film of the soap onto the arm, forming perfect "clubs" to represent the 3 of clubs. The performer then carefully removes the stencil, lets the soap film dry, and pulls down his sleeve.

He is now ready to do the trick, except that he must "force"

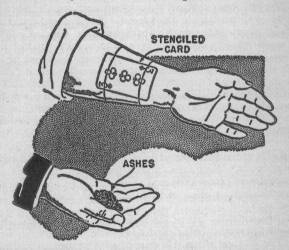

the selection of the 3 of clubs. This is quite simple. He merely places the 3 of clubs to be the tenth card from the top of the deck, and follows the directions as described under Presentation and Effect.

Then, all that the performer has to do is dust the ashes over the part of his arm where the stencil was placed. The ashes will stick to the soap and form three black club marks on his arms.

If the performer does not have a stencil ready, he can write the number of the card and abbreviate the suit of the card on his arm. For example, "C" for clubs, etc. This can be done with the corner of the soap.

In this case the performer may place any card he wants to use in tenth position in the deck.

139. ADD LIB

A puzzling trick featured by Oscar Weigle, the magician from New York.

PRESENTATION AND EFFECT

The performer hands a deck of cards to the spectator to shuffle. The spectator is then told to note any card in the deck, to memorize the name of the card and its position from the top in the deck. (For instance, ace of spades—eleventh card down in the deck.)

The performer places the deck behind his back (no indication of the card or number is given to the performer) and flatly states that he will remove the spectator's card from its original position and place it at another position in the deck. When the performer brings the deck into full view, he asks the spectator to name his card and its position from the top of the deck. The performer counts down to the given number, and proves that the card is not there by turning the card at the chosen number face up. Then the performer names a number, and dealing down to that number, he finds the spectator's card.

THE SECRET

The spectator notes a card and its position from the top of the deck—either by personal observation with the deck in his own hands, or the performer may deal off cards face up on the table from a shuffled deck, counting as he does so and requesting the spectator to identify any one of the cards with its number. In the latter procedure, the order of the cards remains the same, so that there is no change when the cards are picked up and replaced face down on the deck.

Placing the deck behind his back, the performer transfers an arbitrary number of cards—twelve is about right—from the bottom of the deck to the top. As this is done, he states that he is removing the spectator's card and placing it at another position in the deck.

When the deck is brought forward, the performer, ostensibly to prove that the card is no longer at its original position, asks how far down the spectator's card was. We will suppose that the answer is seven. The performer immediately says, "Your card is no longer the seventh card. It is now the *nineteenth card* from the top." The performer has mentally added the number of cards transferred (12) to the spectator's number (7), and arrived at the number (19) which, he now claims, is the position of the spectator's card.

It remains only to count down to the spectator's original number to show that his card is no longer there, and then continue the count to the larger number, where it must inevitably be.

Despite the obvious method (when known), the principle is rather well hidden by the presentation, which "throws off" even astute observers.

140. SEEING THROUGH THE DECK

This trick was originated by Dr. Ed Costello, Bill Simon, and the author during a luncheon session just prior to the writing of this book.

PRESENTATION AND EFFECT

The performer places a deck of cards on the table and requests a spectator to cut the deck to form two groups of cards. Leaving the two piles on the table as cut by the spectator, the performer concentrates and looks at one of the piles, then says, "I see the six of diamonds in this pile. Let me see, it is exactly the fifth card from the top of the pile." He then counts down to that number, counting each card as he takes it off, and puts the fifth card to one side. The four cards taken off the top of the deck are also put to one side (incidentally, the piles are never picked off the table, instead the performer picks the cards off the deck one at a time). The performer now looks at the second pile and says, "The fifth card down in that pile is the ten of diamonds." Counting as described above, he also puts the fifth card on top of the other named card (all the cards picked off the deck are never turned face up).

When both cards are faced up, they turn out to be those named by the performer.

These two cards are placed on the bottom of one of the piles and both piles are brought together. The remaining cards, those picked off the two piles when counting down to the number called, are now placed on top of the deck.

The performer then says, "Let me try it again." He requests the spectator to cut again, leaving two piles on the table. "I see a two of spades," he says, looking at one of the piles. "I think it is exactly the eighth card down from the top of this pile." (The performer points to a pile.)

Picking the cards off face down one at a time, he puts seven to one side, and the eighth card he puts aside separately, taking a little peek at this card before putting it face down on the table.

THE SIX OF DIAMONDS IS EXACTLY THE FIFTH CARD FROM THE TOP OF THE PILE

Then, looking at the other pile, the performer says, "I see a four of spades, and it is at the eighth card he puts aside separately, taking a little peek at this card before putting it face down on the table.

Then, looking at the other pile, the performer says, "I see a four of spades, and it is at the eighth position." Picking seven cards off one at a time and counting them as they are picked, he puts them on top of the other seven picked cards. Then he takes the eighth card without peeking and places it on top of the previously called card. Turning both up at the same time, they again prove to have been correctly identified.

THE SECRET

The performer secretly notes and memorizes the fifth card from the top of the deck. Then he puts the deck face down on the table close to the edge of the table nearest himself. The reason for this is that it will compel the spectator to cut the cards away from the performer, placing the top half of the deck away from the performer. The performer, for example, has noted the 5 of diamonds. It is the fifth card from the top of the deck. When the deck is cut, the performer looks at the nearest packet to himself (bottom half of deck) and calls the 4 of diamonds. Naturally, the 4 of diamonds is the fifth card down in the other pile. Now, when he picks the cards off one by one, he slightly tilts the fifth card a little higher than the rest, and catches a glimpse of the fifth card. Let us say it is the ace of spades. He puts it to one side face down, and looking at the other pile, he calls the ace of spades, putting the fifth card (which is actually the 4 of diamonds) next to the card placed aside from the other pile. He mixes these two cards on the table face down without calling attention to them.

The performer inquires of the spectator, "What was the name of the two cards I called?" Turning both over together, the spectator cannot keep track of which was which. The cards turned over prove to be the cards the performer called.

These two cards are placed on the bottom of one of the piles and both piles are put together. The performer then picks up the eight cards that were placed to one side, and tilts them slightly when putting them on top of the deck, so that he catches a glimpse of the eighth card. The performer now repeats the procedure he used when calling the fifth card. This time he calls the eighth card instead.

This trick can be continued once again, locating the fourteenth card in the same manner, if the performer desires.

141. GENERAL ARNOLD'S MASTER SPELLER

During the author's tour of Army camps during World War II, where he was giving lectures to GI's on how to avoid being cheated in gambling, he had the extreme pleasure of meeting General Hap Arnold, Commander in Chief of the Army Air Force. At this meeting the General asked Scarne if he could spell out the entire deck of cards by taking a card from the top of the deck and placing it on the bottom for each letter spelled, then turning face up the deck card after the word had been spelled.

Scarne told the General that if he gave him an hour's time, he would do the trick for him. An hour later, he did do it, and that is the reason this trick is called "General Arnold's Master Speller." Following is the exact method Scarne used that day at Bolling Field, Virginia, when he gave a card exhibition for General Arnold and his entire staff.

PRESENTATION AND EFFECT

After doing one or more card tricks, the performer puts the deck back into the card case and places it in his pocket, saying, "That's enough for one night."

Then a few seconds later, he changes his mind, and says, "I'll do one more." Taking the pack out of his pocket, he spreads the deck on the table and has a spectator cut the deck several times, completing the cut each time. It is then noticed that a card is turned face up in the deck. It is the 7 of hearts. The performer turns the card face down in its proper order. He then places the deck face down in his left hand.

He starts spelling ace of spades. A-C-E O-F S-P-A-D-E-S, removing one card from the top of the deck and placing it on the bottom of the deck for each letter spelled. He removes the cards one at a time as he pronounces each letter out loud. When he finishes spelling the name of this card, he turns the next top card of the deck face up and places it on the table. It proves to be the ace of spades. The spade cards are all spelled in their proper sequence: for instance, ace of spades, 2 of spades, 3 of spades, etc., ending with king of spades.

Then he spells out the heart suit, follows with the diamond suit, and ends with the spelling of the club suit. This exhausts the entire deck in the performer's left hand; all the cards are on the table, face up, and this remarkable trick is now completed.

THE SECRET

To present this trick properly, two identical decks of cards must be in the performer's possession. One is secretly arranged in the following manner. Reading from left to right, the 2 of clubs would be the top card of the deck and the 7 of hearts the bottom card of the deck. 2C-9C-AD-8S-QH-AC-3C-2H-10H-6D-5H-AS-5S-QS-KC-3D-JD-QD-9S-10D-8H-KD-4C-2S-JC-6S-5D-3H-KH-KS-6H-9D-10S-JH-2D-10C-5C-3S-7C-8D-7S-9H-8C-6C-AH-4H-4D-JS-QC-7D-4S-7H

With the deck arranged as bove, the performer turns over the last card of the setup, which is the 7 of hearts, and leaves it face up on the bottom of the deck. Then he cuts the cards and completes the cut. He inserts the deck, properly arranged, into the card case, and puts the card case into his pocket.

The performer has just completed one or more tricks, saying, "That's enough for one night." He puts the cards back into the card case and the case into his pocket. A few seconds later he decides to do another trick. Out comes the deck again, but this time the performer takes out the prearranged deck. Taking the cards out of the case, he has the deck cut one or more times, then notes that a card is turned face up in the deck. Naturally, it is the 7 of hearts. The performer turns this card face down, but cuts the deck at the exact spot to bring the 7 of hearts to the bottom and the 2 of clubs to the top of the deck. Now the performer is all set to work the trick.

142. THE PSYCHIC NUMBER SEVEN

Here is a method of performing a long distance mind reading mystery in which seven cards are used. The simplicity of this method will appeal to any performer. From Louis Tannen, the New York magic dealer.

PRESENTATION AND EFFECT

To demonstrate the long distance mental powers of his assistant, the performer asks someone to supply a pack of cards—then he asks for a spectator, who is to telephone the assistant. Over the phone, the assistant instructs the spectator to shuffle the pack, remove any seven cards, and discard the balance of the pack. The spectator is next instructed to set aside one card out of the seven, and then to call successively the names of the other six cards. Immediately thereafter the assistant names the card that was set aside.

THE SECRET

Only a pack of cards and a simple code are required. The assistant might have paper and pencil handy to aid a faulty memory.

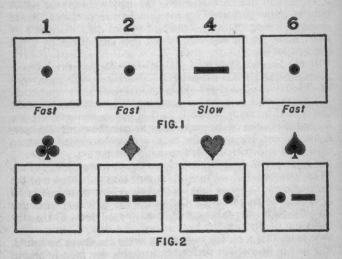

FIG. I

FIG. 2

The performer never says another word after the spectator contacts the assistant. The spectator (Mr. S) speaks to the assistant (who may be called the Medium), the latter giving Mr. S further instructions over the telephone—or the Medium may be in an adjoining room and simply speak loudly and clearly enough so that Mr. S will understand what is to be done. The performer appears to be merely a silent observer as Mr. S follows the instructions given him by the Medium. However, it is the performer who holds the six cards, and by exhibiting them to Mr. S one at a time, quickly or slowly, he causes the spectator to name the cards quickly or slowly, as desired for coding purposes. Mr. S thus unwittingly conveys the code. Although the performer never says a word, he must know the name of the chosen card (the one that is set aside).

This is the secret code used to determine the rank of the unknown card. A dot (.) indicates *fast,* a dash (-), *slow.* The speed with which the first four cards are named will enable the Medium to calculate the value of the unknown card. To accomplish this, assign to the first four cards, regardless of their actual ranks, four digits, which singly, or in combination, can be made to total any sum from 1 (ace) to 13 (king). The four digits are 1, 2, 4, and 6. Only *fast* cards are used to make up the value of the unknown card. For example, suppose the Medium has written down four digits and has marked a dot or dash under each of them to indicate the speed with which the first four cards were named (as in Fig. 1). Adding the *fast* ones, the dots, a total of 9 is reached, which is the value of the card. Now for the suit— use the same dot-dash code for the last two cards of the six that are named. Clubs are indicated by two dots; diamonds by two dashes; hearts by a dash and a dot; and spades by a dot and a dash (is in Fig. 2).

If the 9-spot coded in the above example happens to be a diamond, the fifth card would be given *slow;* the sixth card would also be *slow*—these two dashes indicating diamonds. King of spades would be coded as follows: four *fast* cards, totaling 13 for king, and then one *fast* and one *slow* for spades.

Now let us run through a complete performance. The performer instructs the spectator to phone the Medium, or call to the Medium in an adjoining room. The Medium gives Mr. S the necessary instructions—to shuffle the pack as much as desired; withdraw any seven cards and discard the balance of the pack; shuffle the seven cards; withdraw one of them and lay it on a table or stand "so all can see it." Mr. S is told to shuffle the remaining six cards and hand them face down to the performer.

Now the Medium instructs Mr. S to do exactly as he is told. The performer knows the withdrawn card is, say, the 5 of hearts, and he is holding the packet of six cards, face down, ready to expose the top card to Mr. S, who is at the telephone. Since he wants no lapse of time when Mr. S names this first card to the Medium, the performer has it already exposed to Mr. S, who sees it and names it the moment the Medium tells him to call off the first card—thus this first card is a *fast* call for the number 1. The Medium always waits about three seconds after he gets the name of a card (putting down the mark—dot in this case) before asking the name of the next card. Since this is to be *slow*, the performer takes his time in lifting and exposing it, or he may lift and glance at it himself before exposing it to Mr. S, which delays the naming and thus makes it a *slow* card for a dash; the next is given *fast* (dot); and the fourth card *slow* for a dash; and thus the 1 and 4 added give the value of 5.

The fifth card is given *slow* treatment; the sixth and last of the packet of six cards is a *fast* call, the dash and dot indicating hearts. The 5 of hearts is now known to the Medium, and is disclosed to Mr. S in the usual manner. "I am getting an impression of the color, red . . . a heart, yes . . . and a spot card with one, two, three, four, and five spots—the five of hearts."

Note: The performer and Medium can practice this without a third party until the code is fixed in their respective memories and is recognized easily from the manner of sending, fast or slow, as the case may be. If the Medium doubts his ability to remember the successive codes sent, he may tabulate them on a slip of paper, for he is never visible to the spectators.

The performer's function lies in making the *fast* and *slow* actions seem nonchalant and natural, thus avoiding suspicion. He may be intently looking in another direction to delay the action; he may drop a pencil; may be getting out his handkerchief; may first glance at the card before exposing it, etc. For *fast* action, it is only necessary to have the card exposed ahead of time.

And a final recommendation—we restate the advisability of the Medium's waiting about three seconds before asking for the name of the next card, thus permitting better timing all around.

143. ON THE SQUARE

Originated by the author and Eddie Joseph, one of India's cleverest magicians.

PRESENTATION AND EFFECT

The performer removes a dice shooter's die (the familiar type with one to six spots on its faces) from his pocket and places it on the table next to a pack of cards. To a spectator he says, "I am going to turn my back to do this trick. While my back is turned I will tell you what to do. Please do exactly as I ask you."

Turning his back, the performer instructs, "Shuffle the deck thoroughly, cut the cards and place the deck on the table. Now pick up the die, roll it out onto the table and note the number of spots shown on top of the die. Put the die to one side, keeping the same face of the die uppermost so that you can refer to the number in case you forget it. Pick up the deck again and deal as many cards in a row face up on the table as there are spots facing up on the die. In other words, if you threw a five, deal five cards face up on the table, side by side.

"In this trick, jacks, queens, and kings have a numerical value of ten; all other cards have the value of the number of spots on them, an ace counts one, a deuce is two, etc.

"Look at the first face-up card on the table and note its value. Now take the rest of the deck and deal cards face down on top of this card, adding one to the value of the face-up card for each card dealt until you reach a total of twelve. For example, if the first card is a two-spot, deal one card face down on top of it and count this as three; the next is four, etc., until you reach a total of twelve. Please do not count out loud. Do the same with each of the face-up cards.

"After you have done this, pick up the piles which you have built on the row of face-up cards and put them in your pocket, keeping the original cards face up. Place the rest of the deck on the table."

Facing the spectator, the performer deals the remaining cards of the deck into four piles so as to form a square, dealing the cards face up. Picking up the die, he touches it to the four corners of the square and turns it over slowly as if receiving an impression from the die. He stops handling the die, and removes a card from one of the four piles. We shall assume that it is a 3-spot. He follows the same procedure, and now removes another card from one of the piles and places it face up on the table next to the face-up 3-spot. We shall assume that the second card is a 7.

Calling attention to these cards, he says, "You will notice that we have a three and a seven face up on the table. Three and seven; three, seven; *thirty-seven*. These two cards tell us that the total of the face-up cards in your pocket is thirty-seven."

The spectator removes the card from his pocket and adds the numerical value of the face-up cards. They are found to total thirty-seven.

THE SECRET

This trick is based on a mathematical concept. First, the performer must ascertain the number of face-up cards or piles that has been dealt onto the table. This is found by glancing at the uppermost number on the die before picking it up. The performer remembers this number.

The procedure of dealing the cards into a square and then touching them with the die is just a bit of misdirection, but it is an essential bit of business, for it gives the performer an opportunity to count the cards remaining in the deck. The performer thus determines the number of those cards and the number of face-up cards in the spectator's pocket. These two numbers are employed in a very simple formula.

The number 13 is the key number in this formula:

If the die shows a 1-spot, subtract 39 from the remaining cards
" " " " " 2 " " 26 " " " " "
" " " " " 3 " " 13 " " " " "
" " " " " 4 " " 0 " " " " "
" " " " " 5 " add 13 to " " " "
" " " " " 6 " " 26 " " " " "

As can be seen from a study of the above table, if four piles are used the total of the face-up cards in the spectator's pocket is equal to the number of cards remaining. If less than four piles are used, the performer subtracts 13 or multiples of 13 from the number of remaining cards. If more than four piles are used, the performer adds 13 or twice 13 to the number of remaining cards.

For the final step, the performer removes the two cards which when placed side by side will give the total arrived at through the use of the formula.

If the performer has too few cards to deal out into a square, he merely lays out the remaining cards and announces the total of the face-up cards in the spectator's pocket. The same holds true if he cannot locate the cards which will form the total.

It may also occasionally happen that the spectator will lack sufficient cards to bring all his piles up to a total of 12. This will happen only in the event that a 5 or 6 shows up on the die, and the face-up cards are aces and deuces. In this case, the performer instructs the spectator to bring as many piles as possible up to a count of 12, and to leave the remaining card or cards on the table. In this situation, the performer subtracts the number of remaining face-up cards from the number on the die and uses the formula, as described.

Naturally, in performing this effect a full deck of fifty-two cards should be used.

144. SCARNE'S SYMPATHETIC CARD TRICK

Created by the author. A trick which has fooled many of the nation's top magicians.

PRESENTATION AND EFFECT

The performer introduces a red-back deck and a blue-back deck in their card cases. Dropping these two decks onto the table, he asks a spectator to select one of the decks; the performer takes the remaining one.

The performer then says, "Before you remove your cards from the card case, I want you to think of a number, but it must be one of a group of numbers that I am about to call out." The performer then calls out, "Five, six, seven, eight, thirteen, fourteen, fifteen, sixteen, twenty-nine, thirty, thirty-one, thirty-two—" And he pauses to ask, "Have you thought of one of these numbers yet?"

After receiving an affirmative answer, the performer says, "What number are you thinking of?" We will assume that the number selected is 16. "Very well," continues the performer, "please give me another number from ten to thirty-five. I could say any number from one to fifty-two, but, frankly, I would prefer a number between ten and forty. You can understand why. I don't want too small a number, because that would mean that I would have to take too few cards from the deck, and too large a number would give me so many cards that the trick would be prolonged unnecessarily." We will assume that the spectator names the number 22.

The performer then says, "Remember the first number that you thought of? I believe it was sixteen. Well, take the deck which you selected, remove it from the card case, and deal sixteen cards face down on the table on the top of the deck. I will take the other deck, remove it from the card case, and deal off the top of the deck the other number of cards which you called. I believe the second number was twenty-two."

After the spectator and performer have finished dealing the proper number of cards face down onto the table, the performer says, "Pick up the cards which you have dealt onto the

275

table and hold them face down in your left hand. Then deal the top card face down onto the table; the next one place on the bottom of the deck; the next one on the table; the next on the bottom of the deck, and continue doing this until you have only one card left in your hand. I will do the same thing with my cards. Don't turn over your last card until I tell you to." The performer and spectator both deal the cards which they have until each has only one card left. "Now," says the performer, "let's both turn over the cards we hold in our hands." When they do, they find that they are both holding the same card; let us assume that it is the ace of spades.

The Secret

A bit of preparation is necessary. The performer secretly places the ace, 2, 3, and 4 of spades on top of each deck, with the ace as the top card of the deck and the 4 as the fourth card of the deck.

While presenting the trick, the performer has three essentials to consider.

1. He must learn to use a simple mathematical formula. The key numbers in this formula are 2, 4, 8, 16, and 32, although the 2 and 4 are usually not used, since they would result in too small a number of cards being used in the trick to be really effective. Therefore, the performer actually has only three key

numbers to remember: 8, 16, and 32. With these three key numbers and the arrangement of cards on top of the decks, the performer instantly can determine which card will be left in the spectator's hand.

2. Should the spectator call 8, 16, or 32 for the first number,

the performer knows that the top card of the deck will be left in the spectator's hand, and that this card is the ace of spades. Should the number be one less than these key numbers, the card is the second one, the 2 of spades. If the number is three less, the card is the 3 of spades; four less, the 4 of spades.

For example, should the spectator select number 6, 14, or 30 (one of the numbers called by the performer) for his number, the performer knows that this number is two less than any of the three key numbers. Therefore, the third card from the top of the deck will be left in the spectator's hand. This card is the 3 of spades.

Consequently, the first requirement of the performer in the handling of his deck is to bring the 3 of spades in his deck to the top. This is accomplished in full view of the spectator, as follows: The performer casually removes the two top cards of his deck and inserts them into the center of the deck. Should the desired card be the 4 of spades, he removes the three top cards. Should it be the 2 of spades, the performer removes the top card.

3. After ascertaining which card will be left in the spectator's hand, and having his corresponding card on top of his deck, the performer must then bring the corresponding card to the proper position in his pile to retain it as the last card in his hand. To accomplish this, he again uses the three key numbers previously mentioned. In our example the spectator selected for his second number the number 22. The performer subtracts the nearest lower key number from the number which is called out. He doubles the difference, and that determines the position to which the selected card must be brought from the top of his pile. In this case he subtracts 16 from 22, his remainder is 6, he doubles this and gets 12. He remembers this number.

When the spectator deals sixteen cards onto the table, he brings the ace of spades to the bottom of the pile. With eight, sixteen, or thirty-two cards, this is the proper position for the ace of spades in order for it to be the last card held by the spectator. The performer, on the other hand, has to do just a little work to bring his ace of spades to the proper position in his deck. The number which the spectator called was 22; the number the performer is remembering is 12. To bring the card to the proper position, the performer holds the deck in his left hand and counts the first twelve cards into his right hand by placing one on top of the other. This establishes the ace of spades as the twelfth card from the top of the deck. He stops counting momentarily, and by way of subterfuge asks the spectator to repeat the second number he named. Naturally, the spectator says, "Twenty-two." The performer then continues dealing the remaining ten cards, not on top of the first twelve, but under them. This change of procedure is not noticed by the spectator because of the performer's stopping to ask him to repeat the number, and because the spectator is engrossed in counting his sixteen cards onto the table at the same time. Both cards are now in the proper positions to be the last cards remaining when the cards are dealt alternately onto the table, and onto the bottom of the packets. If the performer follows the directions as described above the trick must work out successfully.

145. THE SECOND-GUESS CARD TRICK

Originated by magician Paul Rosini and by W. F. (Rufus) Steele, the magic writer and Bridge expert.

PRESENTATION AND EFFECT

The performer requests a spectator to shuffle a pack of cards, and to think of any number between 5 and 30. Turning his back, the performer instructs, "Count a number of cards from the top of the deck equal to the number which you have thought of. Look at the card at that number, remember it, and place all the cards back in the deck in their original positions." Facing the spectator again, the performer takes the deck, cuts it and completes the cut. He then places the cards behind his back and states that he is going to remove the selected card from the deck while the cards are behind his back.

He brings a card forward, places it face down on the table, and says, "You may not believe it, but the face-down card is the card which you selected. I'll prove it to you. Here, take the cards and deal them face up on the table, one at a time from the top of the deck, making a neat pile on the table." After a number of cards have been dealt, the performer asks, "Have you seen your card yet?" The spectator answers that he has not seen his card. "Incidentally," continues the performer, "what was the number you thought of?" We will assume that the spectator answers that his number was 10. "Well," says the performer, "to prove beyond a doubt that your card is gone from the deck, continue dealing the cards face up one at a time until all the cards have been dealt."

After all the deck has been dealt onto the table, the performer asks, "Did you see your card in the deck?" The spectator answers, "Yes."

"That's strange," says the performer. "I thought that I had removed your card from the deck and placed it on the table. Well, suppose you pick up the deck and place that card which I thought was yours back in the pack and shuffle the cards again. Now, give me the deck."

Scanning the cards rapidly, the performer removes a card

from the deck and places it face down on the table. "This," he says, "must be your card. What was the card you selected?" After the spectator names his card, the performer turns the card on the table face up. It is the selected card.

THE SECRET

The performer, prior to, or in the act of, cutting the cards, glances at and remembers the bottom card of the deck. Let us suppose the bottom card is the ace of spades; this card is the performer's key card. In cutting the cards, he cuts the deck about two-thirds of the way down, thereby putting approximately seventeen cards on top of the original top of the deck.

The selecting of the first card behind the back is part of the subterfuge employed by the performer. The purpose of this action is to induce the spectator to deal the cards face up onto the table. In removing a card from the deck behind his back, the performer merely takes the top card of the deck. Were he to remove a card from the center of the deck, the trick might not work, for he would then run the risk of removing one of the cards which the spectator had counted. The performer would then miss finding the correct card by one card.

When the spectator is dealing the cards face up onto the table one at a time, the performer permits him to deal about twelve cards, then he casually asks if the spectator has seen his card. Receiving a negative answer, he instructs the spectator to keep dealing until he has looked at all the cards in the deck. Before the spectator begins dealing again, the performer asks, in an offhand manner, what number the spectator has in mind. In our example this number is 10.

The performer has now learned the second and final essential needed to complete the trick successfully. Watching the cards as they are dealt onto the table, he waits until he sees his key card (the ace of spades) dealt onto the table. Beginning with the next card, he counts to the number which the spectator named (10). The card at this position is the selcted card. Let us suppose that the tenth card after the ace of spades is the king of clubs. The performer remembers this card. It is not advisable for the performer to turn his attention away from the deck at this point; he must continue to watch the deck as the cards are dealt. Psychologically, if the performer were to turn his attention away from the deck, the spectator might receive some inkling of the true significance attached to his looking through the cards. When the spectator finds his card still in the deck, he then thinks that the performer actually missed his card on the first try; he doesn't realize that the performer was attempting to discover the identity of the card.

Knowing which card the spectator had selected, the performer

279

can then ask the spectator to reshuffle the deck. Scanning the cards rapidly, the performer removes the selected card (king of clubs), places it face down on the table, and concludes the effect, as described.

146. THE ATOMIC LOCATION

The basic principle of this trick was conceived jointly by Audley Walsh and Al Baker.

PRESENTATION AND EFFECT

The performer hands the deck to a spectator and instructs him to shuffle it thoroughly. The spectator is then told to hold the deck in his left hand and deal off one card at a time face down forming a pile on the table. He may deal as many cards as he wishes. When he has finished dealing to his own satisfaction, he is told to look at and remember the top card of the pile on the table. Then he is to deal on top of that card as many cards as its value. For instance, if the card is an ace, he deals one card on top of it; a 9, he is to deal nine cards on top; a jack, he is to deal eleven cards; queen, twelve cards; and king, thirteen cards.

He is now to place the remaining cards in his hand (those which have not been dealt off) face down next to the other pile. The performer tells the spectator to cut as many cards as he wishes off this pile (undealt pile) and hand the cut-off packet to the performer. The spectator is then instructed to place the packet with the selected card on top of the remaining packet on the table. The performer shuffles the packet he is holding and then drops the packet on top of the remainder of the deck. The spectator is now requested to cut the cards and complete the cut.

The performer takes the deck, looks through it, removes a card and places it face down on the table. This card proves to be the spectator's selected card.

THE SECRET

The performer, after shuffling the packet which he places on top of the remainder of the deck, glances at and remembers the bottom card of this packet. This is his key card.

Then, when the performer picks up the deck and looks through it to remove the spectator's selected card, he actually looks for his key card. Then he skips one card to the right of the key card and starts counting the next card as 1, the next as 2, etc. When the performer comes to a card which has the same value as the number at which it is counted, he remembers that card, and continues counting to 13, remembering all such cards.

If there is only one card to be remembered, that is it, the spectator's selected card.

However, there may possibly be two or three. If there are two, the performer places one on the top of the deck and one on the bottom and holds the deck face down in his hand. Should the spectator name the top card of the deck, the performer removes the top card of the deck. Should the spectator name the bottom card, the performer turns the deck face up.

Should there be three such cards, the performer eliminates one or two, by asking the spectator if his card is red or black.

If the cards have been cut in such a manner that when the performer counts the cards he finds that there are less than thirteen cards at the bottom of the deck, he continues his count from the top of the deck.

147. SCARNE'S POWER OF THOUGHT

A surprising and sensational mental effect. One of the author's top creations.

PRESENTATION AND EFFECT

The performer produces a sheet of paper about six inches square, and with a pen or pencil writes a message on this sheet of paper. Without anyone's seeing the message, the paper is placed face downward on the table. The performer does not give the spectators any hint of what is written on the paper.

Handing a pack of cards to a spectator, he says, "Will you please shuffle the cards. Shuffle them real well. Now place the pack face down on the table." Turning to a second spectator, he asks, "Will you please cut the cards and deal five cards face down on the table in a straight line. Thank you. We now need the help of a few other people."

The performer then states that the spectators may, if they wish, exchange one or more of the cards from the five-card packet for any other card or cards in the deck.

Pointing to different spectators who are standing in front of the table, the performer says, "I want to make up a five-man team. Will you, sir, please be number one; and you are number two; you, sir, are number three; the next gentleman is number four; and will you, sir, please be the fifth member of the team."

Pointing to the first card in the row of face-down cards, the performer says, "This is card number one; the next is card number two; this is card number three." (The performer pushes the third card forward about two inches, saying that this is the captain's card.) "The next one is card number four; and the last one is card number five. We now have five cards, and a five-man

281

team. All good teams have a captain—so why should we be any different? Who'll be the captain of the team—number one, two, three, four or five?" For the purposes of our story, the spectators select the third member of the team as the captain.

The performer turns the first card face up (let us assume that it is the ace of spades). "Number one," he says, "will you please remember that your card is the ace of spades." Looking at the next card, he says, "Number two, your card is the five of clubs." Looking at the third card, he says, "Number three, you're the captain, aren't you? Please remember that your card is the ten of diamonds." (The performer does not turn up the captain's card but merely peeks at it.) Turning the remaining cards face up one at a time, the performer says, "Number four, please remember the eight of hearts. Number five, your card is the queen of clubs. Please don't forget your cards."

After each card is named, the performer returns it to its original position on the table face down before naming the next card.

Picking up the face-down cards one at a time, in their numerical order, the performer arranges the cards in a small pile, the first card on the bottom of the pile and the fifth card on top of the pile. This pile of cards is then placed in the performer's right-hand coat or jacket pocket.

The performer then looks at the first spectator and says, "You are number one on our team, am I correct? What is the name of your card?" When the card is named, the performer removes it from his pocket and places it face up on the table in front of spectator number one. He does the same with the second spectator's card. Turning to spectator number three, he says, "Captain, what is the name of your card?" When it is named, he removes the 10 of diamonds from his pocket and places it face down on the table. The fourth and fifth spectators then name their cards. These cards are removed from the pocket and placed face up on the table.

The performer removes the four face-up cards and places them to one side. Facing the captain again, he asks, "Captain, what is the name of your selected card?" The captain answers, "The ten of diamonds." "Will you please turn your card face up," asks the performer. The captain does so, and, naturally, reveals the 10 of diamonds. So far, nothing has happened. Some of the spectators may even be thinking that the performer is pulling their legs.

The performer then says, "Captain, before we began this trick, I wrote a prediction on this piece of paper which has been in full view all this time. Will you please read what is written on the paper." The captain does so, and finds that the paper contains the prediction:

THROUGH THE POWER OF THOUGHT

I

WILL CAUSE THE

CAPTAIN OF THE TEAM TO

SELECT THE

TEN OF DIAMONDS

This invariably takes the spectators completely by surprise.

Should there be less than five spectators present, a spectator is told to jot down the position and the name of each card on a piece of paper as it is called. In order to remember the captain's numbered position and the name of his card, the spectator is told to draw a circle around that information.

THE SECRET

Before performing the trick, the performer secretly removes a card from the pack and memorizes it. This card he places in his right-hand coat or jacket pocket, with the face of the card toward his body. Let us suppose that this card is the 10 of diamonds. At the start of the trick, he writes the message on the piece of paper, using the name of the card in his pocket for the selected card. This paper is then folded and placed on the table.

The cards are well shuffled by the spectator, and any five cards may be withdrawn from the deck. This is what makes the trick so baffling.

283

Assuming that the card in the performer's pocket is the 10 of diamonds, and that the third spectator is elected captain, the performer picks up the first card that is on the table, turns it face up, names it, and asks the first spectator to remember it. Then he turns the card face down again. The same procedure is followed with the second, fourth, and fifth cards. When he looks at the third card (the captain's card), however, he does not show its face, he merely peeks at it. Regardless of the actual value of this card, he asks the captain to remember the 10 of diamonds.

When he places these five cards in his pocket, the first spectator's card is on the bottom of the pile. This card is closest to his body. The hidden card falls on top of the pile.

When the cards are removed from the pocket, the performer takes the first spectator's card from the bottom of the pile. The second spectator's card is also removed from the bottom of the pile. The captain's card is taken from the top. This is the predicted card; in our example, the 10 of diamonds. After removing the captain's card, the performer secretly removes the bottom card of the pile and places it on top. He can then continue to remove the fourth and fifth spectator's cards from the bottom of the pile.

Naturally, if one of the other spectators is elected captain, the performer switches the corresponding card in his pocket for the predicted card, and continues the effect as above.

When doing this trick for the first few times, the author suggests doing it with less than five spectators. Merely have a spectator write down the names and numbered positions of the cards as they are called. The spectator is busy writing and will be baffled more easily.

148. THE CARD THROUGH A HANDKERCHIEF

This trick, in which a selected card mysteriously passes through a handkerchief, is a favorite with two well-known performers: Harlan Tarbel, magician and writer of magic books; and Jimmy Grippo, noted hypnotist and card manipulator.

PRESENTATION AND EFFECT

The performer has the spectator shuffle the deck of cards. Then he explains what the spectator is to do while the performer's back is turned. "Think of any number between five and thirty," says the performer. "For example, you are thinking of number six. Deal off that number of cards into a pile on the table face down. Then look at and remember the top card of the face-down pile. Then drop the entire deck on top of those dealt cards and cut the deck."

To illustrate this, the performer deals six cards onto the table, peeks at the last dealt card, and drops the remainder of the deck on top of the six-card pile. The performer now turns his back and instructs the spectato 'o do exactly as he did.

After the spectator has selected a card, the performer faces the spectator, takes the deck, and looks through the cards for a moment; then he squares up the deck.

Placing the deck face down on the table, the performer says, "I'd like to borrow a handkerchief, if I may." Upon receiving the handkerchief, he places the deck in the center of the table and covers the cards with the handkerchief. The handkerchief is opened flat before being placed over the deck. One corner points toward the performer. The deck is centered under the handkerchief (see Fig. 1).

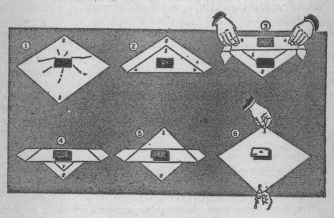

The performer folds the corner nearest him toward the corner furtherest away from him. He continues folding these two corners back and forth over the deck until the handkerchief is folded neatly. He then looks at the spectator and says, "Concentrate on your card and stare at the handkerchief. I hope to cause an image of your card to appear on the handkerchief. Ah, yes, I'm beginning to see your card already. Do you see it? No? Oh, you must see it! Look, I'll show you." So saying, he opens the folded handkerchief, and reveals the selected card face up on top of the cloth, while the deck remains underneath. "How do you like that?" he says. "You concentrated so hard you made the card pass right through the handkerchief!"

285

Before presenting this effect, the performer must obtain some magician's wax. This is a soft pliable wax which can be obtained in any magic shop. If he is unable to obtain magician's wax, beeswax, obtainable at any drugstore, will do. This wax can be carried conveniently in a small tin box. If the top of the box is dented slightly, a small pellet of wax can be carried in the small recess in the bent top until needed. The performer places the box in his jacket or coat pocket where he can obtain the pellet of wax without difficulty.

When the performer deals the six cards face down into a pile on the table—to illustrate to the spectator what he wishes him to do when hs back is turned—he quickly glimpses the sixth card and remembers it as his key card.

Now, when the performer faces the spectator who has selected a card while the performer's back was turned, he takes the deck and looks for his key card. He loctates it and secretly counts back six cards to the right of the key card. This must be the selected card.

The performer cuts the deck, bringing the selected card to the top, and places the deck face down in the center of the table.

While asking for a handkerchief, the performer lets his hand drop into his pocket as if looking for one also, and obtains the small pellet of wax. Holding the wax between his thumb and first finger, he places it on top of the deck while moving the deck into the center of the table. He then spreads the handkerchief over the face-down deck, as in Fig. 1. He folds the corner nearest to him (marked number 1 in the illustration) to about four inches from the diagonally opposite corner (Fig. 2). While his left hand is adjusting the corners, the performer's right hand presses against the top card of the deck through the handkerchief. This action causes the wax on the back of the top card to adhere to the handkerchief.

The performer then picks up both layers of cloth at the points marked A and B. The left hand grasps point A, with the thumb on top and the first and second fingers under the handkerchief. The right hand grasps point B in the same manner. Holding the handkerchief in this way, the performer lifts the cloth so that corners A and B fall behind the selected card which is now fastened to the handkerchief by the wax. The third finger of each hand presses against the back of the handkerchief, holding the fold taut. When the handkerchief is replaced, corner 1 becomes the bottom. Fig. 3 shows how the handkerchief looks to the performer at this time. Placing the handkerchief on the table so that the corners numbered 1 and 2 are over the deck (Fig. 4), the performer then pulls out just enough of corner number 1 (Fig. 5) so that the card is now wrapped in the handkerchief with three layers of material under the card and two over it. The card is once again over the deck.

When he is ready to reveal the selected card, the performer grasps corner 1 in one hand and corner 2 in the other hand (as shown in Fig. 6) and pulls them apart. The card is now found face up on top of the handkerchief, while the deck remains underneath. The performer then removes the card from the handkerchief and secretly scrapes the wax off the back of the card with his thumb nail.

149. THE CARD IN THE WALLET

Created by the author, and much favored by magicians Bill Pawson and Howard Wurst.

PRESENTATION AND EFFECT

After performing several card tricks, the performer shuffles a pack of cards and, placing the deck face down on the table, asks, "Will someone please cut the deck into two piles." Picking up one pile of cards and placing it crosswise atop the other part of the deck, the performer selects two spectators to assist him in the trick.

Calling attention to the pack of cards, he says, "The cards have been shuffled and cut. At the point where the cards were cut I have turned the top part of the deck at right angles to the rest of the deck. You will notice that two cards have been selected by this cut: the bottom card of the top portion of the deck, and the top card of the bottom portion of the deck.

Turning to the first spectator, he says, "Look at the bottom card of the top portion of the deck. Please remember the identity of this card." To the second spectator he says, "Look at and remember the top card of the bottom part of the deck, please. Now place your cards back in the deck." The performer then picks up the deck and shuffles the cards.

Picking up the card case, the performer says, "So that I can't possibly manipulate the cards, I shall place them back in the card case. Now I'll just place the card case in my pocket. Do you gentlemen still remember your cards?" After receiving an affirmative answer, the performer says, "Remember, your cards were placed in the deck and the deck was shuffled. Then, to prevent me from manipulating the cards, we placed the deck back into the card case. Yet, despite all these precautions, I have caused your cards to turn face up in the deck."

Reaching into his pocket, he removes the card case and takes the pack of cards from the case. Spreading the deck face up on the table, one card is seen to be face down in the middle of the deck. Sliding this face-down card into the center of the table, the performer says, "Here's one card. Now, where's the other?" He looks through the entire deck, and fails to find the other reversed card. Turning the face-down card face up, the performer says, "Here's the three of clubs anyway. Who selected the three of clubs?" One of the spectators answers that he did.

Turning to the other spectator, the performer says, "I can't understand what happened to your card. I could have sworn that I had turned yours over in the deck, also. In fact, I would have been willing to bet money on it." Saying this, the performer reaches into his pocket for his wallet and places it on the table. Turning to the spectator again, he asks, "What was your card?" We will assume that the answer is "The seven of diamonds."

The performer says, "Please take your card out of the deck." The spectator looks for the 7 of diamonds and fails to find it. "In that case," says the performer, "look in my wallet." The spectator does so, and finds his card in the performer's wallet.

THE SECRET

Two packs of cards, identical in appearance, are used. From one deck the performer removes a card; in our example, the seven of diamonds. He places this card in his wallet. He then takes another card (in our example, the three of clubs) from the same deck and places it face up in the center of the deck. This deck is placed in the card case and then placed in a jacket or coat pocket, and the wallet is placed in a trouser pocket. This is, of course, done secretly.

Using the other pack of cards, the performer can then perform any number of card tricks before presenting this one. When ready to perform this trick, he brings the seven of diamonds to the top of the deck, and the three of clubs to the bottom of the deck. He then shuffles the cards without disturbing the top or bottom cards.

When the deck is cut into two piles, the performer actually completes the cut, but places the packets at right angles to one another. That is, he places the packet which was originally on the bottom of the deck crosswise on top of the packet which originally constituted the top of the deck. This brings the two previously determined cards next to one another. The spectators are then instructed to look at these cards. This method of forcing two cards is a perfectly natural one, and the performer's actions are concealed by his talking and by the inability of the spectator's minds to follow this subterfuge.

After the spectators look at their cards and return them to the deck, the performer places the pack back into the card case and places this deck into the pocket with the other deck. When he removes the cards from his pocket, he switches decks, bringing forth the deck which had been hidden in the pocket before beginning the trick. He then concludes the effect, as described.

Note: The force employed in this trick is a very effective one. If the performer has used this force in another trick, he may vary the method by riffling the edges of the cards and asking a spectator to insert his finger any place in the deck while he riffles. He then shows that he has split the deck exactly where the spectator inserted his finger. He then places the cards on the table in the same manner as described in the effect above.

150. THE CARD CLOCK

The spectator, through a process of elimination, removes all but his selected card from a circle of twelve cards. Created by the author, the basic idea was suggested by magicians Bill Pawson and Howard Wurst.

PRESENTATION AND EFFECT

The performer removes a pack of cards from a card case, shuffles the deck, and requests a spectator to "select a card, look at it, and place it on top of the deck. Now, please give the deck a complete cut." Looking through the cards, the performer removes the joker and places it face up in the center of the table. He then deals a clock around the joker. That is, he deals one card in the position of each number on a clock's face.

After doing this, the performer turns to the spectator and says, "I want you to turn any three cards in this circle face up.

Now, select any one of these three cards. Leave this selected card face up, and turn the other two face down again. If your card should happen to be among those that you have turned face up, please be sure that it is one of the two which you turn face down again." If the face-up card is a spot card, it carries the same numerical value: jack counts 11, queen counts 12, and king counts 13.

The performer instructs the spectator to start counting "one" with the card next to the turned-up card. The count is continued until the count equals the numerical value of the face-up card. This procedure is continued until all but one card is left. When the count stops on the face-up card, it is removed.

We will assume that the spectator leaves the 8 of spades face up. The performer continues, "You have left an eight face up Beginning with the next card, I want you to count eight cards around the clock and remove the card at that position (eighth) and place it face down on top of the joker. Then, continue counting around the clock from that point, eliminating every eighth card until you have only one card left in the clock."

The spectator counts around the clock, removing every eighth card until only one card is left. "Now," says the performer, "what was your card?" The spectator names his card. The performer then says, "Turn that last card face up." The spectator does so, and finds that it is his card.

THE SECRET

This trick requires a twelve card set-up. On top of the deck, the performer secretly places a red 4, a black 3, a black 2, a black king, a red 3, and a red jack, with the red 4 on top of the deck. On the bottom of the deck he places the joker, a black 8, a red king, a black 6, a red 3, and a black 4, with the black 4 on the bottom of the deck. He then places the cards in the card case, where they will be available when he is ready to perform the trick.

At the start of the performance, he removes the cards from the card case and riffle shuffles them without disturbing the top six cards or the bottom six cards. If the performer desires to dispense with the shuffle, he may do so. He has a card selected from the center of the deck, looked at, and placed on top of the deck. The deck is then cut by the spectator.

The performer looks through the deck until he finds the joker. When he finds this card, he takes it and all the cards below it in his right hand, and holding his left hand stationary, moves his right hand forward, dropping the joker face up in the center of the table. He then places the cards in his right hand on top of those in his left hand. This action serves to cut the deck so that the black 8 is now the top card. The move is a perfectly natural one and does not arouse any suspicion in the minds of the spectators. This cut also serves to bring the selected card to a position sixth from the top of the deck.

When the cards are dealt in a circle, they should be dealt in a clockwise direction. The performer has the spectator turn up three cards to show him that all the cards are different, but he does not mention this. The performer always says that if the selected card is among the three turned face up it should be turned down again, although he can tell if the card is among these three, for he knows that it is the sixth card dealt in the circle. The reason for his saying this is to convince the spectator that he does not know the location of the selected card.

Should the card which is left face up be black, the performer signifies, by swinging his finger clockwise over the deck, that the count should be done in a clockwise direction. If the card is red, he signifies that the count should be in a counter clockwise direction.

If the instructions above are followed exactly, the spectator will always be left with his card, for the trick is mathematically perfect.

151. AUTOMATIC PENCIL WRITING

Originated by the author, based on an idea given him by magician Frank Garcia.

PRESENTATION AND EFFECT

The performer produces a piece of paper about four inches square. Placing this piece of paper on the table, he takes a wooden pencil from his pocket and says, "I would like to give you a demonstration of automatic pencil writing. All that is needed to effect this phenomenon is a piece of paper and a pencil. In fact, we don't even need the whole pencil, just the point; so, I'll break the point off this pencil. Then, we place the pencil point on the paper, and crumple up the paper into a little ball." Placing the ball of paper on the table, the performer removes a handkerchief from his pocket, opens it, and says, "In order not to disturb the automatic writing by watching it, we will cover the paper with this handkerchief." The handkerchief is placed over the paper so that the paper makes a small bump in the center of the cloth.

Handing the spectator a pack of cards, the performer says, "We need a message for the experiment. Suppose we use the cards to determine the message. Cut off a bunch of cards from the top of the deck and shuffle these cards. Select any three cards and place them face up on the table." (We will assume that the spectator turns up a 4, a 7, and a 6.) "Now," says the performer, "I want you to deal cards face down on these three face-up cards. When you deal, start with the value of the face-up card and count cards face down on top of it until you have reached a total of ten. For example, the first card on the table is a four. Deal cards face down on top of this card one at a time, counting the face-up card as four, the next as five, then six, and so on, until you reach a total of ten. Do this with each face-up card."

After this has been down, the performer instructs, "Place the cards which you still have in your hand on top of the deck. Now, add up the value of the three face-up cards." (In our example, this total is 17.) "Count down that many cards from the top of the deck and place the next card face down on the table without looking at it. Then, slide it under the crumbled ball of paper which lies under the handkerchief.

"Now, let's see if any automatic pencil writing has taken

place." So saying, the performer removes the handkerchief which is covering the ball of paper and the card. "Open the paper, " says the performer. The spectator does so, and finds, in addition to the pencil point, the words "Ace of Clubs" written on the paper. "Turn over that face-down card," says the performer. The spectator turns the card face up and finds that it is the ace of clubs. "This automatic pencil writing is pretty good stuff," concludes the performer.

THE SECRET

Before presenting this trick, the performer takes a duplicate piece of paper and writes the name of a card on it. He then places a pencil point on the paper and crumples it up with the graphite and the message on the inside. This paper is placed in a pocket where it can be easily obtained. In our example, he wrote "Ace of Clubs."

Taking the pack of cards, he places the ace of clubs as the twentieth card from the bottom of the deck. He is then ready to perform the trick.

After the blank piece of paper is crumpled and covered with the handkerchief, the performer tells the spectator what to do with the pack of cards. This is a mathematically certain method of forcing the card, which in this case is the twentieth from the bottom of the deck. If the instructions are followed exactly, the spectator will allways push out the card to be forced. Should one or more of the three cards which the spectator turns face up on the table be a picture card, he does not deal any cards on top of them. Picture cards in this trick have a value of 10.

The performer has nothing to do until the time comes to re-move the handkerchief from the paper. While the spectator is counting down through the deck, the performer obtains the pre-pared paper from his pocket. He holds this paper in his right hand by curling his third and fourth fingers slightly. Held in this position, the paper is not seen by the spectators. In picking up the handkerchief, he grasps the first ball of paper through the cloth with his right thumb and first two fingers. This ball is kept inside the handkerchief. As the handkerchief is raised, he shakes it slightly and drops the concealed piece of paper onto the table. Thus, he has switched papers, but to the spectators it appears as if he has merely shaken the first ball of paper out of the handkerchief—and he places the handkerchief, with the blank piece of paper concealed, in his pocket.

152. THE FOUR DEUCES

Created by the author, based on a suggestion given him by magician Frank Garcia and mentalist Dr. Jaks.

PRESENTATION AND EFFECT

The performer asks a spectator to shuffle a pack of cards. "Now," says the performer, "cut the deck into two packets. Put one packet in your pocket, and I'll take the other packet (remainder of deck) and place it in my pocket." After this has been done, the performer seems to have a change of mind. "On second thought," he says, "it's more convenient to do this trick behind our backs. Please take your packet of cards out of your pocket and place it behind your back. I will do the same with my packet."

After this has been done, the performer continues, "Now, reach behind your back and remove a card from your packet, and I will remove a card from my packet. Bring your card forward face down, and I will bring my card forward face down. Let us now exchange cards." The performer takes the spectator's face-down card; the spectator takes the performer's face-down card.

The performer instructs the spectator to place this card behind his back without looking at its face value, and to insert it

face up into the deck. The performer says that he will do the same with the spectator's card which he now holds.

A second card is removed by spectator and by performer, exchanged, and turned face up in the deck, in the same manner as described above. The spectator is now instructed to bring his packet forward, and the performer does likewise. The spectator is asked to spread out the cards that he has, and the performer spreads out his own packet. This is done—and face up in the center of each packet is a red deuce and a black deuce.

The performer secretly removes the four deuces from the pack. He places the two red deuces on top of the two black deuces, and places the four deuces in his irhght-hand coat pocket so that the faces of the deuces are toward the performer's body. This is all that is required to prepare for this trick. The remainder of the deck is placed in the card case.

After the spectator has shuffled the deck and cut the cards into two groups, the performer places his packet of cards in the same pocket with the four deuces. These cards are placed in the deck so that the faces of the cards are toward his body and so that the four deuces are atop the packet.

When the performer changes his mind and decides to do the trick behind his back rather than in his pocket, he removes the packet with the four deuces on top. Now, when he removes a card from the packet behind his back, he takes the first deuce from the top of his packet. This card the spectator reverses and inserts into his packet. The performer does not reverse the spectator's card. He places it instead on the bottom of his packet, then removes the second deuce from the top of the packet, reverses it, and inserts it into his packet. The same procedure is followed with the other two deuces.

Naturally, when the spectator removes the second card from his packet to be exchanged for the performer's, if he should happen to remove the face-up card he just inserted in the packet, he is told to replace that card and choose another one.

Note: If the performer does not wish to place the cards in his pocket, he can secretly hide the four deuces under his belt at the rear. In this version, the cards are placed behind the back by the performer and spectator at the start. The method is exactly the same as in the above trick. When the performer places his cards behind his back, he removes the deuces from under his belt and places them on top of the packet he holds. The effect is presented exactly as described, with the substitution of "behind the back," for "in the pocket."

153. WILD BILL HICKOCK'S HAND

Wild Bill Hickock's historic Poker hand—created by magician Henry Christ, with a few twists added by the author.

The performer picks up a pack of cards and says, "Probably everyone here has heard of 'Wild Bill' Hickock—but do you know how he died? It happened in the Mann and Lewis Saloon in Deadwood, South Dakota, where Wild Bill was playing Poker with some of his friends. Bill made one big mistake that night, he sat with his back to the door. Just as Bill was about to discard one card, Jack McCall stepped into the doorway behind him and shot him in the back. Suppose we reenact that last game played by Wild Bill."

Indicating the spectator whose back is to the door, the performer says, "Will you please play the part of Wild Bill. I'd like you to remove the same cards that Bill held in his hand when he was shot—but I don't think we should. Some people have a superstition about holding the dead man's hand. In fact, some players have been known to throw in the hand if they happen to be dealt those same cards which Wild Bill held on that fateful night. So, instead, shuffle the cards and deal out four Poker hands face down on the table."

This being done, the performer says, "So that it will be easy for you to remember your hand, look through the hands which you have dealt, and pick out five cards that will be easy to remember. Don't let me see the cards which you are selecting for your hand. These five cards which you select will represent the dead man's hand, the cards which Wild Bill held before he died."

When the spectator has selected his hand, the performer drops the deck on the cards which remain on the table, and squares up the deck. He then places the deck face down on the center of the table.

"Memorize the cards which you have selected for your dead man's hand," says the performer. "Remember, just before Wild Bill was shot, he was contemplating discarding a card. Will you please select one of the cards to discard, and please remember which card this is. Place this card face down on top of the deck. Now place the four remaining cards of your Poker hand on top of the deck and cut the cards.

"It is said that every time the dead man's hand is played, Wild Bill's ghost is present. If this is true, perhaps we can persuade the ghost of Wild Bill to find that card which you wanted to discard. I'll hold the deck under the table, and without looking at the cards, reverse a card in the center of the deck. If Bill is with us, the face-up card should be the one you discarded."

The performer places the deck under the table, and in a short time brings it back into view again. Holding the deck face down, he begins dealing cards face down onto the table one at a time, making a pile of cards on the table. He stops dealing when he comes to a face-up card. Dropping the remainder of the deck on top of the dealt cards on the table, the performer asks, "Is this face-up card the one which you discarded?" The spectator signifies that it is not his card. The performer places this card face down on the bottom of the deck.

"Wild Bill seems to have let me down," continues the performer. "I guess we will have to force him to find your card. You had the dead man's hand, didn't you? Using those words, we should find the card."

Taking the deck in his hands again, the performer deals four cards face down onto the table in a row from left to right. As he deals each card he spells the word D-E-A-D, dealing one card for each letter. On top of these cards he deals another four, spelling the word M-A-N-S. Four more cards are dealt on top of these cards, one for each letter of the word H-A-N-D.

"Now," says the performer, "we will have to call upon Wild Bill." He deals more cards on top of the four piles as he spells the words W-I-L-D and B-I-L-L. Thus, the performer has dealt out four piles of five cards each, each deal of four cards having been dealt on top of the previously dealt cards.

Placing the remainder of the deck face down on the center of

D-E-A-D

the table, the performer asks the spectator to name the card he discarded. When the card is named, the performer turns the top card of the deck face up and places it face up in front of the spectator. It is the selected card. "The ghost of Wild Bill never disappoints those who call upon him."

The performer assembles the four dealt piles into one pile by placing one on top of the other, and then drops the large pile face down on top of the remainder of the deck. He then deals five Poker hands around the table, placing the first card dealt on top of the face-up card. He continues to deal until there are four face-down cards on top of the lone face-up card. (If the performer wishes to deal five cards to each Poker hand, he skips the first hand on the last deal around, as this hand already has five cards.) To the spectator he says, "Do you remember the hand which we were using for the dead man's hand?" After receiving an affirmative answer, he asks that the hand be named. Turning the four face-down cards face up, he shows that they are the remaining cards in the dead man's hand, as memorized by the spectator.

THE SECRET

There is only one subterfuge employed in this trick. While the spectator is deciding which cards he wants to have in the dead man's hand, the performer is holding the pack of cards. He secretly reverses the second card from the bottom of the deck. When he drops the deck on top of the fifteen cards which remain on the table after the spectator has selected his hand, the face-up card becomes the seventeenth card from the bottom of the deck. When the performer places the cards under the table, he does not reverse any card. He merely holds them there and fumbles slightly as if he were turning a card face up. If he follows the procedure of the trick exactly as described above, he will always reassemble the dead man's hand, for the trick is automatic.

Note: The hand which Wild Bill held before he was shot consisted of the ace of clubs, the ace of diamonds, the 8 of hearts, the 8 of spades, and the queen of hearts. It is advisable that the performer memorize these five cards in case someone should ask what the original dead man's hand was.

154. EINSTEIN AND THE MAGICIAN

A novel effect by magician Warner Perry, with suggestions by magician Edward Dart and the author.

PRESENTATION AND EFFECT

After concluding a trick, the performer says, "There's a very unusual story behind the trick which I just showed you. It seems that several years ago the magician who invented that trick was performing at a scientists' convention. He had just shown this trick to Dr. Einstein, and he thought that he had amazed the physicist; but Einstein just looked at him and said, 'Very clever, my boy, but in the ultra-dimensional theory of hyperbolic equations based upon the elliptic paraboloid, there is a simple formula that when applied—for instance, to cards—would enable you in advance to calculate any card that may be selected from a deck. Lay your cards aside for a minute, while I explain the formula to you.'

"Then the scientist took a piece of paper from his pocket and wrote the words 'The Card Is.' He drew a line underneath this, and then proceeded to write the digits from one to nine consecutively under each letter of the words. On the paper it looked like this:

$$\frac{\text{T H E} \quad \text{C A R D} \quad \text{I S}}{1\ 2\ 3 \quad 4\ 5\ 6\ 7 \quad 8\ 9} =$$

"The magician just looked at him. 'This is a formula?' he asked.

"'Yes, that is a formula!' Einstein replied. 'The ultra-dimensional theory of hyperbolic equations based upon the elliptic paraboloid states that the simplest and most direct method is the best. For instance, we want to know what the card is that you will choose—so what could be more natural and direct than to state simply what we wish? And since this is a mathematical interpretation, we must make use of the nine known digits. We therefore simply write them under our statement. Zero has no meaning in the ultra theory, so we do not use it.'"

Handing the spectator a pack of cards, the performer says, "We need a card for this experiment. Suppose you cut off about twenty cards from the top of the deck and shuffle these cards. Select any three cards and place them face up on the table." (We will assume that the spectator turns up a 7, a 7, and a 6.) "Now," says the performer, "I want you to deal cards face down on these three face-up cards. When you deal, start with the value of the face-up card and count cards face down on top of it until you have reached a total of ten. For example, the first card on the table is a four. Deal cards face down on top of this card one at a time, counting the face-up card as four, the next as five, then six, and so on, until you reach a total of ten. Do this with each face-up card."

After this has been done, the performer instructs, "Place the cards which you still have in your hand on top of the deck. Now, add up the value of the three face-up cards." (In our example this total is 20.) "Count down that many cards from the top of the deck and place the next card face down on the table without looking at it. Now slide it to the center of the table and leave it there."

The performer says, "Dr. Einstein continued as follows, 'To apply the formula the answer must be expressed in words so that we will be able to interpret it. This, therefore, means that some relationship between the letters and the numbers must be found. To find this relationship, we must introduce a quantity similar to one of those used in the formula—and since numbers are easier to work with than letters, we shall introduce a similar nine-digit number.' "

Turning to the spectator, the performer says, "Let me demonstrate what Einstein did. Will you please name any nine-digit number." We will assume that the spectator names the number 831643232. The performer writes this number on the paper.

The performer continues, "Einstein then said, 'Now let's make a column of large numbers.' So Einstein wrote the number 543235621 on the paper under the first number given. 'Yes.' said Einstein, 'we need a large column of figures.' So he wrote another number under the first two." The performer writes the number 168356767.

Turning once again to the spectator, the performer says, "Give me another number so that you won't think I'm using my own numbers." (We will assume that the spectator names 328642176, which is also written in the column.) " 'One more ought to be enough,' remarked Dr. Einstein, as he added another number to the column." The performer writes the number 671357823. "Then he drew a line under the last number, handed the pencil and paper to the magician, and asked him to add them up. Will you please add these numbers up?" The spectator adds the column and writes the total, 2543235619, underneath the column.

" 'How many digits do you have in the total?' Einstein asked. 'Ten? Well, we can only use nine. Cross out the first digit, the two there. Now, what have we? Well, we have a third quantity similar to the one in the formula and therefore by simple substitution we can arrive at an answer.

" 'Look at the first digit in your total number—it is a five. Now, in the formula what letter is directly over this number? It is A. Therefore, write the letter A under the number five in your total. Now, take each of the remaining digits and substitute for it the letter for which it stands in our formula.' "

The spectator does the same with the remaining digits in the total. When all the letters have been placed under their corresponding total digits, the spectator finds that they spell out the words, "Ace, hearts." The spectator is then instructed to turn his card face up. It is the ace of hearts.

THE SECRET

The performer must first memorize the number 543235621.

This is the second number in the column, and should be written in an offhand manner, as if any numbers were being selected. The performer writes such digits in the third row as to total 9 when added to the digits directly above in the first row. For example, if one of the digits selected by the spectator is 8, the performer writes the number 1 in the corresponding position in the third row. The magician likewise writes digits in the fifth row to total 9 when added to those in the fourth row. If these instructions are followed exactly, the total will always be 2543235619. The steps in writing the numbers are as follows:

1st row—spectator names numbers.
2nd row—performer writes memorized number 543235621.
3rd row—performer writes numbers to total 9 when added to first row.
4th row—spectator names number.
5th row—performer writes numbers to total 9 when added to fourth row.
Spectator adds total
Letters substituted by spectator.

The card is, of course, forced, and it must be the ace of hearts. To do this, the performer must secretly place the ace of hearts to be the twentieth card from the bottom, and must follow instructions as described in Presentation and Effect.

Note: By not having the spectator look at his card when he selects it, the element of surprise at the end of the trick is much stronger. This trick is mathematically perfect, provided the instructions are followed exactly. In this effect, the patter is all-important. The performer should attempt to sound as learned as possible when playing the part of Einstein.

155. SCARNE'S COLOR CONTROL

A card trick in which the spectator mysteriously separates the red-face cards from the black-face cards. A top creation by the author, who has kept the method a secret for many years.

PRESENTATION AND EFFECT

After having completed several card tricks, the performer places the cards back into the card case, and puts it into his pocket, saying, "That's enough tricks for one session."

Several minutes later he says, "You know, cards are used for a few other things besides card playing and tricks. You've probably heard about the experiments being conducted by Doctor Rhine of Duke University. He's a psychologist who has been trying to prove that there may be something to telepathy, but he calls it extra-sensory perception. In these experiments he uses a special pack of cards having five designs repeated five times each. Without seeing the faces of the cards, the subject of the experiment attempts to determine which design is printed on the face of each card.

"Well, at several other universities, similar experiments are being conducted with ordinary playing cards. These are experiments in color control, as the experimenters call it." Removing the pack of cards from his pocket and taking the cards out of the card case, the performer says, "The experiments are run something like this."

Sitting directly opposite the spectator at the table, the performer looks through the deck and removes two red-face cards, and two black-face cards from the deck. He places these cards face up on the table, with the two red cards in front of the spectator, and the two black cards in front of himself. The cards in front of each person are separated by about ten inches. The black cards, in turn, are placed directly in front of each red card, about ten inches from the red cards.

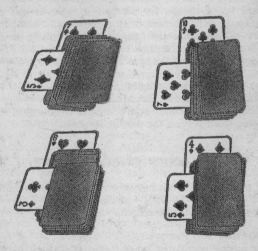

Holding the deck face down in his left hand, the performer says, "I'd like to demonstrate what you should do in this experiment." Dealing the top card of the deck face down into his right hand he says, "If you think this card is red, you place it face down on the top of either of these two face-up red cards in front of you. If you think it is black, place it face down on top of either of the two black cards in front of me." Looking at the face of the card, he says, "This card is black, so we place it face down on top of one of these two black cards."

Dealing another card from the top of the deck, the performer says, "I think this card is red." Turning it face up, he shows that it is red, so he places it face down on top of one of the face-up red cards. He then deals off the next two cards, and guesses their colors. Looking at the faces of the cards to see if he is correct, he places the cards on the properly colored face-up card. These cards are placed on the face-up cards so that the spectator can see his indicators and place his cards on the proper piles.

Handing the face-down deck to the spectator, the performer says, "You see what I want you to do. Deal the cards one at a time from the top of the deck. If you think the card is red, place it on one of the red-face cards. If you think it is a black card, place it on one of the black piles. So that we can make this a real psychological test, do not look at the faces of any of these cards. This experiment relies on your subconscious mind's determining the color of the cards. If you look at the faces of any of the cards, you will be consciously attempting to place the cards on the proper piles. The results of the experiment would not be valid, for you would then be forcing the cards to be placed on the proper piles. Deal the cards slowly and concentrate on the color which you think the card is. I'll try to help you by doing a little thinking myself."

While the spectator is dealing and concentrating, the performer keeps up a running line of talk, reminding the spectator to deal one card at a time, not to deal too fast, and to deal cards onto all four piles. Should one pile have too few cards compared to the others, the performer asks, "What's wrong with this pile? Are you afraid of it? You can deal some cards on this pile too, you know. Try to keep all the piles pretty even."

The spectator continues to deal the cards one at a time onto each pile—when suddenly he comes across a face-up black card. The performer reaches over and places this card face up on one of the black piles. "You know," he says, "I think the next card is also a black card. Turn it face up and we'll see." The card is turned up, and proves to be another black card. The performer places this card face up on top of the other black pile.

The performer than says, "Let's see how you have been doing with the red cards. Turn up the top card of each pile in front of you." The spectator does so, and finds these cards are both red. "To make the experiment a little more complex," says the performer, "We'll transpose the face-up cards on top of each

303

pile. We'll place the face-up red cards on top of the black piles, and the black face-up cards on top of the red piles."

The changes are made, so that on top of each black pile we now have a red card face up, and on top of each red pile we have a black face-up card. "And now," says the performer, "to make it more difficult to control the colors, please shuffle the cards which you have in your hand." This being done, the performer says, "The remainder of the deal will be controlled by the cards which are now face up on top of each pile. If you think a card is black, deal it face down onto a new face-up black card, placing it on a pile which was previously reserved for the red cards. The red cards are to be dealt face down on top of a pile formerly reserved for the black cards."

The spectator deals the remainder of the deck onto the new indicator cards. When the entire deck is exhausted, the performer says, "It would be asking too much to believe that you have dealt all the cards onto the proper piles, so we will just look at the cards in front of you. These cards in front of me we'll just push aside." As he says this, the performer picks up one of the piles in front of himself, places it on top of the other pile, and pushes the group of cards to one side, without disturbing the order of the cards.

Turning to the spectator, the performer points to one of the piles in front of the spectator and says, "You think that all the cards above that black-faced card are black. Well, let's see if you're right." The spectator turns these cards face up, and finds that they are all black.

"Not bad for a beginner," says the performer, "but let's see how you did on the other cards. You think that the rest of the cards in that pile are red, don't you? Well, let's take a look." Once again the spectator turns over the cards, and finds he called the colors correctly.

Indicating the other pile in front of the spectator, the performer says virtually the same things as with the first pile. The spectator turns these cards up and finds that he correctly guessed the colors of the cards.

The performer says, "You have pretty good color control. You did a lot better with those cards which we weren't going to consider." Picking up the pile of cards which he had previously pushed to one side, the performer or the spectator turns the card face up one at a time. All the cards in this pile are also found to be the same color as the indicator card for that group. "You guessed the color of each card correctly. You are really a color controller. I would suggest that you contribute your services to the research being carried out in color control."

In performing this trick, as described in Presentation and Effect, the performer requires two packs of cards of the same color and back design. After the performer has completed a series of card tricks, he places the deck which he has been using in his pocket. When he begins to do color control, he switches decks, removing the prearranged deck from his pocket.

The deck is arranged as follows: first, the performer separates the red cards from the blacks, *turns the top card of the black portion face up,* removes two red cards and places them in the black group, one on the bottom and the other third from bottom. He then places the red group on top of the black group, places the deck into the card case, and places the card case in his pocket.

At the proper moment he removes the deck from the card case and, turning the deck face up, removes the four bottom cards of the deck, two reds and two blacks. These four cards he places face up on the table, as described above, and turns the remainder of the deck face down in his left hand.

While showing the spectator what to do, he looks at the top card, and without showing its face, calls it black and places it face down on a black face-up card. Of course, it is not black, but the spectator does not know that. The next two cards he calls red. These cards he turns face up to show that they are really red, and he places them face down on a red face-up card. The next card, a red one, he does not show, but calling it black, he places it face down on the remaining face-up black card.

The remainder of the trick is self-working and is performed exactly as described in Presentation and Effect, with just one exception, and that is at the end of the trick. When the performer comments on the two piles in front of him, that they are not going to be used, he uses the only subterfuge necessary in the trick. He picks up one pile and places it on top of the other. In pushing the large pile to one side, he leaves the bottom card, a face-up black card, on the table. After moving the pile to one side, he apparently notices this lone face-up card on the table, and casually picks up the card and places it on top of the entire group of cards.

The spectator is then instructed to examine the piles of cards in front of himself. These two packets are in the order as described in Presentation and Effect. When the performer decides to look through the large packet which he had pushed to one side, he takes the top card (black) and says that all the cards under this one should be black, and turns the cards face up one at a time. This same procedure is followed with each face-up indicator card. The spectator does not notice this change in procedure, and is thoroughly amazed that the cards have been properly separated.

Note: The mathematical chance of anyone's putting all the red cards in the red piles and all the black cards in the black piles, without looking at the face of a single card until the completion of the trick, is exactly—once in 456,935,128,170,-496 times.

Bestsellers from SIGNET